Peer Tutoring

PEER TUTORING

A Guide to Learning by Teaching

by

Sinclair Goodlad

Senior Lecturer in the Presentation
of Technical Information,
Imperial College of Science & Technology,
University of London

and

Beverley Hirst

Research and Project Development Officer,
Imperial College of Science & Technology,
University of London

Kogan Page, London
Nichols Publishing, New York

Copyright © Sinclair Goodlad and Beverley Hirst, 1989

All rights reserved. No reproduction, copy or transmission of this publication may be made without written permission.

No paragraph of this publication may be reproduced, copied or transmitted save with written permission or in accordance with the provisions of the Copyright Act 1956 (as amended), or under the terms of any licence permitting limited copying issued by the Copyright Licensing Agency, 7 Ridgmount Street, London WC1E 7AE.

Any person who does any unauthorised act in relation to this publication may be liable to criminal prosecution and civil claims for damages.

First published in 1989 by Kogan Page Ltd,
120 Pentonville Road, London N1 9JN

Phototypeset in 10/12pt Baskerville by The Castlefield Press, Wellingborough
Printed and bound in Great Britain by Billings & Sons, Worcester

British Library Cataloguing in Publication Data

   Goodlad, Sinclair, 1938–
     Peer tutoring : a guide to learning by teaching
     1. Education. Tutoring by tutoring of other students.
     Students
     I. Title   II. Hirst, Beverley
     371.3'94

   ISBN 1-85091-777-9

First published in the United States of America in 1989 by Nichols Publishing, an imprint of GP Publishing Inc., PO Box 96, New York, NY 10024

Library of Congress Cataloguing in Publication Data

   Goodlad, Sinclair
     Peer tutoring: a guide to learning by teaching
     Includes bibliographic references and an index
     1. Tutoring.   I. Hirst, Beverley
     II. Title
     LC 89-29-39 1989
     ISBN 0-89397-342-4

Contents

Preface and Acknowledgements   9

Chapter 1. What is Peer Tutoring and Why is it Needed?   13

1.1 The need for peer tutoring   15

   (a) Reconciling traditional and progressive approaches to education   15
   (b) Moral education through the exercise of responsibility   16
   (c) Flexibility of education at reasonable cost   17
   (d) Easing the strain on teachers: two vignettes   17

1.2 The arrangement of the chapters   20

Chapter 2. What Uses Have Been Made of Peer Tutoring?   22

2.1 Early uses of peer tutoring: Andrew Bell and Joseph Lancaster   23
2.2 Peer tutoring schemes using college students as tutors   27

   (a) Project Technology Power, University of Minnesota   27
   (b) ASPIRA-MACE Bilingual Tutorial Reading Project, Chicago   29
   (c) The PERACH Project, Israel   31
   (d) Some peer tutoring schemes within higher education   33

2.3 Peer Tutoring schemes using children to teach children   37

   (a) The National Commission on Resources for Youth Inc. 'Youth Tutoring Youth' programme   37
   (b) The New York High School Homework Helper Programme   39
   (c) The Tutorial Community Project, Pacoima School, California   40
   (d) Paired reading schemes   42

2.4 Peer tutoring schemes using adults other than students   43

   (a) Project SEED (Special Elementary Education for the Disadvantaged), Berkeley, California   43
   (b) Senior citizens as tutors   45
   (c) Parents as tutors   47
   (d) Adult literacy programmes   50

2.5. Peer tutoring for special needs   51

   (a) Peer tutoring involving the mentally and physically handicapped   51
   (b) Peer tutoring involving the behaviourally disordered   53

Chapter 3. What Benefits are Expected From the Main Types of Peer Tutoring?   56

3.1. Educational theories underlying the use of peer tutoring   57

   (a) Role-model theory   57
   (b) Behaviourist theory   59
   (c) Socio-linguistic theory   59
   (d) Gestalt theory   60

3.2. General benefits sought for participants in peer tutoring schemes   60

   (a) Benefits to tutors   61
   (b) Benefits to tutees   62

3.3. Specific benefits sought from different types of peer tutoring   64

   (a) Same-age peer tutoring: interactive pairs   64
   (b) The monitor system   64
   (c) Unstructured peer tutoring   65
   (d) Structured peer tutoring   65
   (e) Semi-structured peer tutoring   66

3.4. Benefits to the teacher in using peer tutoring   66

Chapter 4. How Effective is Peer Tutoring?   68

4.1. Problems of conducting research on peer tutoring   69

   (a) Choosing an appropriate method of evaluation: tensions between action and research in evaluating peer tutoring   71
   (b) The particular problem of measuring attitude change   73

4.2. Summary review of some 'classic' studies   76

   (a) Cloward (1967) 16-year-old school-children improve their reading skills by tutoring   76
   (b) Klosterman (1970) Tutoring is more effective than an equal amount of normal classroom instruction   77
   (c) Shaver and Nuhn (1971) Improved verbal skills from tutoring persist over two years   78
   (d) Bausell, Moody, and Walzl (1972) Hour-for-Hour, tutoring is as effective as teaching by trained teachers   79

4.3. Effects on tutors of taking part in peer tutoring   80

   (a) Cognitive gains   80
   (b) Affective gains   80

4.4. Effects on tutees of being tutored   81

    (a) Cognitive gains   81
    (b) Affective gains   82

4.5. Factors which seem important in making peer tutoring effective   83

    (a) Pairing of tutors and tutees   83
    (b) Age and ability differences   84
    (c) Number and duration of tutoring sessions   85
    (d) Number of tutees per tutor   86
    (e) Training of tutors   86
    (f) Structured versus unstructured tutoring   87

4.6. The cost-effectiveness of peer tutoring   88

Chapter 5. A Specimen Peer Tutoring Scheme: 'The Pimlico Connection'   89

5.1. The origin of 'The Pimlico Connection' project   89

    (a) Early experiments   90
    (b) Type of work done by the tutors   91
    (c) The training of the tutors   94
    (d) Logistics of the scheme   95

5.2. Methods of evaluation used   96

5.3. Opinions of the pupils about the peer tutoring   98

(a) What the pupils liked best   98
(b) What the pupils disliked   100
(c) How the pupils thought the peer tutoring could be improved   100
(d) 'In every subject they should have some tudors'   101

5.4. Opinions of the students about the peer tutoring   102

    (a) Benefits of being a tutor   104
    (b) What the tutors liked best   108
    (c) What the tutors liked least   109
    (d) How the tutors thought the peer tutoring could be improved   109
    (e) 'A phenomenal amount of untapped potential'   110
    (f) Ex-tutors' views   110

5.5. Opinions of the teachers about the peer tutoring   112

Chapter 6. A Framework for Peer Tutoring   115

6.1. Types of framework: conceptual and administrative   115

6.2. Peer tutoring in higher education   117
    (a) Study Service in higher education   117
    (b) The value of peer tutoring in higher education   121
    (c) Teaching arrangements which can incorporate peer tutoring   124

6.3. Peer Tutoring in secondary education   126
    (a) Study Service in schools   126
    (b) The training of tutors as a focus for study   126
    (c) Making space in specialist subjects for experience in peer tutoring   128
    (d) The assessment of Study Service in schools   129

6.4. The need for structure   131

Chapter 7. How to Start a Peer Tutoring Scheme   132

7.1. Define aims   133
7.2. Evaluate the tutoring   134
7.3. Structure the content   135
7.4. Ensure proper consultation and define roles   137
7.5. Train the tutors   139
7.6. Support the tutors   143
7.7. Logistics: keep the scheme as simple as possible   144

Chapter 8. Concluding Observations   148

8.1. Peer tutoring as a model for professional practice   148
8.2. The urgent need to stimulate 'volunteering'   149

Appendix A Tutoring techniques: a list for tutors   151

Appendix B Check-list for planning tutoring schemes   155

References   158

Index   181

Preface and Acknowledgements

It is a pleasure to acknowledge the generous help and co-operation of some of the many people who have made this study possible.

My first debt is to Alec Dickson, founder of Voluntary Service Overseas and Honorary President of Community Service Volunteers, who first drew my attention to peer tutoring as an activity by which community service could be linked to the curriculum. Andrew Quarmby and Diana Fussell have helped me greatly in exploring the potentialities of Study Service of which peer tutoring is a subvariant.

To the Leverhulme Trust, I am grateful for a grant which helped to finance a visit to the United States of America to study tutoring schemes; Imperial College also contributed towards the costs. The United States Office of Education kindly provided sponsorship and considerable administrative facilitation. The people in the United States who helped in various ways are almost too numerous to mention; but the following were particularly generous with their time: the late Vernon Allen, University of Wisconsin; James Althof, University of Maryland; Jeanne Carney and Al Johnson, National Student Volunteer Program, Washington DC; Grant Harrison, Brigham Young University; Robert Havighurst, Herbert Thelen, Fred Strodtbeck, and Steve Hansell, University of Chicago; Diane Hedin and Dan Conrad, Center for Youth Development and Research, University of Minnesota; William Johntz and Brian Stecker, University of California, Berkeley; David Klaus, American Institutes for Research, Washington DC; Judge Mary Conway Kohler and Peter Kleinbard, National Commission on Resources for Youth, New York; Peggy Lippitt, University of Michigan, Ann Arbor; Margaret MacVicar, Massachusetts Institute of Technology; Ralph Melaragno, Systems Development Corporation, Floyd Cottam, Pacoima School, California, and Roy Ingerbrigsten, Administrative Consultant, Van Nuys; Donald Moore, Center for New Schools, Chicago; Jack Moran and Sharon Oja, Project Technology Power, University of Minnesota; Gilbert Robinson, Dina Steinberg, and Bob Deggan, San Francisco State University; David Sherertz, La Verne College, California; Gail Soren, ASPIRA-MACE Bilingual Tutorial Project, Chicago; and Ralph Tyler, Center for the Study of Democratic Institutions, Chicago. I am also grateful to the many unnamed teachers, students, and pupils in American schools and colleges who willingly answered my questions and tolerated me lurking in their classrooms watching their peer tutoring in action.

Many friends in the United States generously helped my visit with accommodation; many friends both here and in the United States have helped me to formulate my thoughts by letting me talk at them about peer tutoring. The trustees of the Higher Education Foundation have also been greatly tolerant in this regard. My wife, Inge, has, as usual, borne the main burden – and my daughter, Emily, (eagerly 'tutoring' a young neighbour as I write) must wonder why her father goes on at such inordinate length about what seems perfectly natural to her!

A further debt is owed to the Leverhulme Trust for financial support which made possible the setting up of the peer tutoring project known as 'The Pimlico Connection' (see Chapter 5) and to the Inner London Education Authority and Imperial College for its subsequent running costs. It has been a great pleasure and privilege to work with the teaching staff and pupils of the schools which have taken part, and with the Imperial College students who have acted as tutors there and, since the formation of 'The Pimlico Connection Society', have undertaken much of the detailed administration. To my colleague, David Berry, I owe special thanks for taking over the co-ordination of 'The Pimlico Connection' as I have taken on other responsibilities.

The first version of this book (*Learning by Teaching: An Introduction to Tutoring*) would not have appeared but for the generosity of the Royal Jubilee Trusts – and the detailed care of Alec Dickson, Elisabeth Hoodless, and Ann Griffiths who made very helpful suggestions on the draft text of the original book, and thereby helped to shape the present one.

In 1987, the University Grants Committee made an award to Imperial College under its special initiatives scheme to stimulate the flow into teaching of graduates in science, mathematics, and engineering. This grant has made possible the appointment of my co-author, Beverley Hirst, as Research and Project Development Officer, and Joy Hill who, although on only a part-time appointment, has undertaken Herculean labours of typing to help us to meet the publisher's deadline. Dolores Black of Kogan Page has been unfailingly helpful and sympathetic during this process.

Using this book

In writing this book, we have tried to address the interests and needs both of education researchers and of practising teachers. In particular, we have assumed that practitioners take an informed interest in the validity and reliability of the research which informs principles of good practice. To satisfy both types of reader, we have included substantial material dealing with the research on peer tutoring – we hope in a way which is accessible and interesting. Those with neither the time nor inclination to read the research material may wish to skip Chapter 4. For those in an even greater hurry, we have provided an (executive) summary at the start of each chapter – and an unusually elaborate Table of Contents to reveal the structure of the book!

Further information on peer tutoring

A computerized search of the ERIC database 'DIALOG' revealed that since *Learning by Teaching* was published (by CSV in 1979), over a thousand more papers have been published on peer tutoring; and the references sections of the hundreds of these papers which we have scanned reveal still more papers not picked up by DIALOG! Peer tutoring is a massive field of study which we have only touched on in our attempt to identify some key features of the landscape. We have tried to provide a *map*; the curious traveller will wish to consult the texts we cite to travel further.

Many of the works we cite are American, and not readily available in the United Kingdom. Readers who have difficulty in obtaining any texts cited in this book are warmly invited to contact me at Imperial College (London SW7; telephone 01-589 5111). I would certainly appreciate being given details of some of their peer tutoring schemes. The Schools Advisory Service of Community Service Volunteers (237 Pentonville Road, London N1 9NJ; telephone 01-278 6601) can supplement the ideas in this book with further advice and information.

As senior author, I willingly take responsibility for what is written in this book; but the original book could not have been re-written but for the heroic labours of Beverley Hirst.

Sinclair Goodlad
Imperial College
October 1988

Chapter 1

What is Peer Tutoring, and Why is it Needed?

Summary

Peer tutoring is the system of instruction in which learners help each other and learn by teaching.

In essence, peer tutoring is extremely simple to arrange. However, peer tutoring can, and should, be used more systematically than it is at present. Research shows that not only can peer tutoring make learning more efficient and pleasurable for those who are *taught (tutees)*, but it can also increase significantly the learning of the *tutors* who help professional teachers.

This chapter outlines the purpose and scope of the book. In addition, it argues that tutoring can:

- reconcile traditional and progressive approaches to education, making it possible to combine intellectual structure (the strength of the former) with a socially pleasant experience (the attraction of the latter);
- give tutors the opportunity to care for other people;
- offer flexibility to teachers in, for example, mixed ability classes; and
- ease the strain on teachers: (two vignettes of classroom practice show how tutors can help the teacher to achieve a relaxed atmosphere in which pupils can work effectively).

The arrangement of the chapters in the book is reviewed.

Introduction

Peer tutoring is the system of instruction in which learners help each other and learn by teaching.

Tutoring schemes, known variously as Peer Tutoring, Cross-Age Tutoring, Youth Tutoring Youth, and Each One Teach One, have used students to teach students, students to teach children, non-professional adults to teach adults and children, and children to teach children. For the sake of simplicity, the common phrase *peer tutoring* is used in this book – 'peer' being defined as someone belonging to the same group in society when membership is defined by status. In this case, the status is that of not being a professional. In every case of peer tutoring, a professional teacher organizes the acitivity of the non-professionals (*tutors*) as they minister to the needs of the ultimate beneficiaries of the process (*tutees*).

Pioneered in the late 18th and early 19th centuries by Andrew Bell and Joseph Lancaster, peer tutoring has been revived, particularly in the United States of America and in developing countries, to meet situations of crisis. In the United States alone, schools in 41 out of 50 states were recently found to be using tutoring (Smith, 1983), and many after-school study centers have provided extra tuition to those who need it (see, for example, Brown, 1985; Hamilton *et al*, 1985; Sheley, 1984). In the United Kingdom, many teachers have made informal arrangements, in and out of class, for older and more advanced pupils to help younger or more backward ones. In recent years, very considerable use has come to be made of peer tutoring – for example, in paired-reading projects (see Pumfrey, 1986; Topping, 1987a).

In essence, peer tutoring is extremely simple to arrange. Any teacher can readily arrange for abler pupils to help less able ones within a single class. However, peer tutoring can, and, this book will argue, should be used more systematically than it is at present. Research suggests that tutoring may have more possibilities than was at first realized. Not only can it make learning more efficient and pleasurable for those who are taught (*tutees*) but it can also increase significantly the learning of the *tutors*. Peer tutoring could, therefore, usefully become not only a technique to be used by professional teachers to multiply their effects, but also a method by which those who act as tutors learn information and skills. More importantly, it can be used as a vehicle for reflection about the cultural and structural significance of the central discipline being studied or, indeed, about the nature and purpose of education itself.

Until now, tutoring has been seen primarily as therapy – as a means of helping school-children who are troublesome or who are backward in their studies. Tutoring has been thought of as something extra, something special, something unusual. However, the urge to tell people things, to explain, and to instruct is universal; and, as Comenius observed, 'qui docet, discit' – 'he who teaches, learns'. Learning by teaching, can be part of everyone's experience in education – and helping professional teachers can be an immensely enjoyable and rewarding activity for people of any age from infancy to retirement inclusive.

The purpose of this book is to encourage readers to try it. Specifically the book:

1. Describes peer tutoring as a means of instruction available to teachers which can relieve the strain of trying to teach large (often mixed-ability) classes, and which reinforces and enhances teachers' professional identity.
2. Shows how peer tutoring can improve the learning of students or children who act as tutors and introduce an element of reflection into their own studies.

3. Shows how peer tutoring, as a form of Study Service, can make economically feasible enrichment of education which cannot be achieved by other means.
4. Offers practical advice for people who wish to establish peer tutoring within educating institutions or projects outside formal education, (such as after-school study centres).

The book is an *introduction* and guide to peer tutoring. It is a work of consolidation, rather than a definitive review of research, discussing, and illustrating, how a uniquely effective teaching and learning strategy *which is already being widely practised* can be further developed. To indicate the considerable potentiality of peer tutoring, the book:

- describes peer tutoring projects which have been undertaken in the United States and the United Kingdom;
- discusses the attractions of different peer tutoring strategies;
- reviews research on the effectiveness of peer tutoring in enriching the education of both tutors and tutees;
- gives a detailed account of a British scheme;
- examines conceptual and administrative frameworks to show how peer tutoring could be institutionalized; and
- discusses the practicalities of setting up a peer tutoring scheme.

Throughout the book, research findings are 'cut and shuffled' in ways which we hope will:
- illustrate the range of possible uses of peer tutoring;
- convince readers that they may with confidence adopt and adapt one or other of the modes of peer tutoring to their circumstances; and
- offer practical suggestions about what to do.

If there is one over-riding message from the burgeoning literature on peer tutoring, it is

PAY ATTENTION TO LOGISTICS!

To this theme we shall return.

1.1 The need for peer tutoring

The chapters which follow indicate in detail how peer tutoring can enrich the education of those who take part either as tutors or tutees. There are, however, four general points which suggest the need for peer tutoring.

(a) Reconciling traditional and progressive approaches to education

Education is an end as well as a means: it is an experience to be savoured as well as preparation for the future. To conceive of education in too narrowly instrumental terms is to diminish drastically its human value and importance.

Not only must education be adequate preparation for work; it must simultaneously be intellectually enriching and humanly rewarding.

Unfortunately, conflict has arisen in recent years between traditionalists and progressives who, broadly speaking, champion respectively the views that education is primarily a means to some other end (notably, work) or that education is an end in itself. Manifestly it is both. Too often, the conflict reveals itself in confusion about form and content. The form (the setting, the system of human transactions) through which education takes place should indeed be as pleasant and relaxed as possible; but this does not mean abandoning structure in the content. Nor, if content is to be highly structured (offering intellectual discipline), does the form of social interaction need to be rigidly formal and highly disciplined.

Some strategy is needed which can offer the merits of intellectual structure (for this is above all what professional educators can contribute to people's acquisition of knowledge (see Goodlad, 1976, 1988)) and a socially pleasurable form of transmission of that structure. Tutoring can diffuse the *social* predominance of the teacher while preserving and enhancing the teacher's *professional* responsibility for intellectual structure.

Peer tutoring can also transform learning from a private to a social activity. By involving learners in responsibility for their own, and more importantly, *other people's* education, it increases social interaction within an educating institution and between different types of educating institution, making the *process* of learning, as well as its end product, more rewarding.

To perceive the fundamental purpose of a social institution, and thereby perhaps identify with it, the individual must be given an opportunity to share in the process by which the institution defines itself. In educating institutions, peer tutoring is attractive in drawing the maximum possible number of people into the process of sharing knowledge.

(b) Moral education through the exercise of responsibility

Peer tutoring gives those who act as tutors the opportunity to learn how to care for other people. Moral education can all too easily become teaching *about* responsibility without the learner ever having the opportunity to exercise any responsibility. By involving students and children in the teaching process, peer tutoring can provide a valuable occasion for Study Service which can later be developed into other activities related to the disciplines of various school- or college-subjects (see Goodlad, 1975, 1982). A widely-reported feature of peer tutoring is the immense personal satisfaction enjoyed by tutors, who feel that they are needed. This experience of being wanted can contribute to personal growth. Peer tutoring is, therefore, attractive as a relatively simple way in which learners of practically any age and academic competence can be given responsibility.

(c) Flexibility of education at reasonable cost

At present, one person in five of the entire United Kingdom population is engaged in full-time education as a teacher or as a learner. A similar proportion of the population is involved in full-time education in most Western countries. Education, like all labour-intensive industries involving personal care and resulting in no immediate economic benefit, is sometimes perceived as an economic burden.

Currently, teachers in many countries are having to defend their right to a fair share of economic expenditure. Even if education comes to command a greater share of public spending, it will *never* be possible to achieve a ratio of teachers to pupils large enough to maintain both a wide choice of school subjects *and* the sort of detailed attention to pupils which backward pupils need in order to survive, and which bright pupils need for stimulus.

Typically, for example, a large inner-London comprehensive school may have an overall teacher/pupil ratio of 1:17. Even this ratio does not readily permit detailed attention to individuals. However, the real situation is even worse: the school may be required to offer advanced courses in a wide range of subjects – with each advanced class consisting of only a handful of pupils (five or six). Each class must be staffed, with the result that lower down the school the general courses taken by all pupils have to make do with a ratio of 1:25 or 30 pupils.

Again, in schools which have abolished streaming, mixed ability classes positively require that individual attention be given to pupils of differing abilities and attainments. Some strategy is needed which permits individualized instruction at no extra cost. Even if teacher trade unions succeeded in achieving a national average teacher/pupil ratio of, say, 1:10 (in present conditions a wild and fantastical dream!) it will still be necessary to provide in such classes for children moving at different rates. Peer tutoring offers a possible solution.

(d) Easing the strain on teachers: two vignettes

In many schools, particularly those dealing with the 12- to 16-year-old age group, teachers lead lives of quiet desperation. Peer tutoring can ease the strain of dealing with large and troublesome classes, as the following two vignettes ('ideal type' or composite observations) of classroom activity will show.

Vignette one

Scene: A classroom containing about 20 restless 14-year-olds (there should be 30 but 10 are truanting – having registered at roll-call but then having disappeared into neighbouring streets). The girls present are not troublesome, but they are not paying attention to the lesson. Dressed in clothes of the latest fashion, they are huddled in twos or threes chattering about pop stars and swapping magazines under the table. One or two boys, dressed soberly in the school blazer (which all are supposed to wear but which only a handful do wear), are trying to carry out the class-work assigned by the teacher; they are subjected to sudden unprovoked assaults from more restless pupils who pull away and tear up a worksheet or steal a ruler or some item of clothing when the teacher's back is turned.

Two boys are locked in silent struggle on the floor behind a table. The teacher, calling out instructions to pupils as she crosses the room to reach them, does not notice two girls slipping out of the door to exchange greetings with friends in the corridor (girls who are escaping from similar scenes elsewhere in the school). A paper dart, made from one of the worksheets, whizzes through the air from an indeterminate direction. The teacher, disentangling the fighters with one hand, gestures with the other to two pupils to go back to their seats, and calls for two girls to turn back to their own tables. The teacher's original irritation and anxiety at such scenes has long since changed to a case-hardened resignation. Time was when she reported truants, only to find that when they came back (having been rounded up by 'the welfare') the level of noise and general chaos increased intolerably. She had even prevailed upon the head of the department to provide books so that the pupils could do homework away from the distracting presence of their peers; but in the first year, 60 per cent of the books had been lost or destroyed. So much time had been taken up trying to extract explanations for lost books or failure to produce homework, that she had given up. She knew, incidentally, that most of her charges had evening jobs to go to as soon as lessons ended (some of the truants went to jobs *instead* of attending lessons!). She knew too that after their jobs, they would spend the rest of the evening watching television or listening to pop records.

At first, she had tried to impose strict discipline for the sake of the few children who were really keen to study, but after several months of continual frustration she had settled for armed neutrality and now operated at a level which neither she nor the children found intolerable.

Vignette two
This is based on a simple peer tutoring scheme. Scene: Same teacher, same classroom, same syllabus. The level of noise is still considerable but instead of it consisting of shouts from a few particularly querulous pupils – and her own voice exhorting them to sit down and behave – it is a regular hum of conversation from five huddled groups at the centre of each of which there is a student from the nearby university.

The lesson begins quickly and efficiently with the students going straight to their groups, gently but firmly disentangling a few struggling limbs, distributing worksheets, and then earnestly discussing with one pupil at a time what they had covered in the previous week's lesson.

During the first few weeks, many of the girls have maintained their indifference to the subject and the tutors, but now, in the fifth week of term, they have warmed to their patient and friendly tutor who seems genuinely disappointed by their lack of response to what is a life-interest to her. Being friendly girls, they start to talk with her, largely not to hurt her feelings; now, despite themselves, they are getting drawn into the subject.

Joe, who has been forever trying to draw attention to himself (by attacking other pupils and by asking cheeky questions of the teacher), is getting all the attention he wanted, (perhaps even slightly *more* than he wanted!) and is spending every alternate minute writing. He still gets bored after a minute and looks up for some excitement and some attention, but instead of finding Kevin next to him, he finds the friendly and inquiring face of 'his' student.

Kevin, meanwhile, relieved at last from the frequent and distracting attacks of Joe, is quietly and eagerly beavering through his lesson. He has even (secretly) done some homework, knowing that 'his' student will discreetly collect it and discuss it with him, and that he will not be made to look silly in front of the others by handing it in. Although neither of Kevin's parents have been to college, Kevin is now hearing about a strange place called a university. At first, Kevin's student has been somewhat unclear about what he is doing at university and why, but gradually he has been making it sound more interesting and exciting. (Kevin isn't sure whether that is because he is understanding it better or because his student is explaining it better: but it certainly sounds something worth aiming at.)

The teacher is feeling less exhausted and frustrated. She hasn't done three years at university and a year's Post Graduate Certificate of Education to spend her afternoons yelling at a crowd of bored teenagers. She is genuinely interested in her subject, thoroughly enjoyed college, likes children and is keen to lead those of them who want it to the same sort of experiences she has found rewarding. Somehow with 30 of them at once, (even with 20!) it had seemed impossible to get through to them. Now, even if only for one double-period a week, there is a let up in the battle.

John comes forward to sharpen his pencil and she is able to have three minutes of conversation exclusively with him. Extraordinary – she has somehow never really noticed him before. He doesn't fight every period, like Daniel and Mark, nor does he keep messing about like Joe, nor for that matter does he seem bright like Kevin. But he seems genuinely interested in the subject, and grateful for being able to work undisturbed by the others.

John returns to his seat and the teacher turns to one of the students who has come over with a query about the worksheet. Yes, there is some ambiguity there: clever of him to notice. That is one of the attractions of having the students there; they keep her interest in the subject up to the mark and are really stimulating to talk to. She positively enjoys the ten- minute sessions after the lessons discussing how each child is getting on and explaining her thinking behind the design of the next week's worksheet. They can see her overall strategy even if the children cannot. They also value her superior knowledge of how to involve the children in the work, and how to cope with their tantrums or sudden changes of interest. She has also enjoyed visiting the university and has picked up a few ideas for her sixth-form class from a short discussion with one of the professors there.

It had taken a bit of thought to adjust her teaching style to make use of her five helpers, but it has been really worth it. Not only are the lessons themselves much less exhausting, but she feels much more of a professional as she co-ordinates the work of these lively students. Were the timetable less complicated, she would like to make better use of peer tutoring. She decides to see the Headteacher about that.

As these vignettes indicate, peer tutoring, far from replacing the teacher, emphasizes the unique elements of the teacher's professional training. Properly handled, peer tutoring can free the teacher from routine tasks making it possible to concentrate on strategy – planning the curriculum, pacing the pupils' progress through it, managing all the educational resources, and evaluating the outcome of instruction.

1.2 The arrangement of the chapters

To give some impression of the range of uses of peer tutoring, Chapter 2 gives details of various schemes, describing the social needs they were designed to meet. The early work of Bell and Lancaster, which still has much interest for present-day educators, is described. The chapter then gives examples of schemes using college students as tutors, schemes using children to teach children, and schemes using adults other than students as tutors, and peer tutoring involving the mentally and physically handicapped and the behaviourally disordered.

Chapter 3 offers an analytical review of the major variations of peer tutoring, outlining the educational theories upon which they are based, and listing the advantages to participants which are sought in each system. This classification of potential advantages corresponds to a statement of pedagogic aims, which is a useful stimulus to strategic thinking, whether or not one can demonstrate by evaluative research that the aims are achievable.

Chapter 4 reviews some of the major research on peer tutoring, highlighting what is known about its effectiveness in enriching the education of both tutors and tutees. Because it is unusually difficult to conduct such research, the chapter discusses the problem explicitly, emphasizing the tension between action and research, examining in particular the problem of measuring attitude change, and reviewing some specimen psychometric studies which report positive findings at a (statistically) high level of confidence. For ease of reference, the chapter then groups research findings in terms of the effects on tutors and tutees respectively of taking part in peer tutoring, and highlights factors which seem important in making peer tutoring effective.

Chapter 5 gives a detailed account of a tutoring scheme ('The Pimlico Connection') in which undergraduate students of science and technology have been helping in classes in inner-London schools. The peer tutoring is shown to contribute both to the education of the students and to the education of the pupils, and to be a considerable help to the teachers.

Chapter 6 examines conceptual and administrative frameworks through which peer tutoring may be considered, noting points of similarity and overlap with other types of work. The object is to show how peer tutoring could become a natural extension of work with which readers may already be engaged.

Chapter 7 discusses how to start a peer tutoring scheme. Experience suggests that certain procedures should be followed whatever type of tutoring is envisaged. For example, it is necessary for the planner or co-ordinator of a peer tutoring scheme to: define aims precisely; plan evaluative research, to see if the tutoring is meeting the stated objects; structure the content of the tutoring, so that everybody knows where they are going; ensure proper consultation and define roles, so that communication within an educating institution or between educating institutions is effective and efficient; train the tutors, because non-professionals cannot be expected to do by instinct what professional teachers have had to spend years learning; and, finally, support the tutors by careful attention to logistics, which can make or break the tutoring scheme. All this may sound daunting, but it really amounts to organized common sense. Chapter 7 stresses perhaps the key to all effective tutoring:

LOGISTICS!

Appendix A contains a list of tutoring techniques based on use in the scheme described in Chapter 5. Appendix B contains a check-list of administrative considerations designed to help readers who may be thinking of starting a tutoring scheme.

Chapter 2

What Uses Have Been Made of Peer Tutoring?

Summary

Although monitors were used in Elizabethan grammar schools, the first systematic use of tutoring was by Andrew Bell and Joseph Lancaster who used children to tutor children with a view to educating both the tutors and the tutees. In recent years, many schemes have adopted and adapted tutoring to meet situations of acute need.

In tutoring schemes using college students as tutors, undergraduate students of science and technology have coached secondary school pupils who have tutored younger pupils; college students have given tutoring in reading to Latino pupils who were backward in studies and prone to become dropouts; Israeli university students have taken part in a national peer tutoring project; and peer tutoring has been promoted within higher education itself.

In tutoring schemes using children to teach children, underachieving teenagers have helped elementary-school children from disadvantaged neighbourhoods; secondary-school pupils have tutored in homework helper centres; an entire school has been organized so that each child acted as a tutor for part of each day and was tutored for part of each day; and many schools have started Paired Reading projects.

Adult tutors have included professional mathematicians and scientists from major universities and research corporations who have taught mathematics to disadvantaged schoolchildren; senior citizens who have worked in schools with adolescents who were experiencing failure due to academic, physical, social or emotional difficulties; parents in low-income areas who were trained to tutor their own children; and adults who volunteered to help in an adult literacy campaign.

Examples are given of peer tutoring projects involving the mentally and physically handicapped and the behaviourally disordered.

2.1 Early uses of peer tutoring: Andrew Bell and Joseph Lancaster

Many teachers in different times and places must have used some form or other of peer tutoring if only to relieve the strain of dealing with large classes. For example, we know that monitors were employed in Elizabethan grammar schools (Seaborne, 1966). However, the first systematic use of tutoring must be attributed to Andrew Bell (born 27 March 1753). In 1789, Bell was appointed superintendent of the Military Male Asylum at Egmore and minister of St Mary's Church at Madras. The asylum was a semi-official charity school for the orphaned boys of soldiers.

Bell was dismayed by the obstinacy and resistance to change of his teaching staff. For example, having observed children drawing in the sand on the beach at Madras, he became enthused with the idea of using trays of sand as cheap writing material with which to teach children the alphabet. Having failed to convince the teaching staff of the Military Male Asylum of the economic virtues of trays of sand, he started, in 1791 or 1792, to use monitors to teach with these materials. He soon perceived that the use of children to teach children was an educational discovery far more important than that of trays of sand.

Before he left Madras, Bell presented to the directors of the Asylum an account of his work there. This was published in October 1797 as *Experiment in Education*. Salmon (1932) has reproduced: 'The practical parts of Lancaster's *Improvements* and Bell's *Experiment*': the page numbers in the quotations which follow refer to Salmon's edition.

Bell's scheme was remarkably systematic. Every individual in the school had a specific role with associated tasks. Each class was paired off into tutors and pupils. To each class was attached an assistant teacher to supervise and instruct tutors. He, in turn, reported to the teacher who had charge of the class and was responsible for order, behaviour, diligence, and the general improvement of the class. A sub-usher and usher were appointed to inspect the school, watch over the whole, and give their instructions and assistance wherever wanted. The ushers were the 'agents and ministers' of the schoolmaster whose province was to direct and conduct the system in all its ramifications and 'see the various offices of usher, sub-usher, teachers, assistants, tutors and pupils carried into effect'.

Bell's school was arranged into classes with pupils grouped according to their achievement. If a pupil did well at his studies he could be promoted to a superior class; if he did badly he could be degraded to an inferior one. Each class was paired into tutors and pupils. In a class of 24 boys, the 12 superior were tutors respectively to the 12 inferior. This arrangement, central to Bell's scheme, offered many advantages:

> 'First, the sociable disposition, both in the tutor and pupil is indulged by the reciprocal offices assigned to them. Next, the very moment you nominate a boy a tutor, you have exalted him in his own eyes, and given him a character to support, the effect of which is well known.

> The tutors enable their pupils to keep pace with their classes, in which otherwise some of them would fall behind, and be degraded to lower classes, or else continuing attached to their class, forfeit almost every chance of improvement, by never learning any one lesson as it ought to be learned ... Another advantage, attending this arrangement, is that the tutor far more effectually learns his lesson than if he had not to teach it to another. By teaching he is best taught. 'Qui docet indoctos docet se.'
>
> Still another advantage is that there is a grand stimulus to emulation; for what disgrace attaches to the boy who, by his negligence, is degraded into a pupil, and falls perhaps to be tutored by his late pupil, promoted to be a tutor!'

Next in Bell's hierarchy were the assistant teachers and the teachers – none of whom was less than seven years old or more than fourteen years old! These monitors, as Bell subsequently called them, instructed each class in its lessons. The assistant teacher saw that the tutors not only learned their lesson, but assisted their pupils. The teachers, a more superior form of monitor, directed and guided the assistants, inspected their classes – the tutors and the pupils – and maintained order and discipline. These superior monitors, the teachers, either listened to the class saying their lessons or attended while the assistants heard them. Each teacher might have more than one class under his supervision. Bell used a military metaphor to describe this delegation of authority:

> The introduction of monitors, an extremely important part of the whole scheme, is as great an improvement in schools, as the introduction of non-commissioned officers would be in the army which had before been governed only by captains, majors, and colonels; they add that constant and minute attention to the operations of the mass, without which, the general and occasional superintendance of superiors is wholly useless. An usher hates his task, and is often ashamed of it; a monitor is honoured by it, and therefore loves it. He is placed over those who, if their exertions had been superior, would have been placed over him; his office is the proof of his excellence. Power is new to him; and trust makes him trustworthy – a very common effect of confidence – the extraordinary discipline progress and economy of this school are, therefore, in a great measure, produced by an extraordinary number of non-commissioned officers, serving without pay, and learning while they teach. (p. 63)

Ushers and sub-ushers were, as it were, the junior officers, who acted under the direction of the schoolmaster. By this elaborate hierarchy of offices, the schoolmaster was freed to see that all were employed as they should be.

Bell's monitors not only assisted with the detailed teaching but also helped with the general administration of the school, much as do modern-day prefects or monitors in a school. Bell was immensely pleased with his machine.

> [It] establishes such habits of industry, morality and religion, as have a tendency to form good scholars, good men, good subjects, and good Christians. (p. 68)

Of great interest nowadays is Bell's claim that his system:

> Cultivates the best dispositions of the heart by teaching the children to take an early and well-directed interest in the welfare of one another.

Bell's 'Experiment' was, perhaps, the earliest example of the 'systems' approach to education. He would not have rejected this ascription. 'Like the steam engine, or spinning machinery it diminishes labour and multiplies work ...'(p. 69). Bell rightly saw the psychological benefits of his scheme, particularly for involving pupils more deeply in their learning.

> For, unlike the mechanical powers, this intellectual and moral engine, the more work it has to perform, the greater is the facility and expedition with which it is performed, and the greater is the degree of perfection to which it is carried.

Joseph Lancaster's 'Improvements'

Joseph Lancaster (born 25 November 1778) opened his first school on New Year's Day 1798. He was particularly interested in providing education for children who would not otherwise get it. In June 1801, he moved into a room to accommodate 350 boys in Belvedere Place, Borough Road, London. Three hundred and fifty pupils were too many for him to teach alone; accordingly, he readily accepted the idea of having boys who knew a little to teach boys who knew even less. He acknowledges his debt to Andrew Bell, whom he met in 1804 when Bell was back in England as Rector of Swanage.

Lancaster's whole school was arranged into classes with a monitor appointed to each class. A class consisted of any number of boys whose proficiency was on a par. If the class was small, one monitor could teach it; if it was large, assistant monitors were appointed who, under the direction of the principal monitor, taught sub-divisions of the class. To be precise, and Lancaster emphasizes this point at some length, it was not the monitor's business to teach, but to see that the boys in his class or division taught each other. If, for example, a boy in his class made a mistake in pronouncing a letter of the alphabet, the monitor was not himself to correct the mistake but rather to require the next boy in succession to correct the mistake of his fellow-pupil.

Lancaster used his monitors to teach reading, writing, and elementary arithmetic. Like Bell, he was fully aware of the benefit to the monitor of helping with the teaching: 'He cannot possibly teach the class without improving himself at the same time'. Lancaster does, however, perhaps lay greater emphasis on the benefit to teachers of employing monitors.

> ... it is disgusting to teachers of any description to be continually plodding over the same ground of elementary arithmetic. *Sameness, in every instance, produces listlessness; and variety is ever productive of agreeable sensations.* I have seen a respectable school master, well versed in the mathematics, have a dozen boys standing round his desk waiting for him to attend to their sums, while he has been listening to a slow boy, repeating his sums, *till he has bitten his lips with vexation.* (p. 18)

Lancaster's 'Improvements' involved the use of carefully structured contents. If the teaching materials are properly organized, it should not, in theory, be necessary for a highly trained person to administer them.

> Any boy of 8 years old, who can barely read writing, and numerate well, is, by means of the guide containing sums, and the key thereto, qualified to teach the first four rules of arithmetic, simple and compound, if the key is correct, with as much accuracy as *mathematicians* who may have kept school for 20 years. (p. 21)

By having monitors supervise the detailed drills, Lancaster ensured that none sat idle while others were waiting for the master's instructions. By this early mode of 'individualized instruction', Lancaster ensured that three times the usual quota of sums were done and repeated by every boy.

Lancaster anticipated the later use of 'sets' by having pupils grouped according to their ability in individual *subjects*. That is to say, a boy who was good in arithmetic might be in a superior class while, through incompetence in spelling, would attend an inferior class for the spelling lessons. Within the 'sets', pupils were divided into even smaller groups under the supervision of monitors. For example, every rule in arithmetic was usually considered as a study appointed for a separate class.

Lancaster regarded his principal improvement as being the introduction of the so-called 'key' or closely structured syllabus. This reduced the tutoring to a mere system of reading on the monitor's part.

> If the boys repeat the sum, *extempore*, naming the total, according to the key in the teacher's hand, they are correct; if their account differs, the monitor immediately detects the error, when it becomes the business of the next boy in the class to correct it. On this plan, *any boy who can read, can teach*; and the inferior boys may do the work usually done by the teachers, in the common mode: for a boy who can read, can teach, ALTHOUGH HE KNOWS NOTHING ABOUT IT; and, in teaching, will imperceptibly acquire the knowledge he is destitute of, when he begins to teach, by reading. (p. 33)

In Lancaster's system, highly intelligent boys were rapidly identified and progressed through classes, themselves becoming monitors.

Like Bell, Lancaster was shrewdly aware of the stimulating effect of being a monitor not only on a boy's learning but also on his behaviour. 'Lively, active-tempered boys, are the most frequent transgressors of good order, and the most difficult to reduce to reason; the best way to form them, is, by making monitors of them' (p. 48).

After returning to England, Andrew Bell lapsed into relative obscurity occupying various clerical posts and finally becoming a Canon of Westminster before dying in 1832. He was a much less flamboyant publicist than Joseph Lancaster who succeeded in raising considerable sums of money from the nobility as subscriptions for his schools. Unfortunately, Lancaster's style of spending was as flamboyant as his fund raising. He was, in fact, arrested for debt in 1807 only to be rescued by a self-appointed committee which tried to handle his finances. He seems to have fallen out badly with his committee and to have somewhat dissipated his energies. Nevertheless, his ideas were taken up in America and had a certain currency both there and in England until professional teachers became more widespread. (Dickson (1986) offers a lively biography of this fascinating man.)

2.2 Peer tutoring schemes using college students as tutors

In the United States, in particular, college students have frequently been used as tutors. In some cases, college students give direct instruction to schoolchildren; however, in some of the more imaginative schemes the college students tutor older schoolchildren who in turn tutor younger ones – see, for example, Jason and Frasure (1979).

(a) Project Technology Power, University of Minnesota

The primary objective of Project Technology Power, according to its director, Professor J Moran, was to increase interest in mathematics and science among the low-income and/or minority youth in inner-city schools by training students from these schools to teach mathematics or science to their socio-economic peers one or two grade-levels below their own.

Project Technology Power is of particular interest as a multilevel system of teaching. University teachers trained students who in turn acted as coaches for older schoolchildren who in their turn acted as Associate Teachers for younger pupils in their schools. Both the undergraduate students and the schoolchildren who acted as tutors did so within the context of their respective curricula. Moran and Oja (1977) note that minority groups are vastly under-represented in the scientific and technological professions. The Institute of Technology therefore mounted Project Technology Power in an attempt to attract non-white and low-income students from inner-city schools to the Institute of Technology. The Peer Teaching Programme was established by the Institute of Technology with the goal of motivating the inner-city students towards the mathematics and science courses which would qualify them for entry to the university.

The objects of the Peer Teaching Programme were as follows:

1. To improve the attitudes towards subject matter among the target group of students by
   (a) selecting the Associate Teachers from the target group;
   (b) placing the Associate Teachers in a prestigious position within the class, one which other students would seek out; and
   (c) training the Associate Teachers to use a teaching style which would induce a positive attitude towards the subject matter.
2. Increase individual attention to students.
3. Improve the self-concept, interest in academic studies, and knowledge of subject matter of the Associate Teachers themselves.
4. Improve achievement in subject matter by the students taught by the Associate Teachers.

The target group was, then, the minority and low-income population of the school district, while the subject matter was mathematics and science. The structure of the programme could, however, be readily adapted to other target groups and to other subjects.

The university students who acted as coaches to the Associate Teachers were trained in a course, given by the programme director, which formed part of their studies at the university. The university students then joined in a five-week summer training programme in which the Associate Teachers attended the University of Minnesota (living in its Halls of Residence and using its laboratories) to learn the subject matter, but above all to learn teaching techniques. Each undergraduate was made responsible for between two and six school pupils aged 15 to 18 (grades 10, 11 and 12). During the ensuing school term, the Associate Teachers, one or two to a class of 30 or more younger pupils, assisted the regular class teachers in their duties: responding to pupil requests for help; determining when they needed help in the absence of requests; and leading them into an understanding of the subject matter under study.

The university undergraduates who participated were selected by the programme director. They received academic credit not only for taking part in the training programme, which was similar to a regular university lecture and seminar course, but also for their supervision of the Associate Teachers. This supervision involved some three to four hours a week of contact with Associate Teachers in which the undergraduates helped them to prepare the subject matter for use in the school classes.

The regular teachers of the schoolchildren were involved in the programme at all stages. The regular teachers selected the participants from schools, choosing them for their ability to communicate with their peers; ability to command the respect of their peers: interest (though not necessarily aptitude) in science and mathematics; rapport with the regular teacher; and socio-economic background similar to the target group of pupils with whom they would later be working. The regular teachers took part in the summer training programme in which the Associate Teachers were equipped for their task. The Associate Teachers, that is to say the minority group older pupils, subsequently acted under the direction of the regular class teachers.

Project Technology Power operated with the following division of duties and responsibilities:

1. Programme director – responsible for the overall planning of the scheme; arranging the training programme; co-ordinating the work of the regular teachers; recruiting the university undergraduate coaches and, with the help of the regular teachers, the Associate Teachers; observing Associate Teachers and coaches periodically and generally supervising the scheme.
2. Associate directors – one for mathematics and one for science. They were university personnel who were responsible for: planning the curriculum of the summer training programme and for its execution; seeing that the requisite equipment and supplies were available and arranging lessons and experiments with the participating regular teachers; supervising the daily schedule of activities.

3. Regular teachers – one per subject per school. The regular teachers were responsible for: selecting the Associate Teachers from their schools; overseeing the performance and behaviour of their own Associate Teachers; preparing their Associate Teachers to teach or supervising the work of the university undergraduate coaches in preparing them; conducting review sessions for their own group of Associate Teachers; and meeting regularly with the associate director in their subject area.
4. University student coaches – one per regular teacher in science. Their main responsibility was for meeting their Associate Teachers for three to four hours per week outside of school hours. They studied techniques of communicating scientific ideas in the university course designed for that purpose; met the regular classroom teachers to train the Associate Teachers during the summer programme; and maintained contact with the regular teachers during the subsequent academic year.
5. Associate Teachers – up to six per regular teacher. The Associate Teachers were expected to teach one hour per day in a class of their regular teacher. One or two Associate Teachers were assigned to a class and they moved around helping the pupils with their studies. They met with their university student-coach for three to four hours per week and were required to attend the summer training programme.

Both the university student coaches and the Associate Teachers were paid for participating in the programme.

(b) ASPIRA-MACE Bilingual Tutorial Reading Project, Chicago

The goal of this project was to remedy the problem of low reading-achievement levels in ten Chicago public schools with predominantly Spanish-speaking student populations.

The scheme was set up by a variety of organizations, the principal ones being ASPIRA Inc of Illinois (part of the nationwide organization dealing with the interests of Puerto Ricans in the United States) and the Mexican-American Council of Education (MACE). The main element of this project was to use college students to provide tutorial assistance to selected pupils who had been diagnosed to be backward in reading. The project provided tutors in selected Chicago public schools with predominantly Latin populations. One hundred and fifty tutors were recruited from member schools of the Chicago Consortium of Colleges and Universities.

Between 400 and 500 children were serviced by the programme. About 80 per cent of these children were one or two years behind in their achievement-level in reading. Each college student tutor was assigned a minimum of one child and a maximum of four children. Regular classroom teachers were assigned a minimum of four tutors.

The tutors were bilingual and/or bi-cultural. They were thus equipped to make the sort of personal contact with the pupils being tutored which makes learning more pleasant for all concerned. The need for this sort of close cultural contact is very great in Chicago.

Chicago is the only city in the United States with a large population of both Mexican Americans and Puerto Ricans. It has more Mexican Americans than any other city outside the South West, and more Puerto Ricans than any other city except New York. The Spanish-speaking population of Chicago also includes Cubans and immigrants from various South and Central American countries.

Various factors exacerbated the problems experienced by the pupils. For example, only a very small proportion of teachers in Chicago were of Latino background; few teachers were culturally equipped to understand the backgrounds of the Latino pupils they taught. Again, a disproportionate number of Latino students were placed in grade-levels lower than the pupils' previous attainment in other school systems, and many pupils were classified as mentally handicapped or placed in any one of several 'special educational' programmes. This classification inflicted a particular burden on the Latino students, negatively influencing both their self-concept and how they were seen by others. It marked them down in their school career as 'failures'. Added to these problems was the fact that the primary language of many of the pupils was Spanish.

The problem which the ASPIRA-MACE project tackled was that many of Chicago's Latino pupils were in the position of knowing neither Spanish nor English well. They were suspended between two cultures, unable to participate fully in either. TESL programmes (Teaching English as a Second Language) had not sufficiently eased the lives of these pupils. ASPIRA-MACE cited evidence that over 70 per cent of Puerto Rican students became drop-outs. This percentage was larger than that for any other racial group in Chicago public schools. Pupils came to show lack of self-confidence, defensiveness, and a general revolt against a hostile environment. Lacking interest in school, they left. Some Puerto Rican youths turned to gangs or other peer groups not accepted by society because there they found a congenial environment where they found more acceptance. Hundreds of Latino youngsters had dropped out due to the lack of response to their needs and the deficient reinforcement of their interests and values. Very few Latino students went on to college.

The ASPIRA-MACE project had a variety of complex objectives with associated activities and strategies of evaluation. Priority was, however, given to improving the achievement of selected Latino pupils who were at least one or two years behind in their reading.

Paid co-ordinators recruited tutors from colleges, universities, and high schools. College tutors achieved academic credit and a modest reimbursement of tuition fees in addition to travel expenses for their visits to the schools. Characteristically, the college student tutors offered three hours a week of tutoring for between 13 and 15 weeks. Most of the tutors received approximately 12 hours of training from one of the co-ordinators.

Being a large-scale project undertaken in schools scattered over a huge urban area, the ASPIRA-MACE bilingual tutorial reading project suffered from many problems less commonly experienced in smaller-scale activities. For example, because the college student teachers came from a wide variety of colleges in the area, it did not prove possible to integrate their training with their university studies. Again, scheduling problems were a nightmare for the co-ordinators who had to juggle with both school and college timetables. Communication between co-ordinators, regular classroom teachers and college student tutors was difficult to achieve – not least because all meetings had to take place within school hours: school custodians liked to have the buildings cleared immediately after the school-day ended. Some college student tutors had to travel an hour or more each way, which exacerbated the problem of building tutoring into their class schedules at college.

(c) The PERACH Project, Israel

One of the largest national tutoring projects in operation at present is the Perach Tutorial Project (Eisenberg *et al*, 1981a, 1982). This project is a one-to-one tutoring project operating in Israel, in which university students help socially disadvantaged children. The programme, which started in 1975, operates within every university in the country. The number of tutors involved in the scheme has been steadily increasing, more than 12,000 tutor-tutee pairs are currently involved in the programme.

Most of the tutored children come from grades five to nine, (although approximately 5 per cent of students come from other grades). The children are recommended for participation in the project by their teachers or their school counsellors. These children are then further screened by Perach workers to determine their eligibility on socio-economic factors.

The tutors are university students who volunteer for the project. They are generally undergraduates and are about evenly split as to year of study, male or female, and major subject of study. The tutor is meant to meet his or her child regularly over a seven-month period (tutoring sessions usually last for two hours and occur twice a week). In return for involvement in the Perach Project, each tutor is entitled to a financial reimbursement amounting to about one half of his or her university tuition. Finance for this tuition, as well as the day-to-day operational costs of Perach are provided by the Israeli Ministry of Education, the universities, the Van Leer Foundation, and some private benefactors. The goal given to the university students is to help the tutored children to realize their potential. The main aims of Perach are to increase the motivation, achievement and self-confidence of the children through the establishment of a close personal relationship between tutor and child. The underlying philosophy of the project is that these goals can be accomplished by demonstrating that someone outside the child's immediate family cares about them as individuals. Tutors aim at improving the children's motivation and attitude towards learning in addition to assisting them with their studies.

Perach tutors are not trained for their task beforehand nor instructed, other than in a very general sense (ie in the form of printed guidelines), as to how to proceed with the tutorial sessions. However, the tutors meet collectively with their co-ordinator once a month for guidance and occasionally to hear a lecture on a relevant subject. The emphasis of the project is on individualization. The specific needs of the child are taken into account, and decisions regarding the use of the tutorial sessions are left to the tutor/tutee pair. In this way it is intended that a close interpersonal relationship will develop between the university student and the younger child.

The Perach Project has a hierarchical structure. Each university has a co-ordinator who is responsible for 35 to 50 tutors. These co-ordinators are responsible to a manager at each university. This manager, in turn is responsible to a national co-ordinating office based at the Weizmann Institute of Science. The job of the co-ordinator is to maintain good contact with the schools involved (currently over 100 schools participate in Perach), keep a record of tutors, and ensure that they are fulfilling their duties, do the necessary paperwork concerning the times and places at which the tutors and tutees meet, and finally, provide assistance to the tutors. In addition to directing the monthly meetings, co-ordinators are available for individual consultation a number of hours a week. In addition, each university has a standing list of professionals who are prepared to help the tutors in the case of special problems.

Despite the large scale of the Perach Project, relatively little evaluation seems to have been carried out on the effects of the programme on the tutees. Eisenberg *et al* (1981b) evaluated the academic progress of a sample of tutored children when compared to that of a sample of non-tutored children in mathematics, reading (Hebrew), and English. The tutored children were not found to be at an advantage on the tests employed. However, parents, teachers and tutors (when replying in an interview or through a written questionnaire), reported that most of the tutored children were showing progress in school, participating more in class, doing homework more regularly, and developing more positive attitudes towards school. Other research instruments showed that at the end of the year Perach children were more satisfied with their academic performance in school, were more often described as participating in class, and were doing more leisure-time reading than non-Perach children. Given these findings, one might expect changes in the academic functioning of the Perach tutees.

The Perach Project staff felt that explanations for the lack of apparent positive effects might lie in the methodological difficulties that characterize evaluation of a project of this kind. Two problems which arise are: the difficulty of finding a comparable control group, and the suitability of the tests themselves. It may be that the tests employed were not sufficiently sensitive to detect changes taking place in the children. Files kept by the tutor/tutee pairs maintained over the year in which the study took place indicated that, while many tutors worked in the areas of mathematics, reading and English, they often concentrated on basic skills in these areas rather than on the material taught in class. As Perach is an unstructured tutoring project in which tutors decide themselves the content and the specific goals of the activity, the construction of appropriate cognitive tests is bound to be difficult. The experimenters suggest that, in reality, a different test might be needed for each tutored child in order to detect any changes taking place.

An evaluation of the affective impact of the Perach Project was also carried out (Eisenberg *et al*, 1982). The two main affective areas which it was hoped that the Perach Project would influence were the child's motivation and self-confidence. Results of the evaluation indicate that Perach tutors are having a positive influence on the children with respect to attitude towards school. In general, the Perach children are more satisfied with the school context, are more certain of themselves in the classroom, and are spending more time reading than non-Perach children.

(d) Some peer tutoring schemes within higher education

Peer tutoring is found in many forms within higher education. Goldschmid and Goldschmid (1976) offer a substantial review of some of them. Cornwall (1980) summarizes four basic types of peer teaching at undergraduate level. The forms that peer teaching in higher education can take are not limited to Cornwall's categories but most approximate to one of them. They are:

(a) surrogate teaching;
(b) proctoring;
(c) co-tutoring;
(d) teacherless groups.

The examples which follow will be grouped in these categories.

Surrogate teaching

This involves the delegation of responsibility to selected students (often PhD students) of some of the teaching functions normally carried out by academic staff, ie marking and grading, laboratory instruction, leading small-group discussion, and, in a few cases, large-class teaching.

An example of this type of peer tutoring is described by Carsrud (1984). Undergraduate psychology students conduct independent studies which are supervised by advanced graduate students actively involved in their own research programmes. Each graduate has to submit a proposal to their major professor for approval as a course offering. This has to include a description of the proposed joint research project, an outline of the work to be done including major readings, a description of how the project differs from the graduate student's own thesis or dissertation, a statement for ethical review, and the grade-determination procedure to be used by the graduate student. The programme is designed primarily for well-prepared and highly-motivated undergraduates in the hope of interesting them in long term research. It gives them an appreciation of psychological research, a chance to acquire new skills and the opportunity to complete an original piece of research. Once the undergraduates have selected projects, they work with their post-graduate supervisors over three semesters, meeting at least once a week. At the end of the project, the undergraduates have to write reports as if for a journal or conference presentation. The programme is also an educational experience for the postgraduates in that they are able to supervise research projects and pursue wider research interests and opportunites in their specific fields.

Proctoring
In these programmes, students take on the role of individudal (one-to-one) tutors for fellow students who are at a similar or slightly lower stage in a course.

A special form of peer tutoring, 'Proctoring', has been widely used in American universities and colleges (and to some extent within the UK). Proctoring is associated with the personalized system of instruction (PSI) which was developed by F S Keller (see Keller, 1968; Keller and Sherman, 1974). PSI differs from conventional teaching in at least five ways. PSI courses are:

(a) mastery-oriented;
(b) student-proctored;
(c) self-paced;
(d) use printed study-guides to direct students' learning; and
(e) employ occasional lectures to stimulate and motivate the students.

The work is usually divided into topics or units. At the start of a unit the students receive printed guides to direct their work. They then complete the work at their own pace, (with the help of the proctor if necessary), before taking a mastery test on the unit and, on successful completion, moving on to the next topic. The proctors are students who have demonstrated their mastery of the appropriate course material, ie an older student or one who has completed more units in the course than the majority of students. They help other students to follow each unit of study by answering and asking questions about the work. They are also frequently employed to administer and grade the mastery-tests and give feedback. In addition to tutoring tasks, proctors have a responsibility for providing feedback to the course instructor on the general progress of students, and on the reactions of students to the specific course materials and procedures. Interesting examples of such courses using students as tutors are offered by, for example, Bridge (1975) for physics and Hill and Helburn (1981) for geography.

To compare the effects of PSI with those of conventional teaching, Kulik *et al* (1979) performed a meta-analysis of 65 studies of Keller-plan courses. (A meta-analysis is a statistical analysis of a large collection of results from individual studies for the purpose of integrating the findings.) They identified 75 courses whose directors had compared the effects of PSI with conventional teaching on final-examination scores, instructor-assigned course grades, course ratings, course completions, and student study-time. The major findings of the meta-analysis were that PSI generally produces superior student achievement, less variation in achievement, and higher student ratings in college courses, although it does not affect course withdrawal or student study-time in these courses.

Co-tutoring (or reciprocal tutoring)

Much informal co-tutoring takes place within higher education establishments between pairs of students encountering difficulties in understanding lectures or set texts. Many institutions, recognizing the benefits to students of mutual learning, have formalized this type of relationship so that all students have the opportunity to engage in shared learning.

The benefits of co-tutoring were recognized by Goldschmid who examined the idea of the 'learning cell' (Goldschmid, 1970a, 1970b), in which pairs of students tutor one another. Students prepare themselves for the tutoring by reading assigned material and producing a list of questions. During the formal teaching periods, students are randomly paired in 'cells' and then alternately ask, answer, and comment upon each other's questions. A lecturer or teacher is available in the class as a consultant to give advice on subject-matter and tutoring techniques.

Schermerhorn et al (1976) have shown this technique to be successful with high school students as well as with university students. In a comparative study to look at the effect of the learning cell on tutoring in understanding of probability with both undergraduate and high school students, they found that although students learned from preparing assignments themselves, their understanding further improved after the peer interaction component. The discussion with a peer made a positive contribution to the learning process.

Another form of reciprocal peer tutoring has been used by Hendelman and Boss (1986) in the Gross Anatomy Laboratory at the University of Ottawa, Canada. In this programme, involving approximately 65 medical undergraduates, students were asked to give 15- to 20-minute presentations to their peers during laboratory sessions in place of demonstrations by the faculty. Students were assigned material prior to the laboratory period, (to allow them time for preparation), and then gave presentations to groups of six to eight students in the scheduled laboratory period. The students were not graded on their teaching as the presentations were emphasized as a learning activity. However, evaluative questionnaires showed that as a result of demonstrating in the laboratory, students felt that they had a better understanding of their own topic, had acquired the ability to select relevant information and organize material, and had a better attitude towards learning anatomy and more commitment to self-study. In addition, they felt more like students of medicine and thought that they would be more able to communicate with patients.

An interesting use of reciprocal peer tutoring is employed at the University of Michigan, Flint (Selig and Perlstadt, 1985). The sociology department of the university offers a course in medical sociology on which both health care students with little sociology background, and sociology students with no health care background enrol. Course directors noticed that these two groups of students were often antagonistic towards one another, being unsympathetic towards their different perceptions of a problem. The faculty decided, therefore, to implement a programme of paired-observation. In this programme, health care and sociology students are paired together. Each pair observes the same medical encounter and writes an individual report. The two members of a dyad then review each other's papers. In this way, the course organizers intend to establish a clear link between the concepts of medical sociology and health care practice (specifically the parent-practitioner relationship). They also hope to reduce feelings of antagonism within the class by enhancing the appreciation of fellow-students' viewpoints by teaching them to recognize both the strengths and limitations of different backgrounds in observing the same interaction.

Teacherless groups

Further variations of peer tutoring in higher education take place in peer-led discussion groups which meet in the absence of a teacher. The aim of these is to motivate students to become more involved with their own learning, so that they become more active and self-directed in their work. Typically a discussion group has between four and eight members, the teacher assigns questions together with reading references prior to a meeting, and the group will then discuss these during the next class period, sometimes concluding the work with a summary report. Collier (1980) offers a comprehensive review of this type of work; further case studies are offered in Collier (ed) (1983).

Grafting peer tutoring into higher education

What must be obvious from the above examples of peer tutoring in higher education is that peer tutoring has many points of similarity with other activities in which students support one another. This is, indeed, its very strength because innovations are probably most likely to 'take' if they can be grafted on to existing activities rather than coming in as totally unfamiliar ones.

In teacher-training, for example, peer tutoring has for years been used to offer trainee-teachers the school-experience they earnestly seek (see, for example, Gray, 1983; Janowitz, 1971). It is not a great step from such a basic use of peer tutoring to have trainee-teachers with varying amounts of classroom experience *help each other* (see, for example, Nott and Williams, 1980; Riley and Huffman, 1980). (Similar support groups have also been used in nurse education – see Kammer, 1982.) Even school principals have benefited from peer tutoring on in-service courses (Barnett and Long, 1986).

In work designed to offer students greater autonomy in their learning, (see Boud, 1988), there is a spectrum of activities from those which give students greater control over the *content* of their study, such as the School for Independent Study at North East London Polytechnic, to those which offer greater control of the *mode* of study, such as the 'parrainage' (or mutual support) arrangements described by Goldschmid (Chapter 9 of Boud, 1988). There are numerous similarities between activities designed to teach thinking by discussion (Bligh, 1986), through projects which give students responsibility for planning their work in ways which require them to learn from each other (Goodlad,1977), to the teacherless groups described by Collier (1980). The phrase 'peer tutoring' should, perhaps, be reserved for activities in which there is *systematic* and *explicit* use of students to teach students. The point of this brief excursion, however, is to show that there are numerous points of continuity which can, and should, be explored if best use is to be made of the possibilities of peer tutoring within higher education. Chapter 6 returns to this theme.

2.3 Peer Tutoring schemes using children to teach children

Since the early 1960s, in the United States in particular, many tutoring schemes have been developed which use children to teach children.

(a) The National Commission on Resources for Youth Inc 'Youth Tutoring Youth programme'

In 1967, the National Commission on Resources for Youth (NCRY) was founded by a group of social scientists, educators, judges, and businessmen. Its mission was to promote acceptance by the American public of the idea that youth could be integrated into the adult society at an earlier age. The founders of the NCRY were concerned that modern industrial society provides few opportunities for meeting the needs of young people to prepare for adulthood. If young people remain in school, they are insulated from the real world, their dependancy is prolonged, and their assumption of positions of responsibility in the adult world is postponed. Likewise, when young people leave school early they find that there is little need for their services in the world of work, and that they often remain unemployed.

The NCRY began its mission by identifying activities which gave young people the chance to assume responsible roles, particularly ones involving valuable human service which affected other people and could provide significant change in the community. The commission developed and distributed how-to-do-it materials in the form of print, film, and video-tape about exemplary projects in which youth could participate. It also provided training workshops for people from schools and youth-serving agencies. One of the ideas for youth participation which seemed to show most promise of being widely adopted, and subsequently adapted, by established institutions was the Youth Tutoring Youth programme, in which older children teach younger children.

Youth Tutoring Youth has been massively documented and stands as one of the primary models for tutoring. For example, in the summer of 1967, The National Commission on Resources for Youth organized a pilot programme in Newark, New Jersey and Philadelphia in which two hundred fourteen- and fifteen-year-old children who were not achieving well in school, and who had fallen below grade-level in reading, were trained to serve as tutors for elementary-school children from disadvantaged neighbourhoods. In Newark, non-professional negro women of the neighbourhood acted as supervisors of groups of tutors and tutees; in Philadelphia, the programme was more closely linked with the school system. The idea behind the project was not only that teaching is a most powerful learning experience, but also that teaching gives a sense of being needed. The tutors were paid $1.25 an hour for 22 hours of work each week – 16 hours of tutoring and six hours of training. In Newark, 80 tutors were divided into six groups, each group working under a member of the community who acted as tutor-supervisor. The tutors concentrated on one school with four tutees per tutor. In Philadelphia, 120 tutors, in groups of 20 worked at six schools, each group of tutors being supervised by a certified teacher and a young teacher-aide. Tutoring sessions were two hours long, broken by a 'snack' break. The tutoring went on for six weeks.

The results were quite startling:

> In Newark where the tutors were indeed under-achieving youngsters, significant gains were noted in various reading skills, and reading-age equivalents leapt 3.5 years. Philadelphia's tutors, who did not really fit the programme's criterion of demonstrated reading failure – increased one year in their mean reading age equivalency.
>
> No-one expects the Newark tutors really did gain 3.5 years in reading maturity in a mere six weeks. Although some of the gains may have been genuine, there are many explanations – such as test-familiarity and pressures for improvements – for the startling rise. (NCRY, 1968b)

The experiment was valued not because of its quantitative effects (whose statistical significance was not systematically explored), but rather through the qualitative changes which were noted. These included, the care and excitement with which these tutors led their tutees though the lessons; the lessons themselves in which tutors learned alongside their charges; the tutors' sustained interest and participation (only seven out of 200 dropped out – through illness or to go to a better-paid job); the changed aspirations of the tutors and their greater sympathy for classroom teachers; the rapport between tutors and tutees; and the increased use of books by tutors and tutees as the written word came into their lives in a meaningful way for the first time. In short, as a later subjective evaluation of the experiment noted, (NCRY, 1969) 14- and 15-year-old underachieving youths made progress in gaining a sense of work-responsibility, an appreciation of learning, improved literacy skills, and the motivation to work and to stay in school.

Following the success of the 1967 experiment, Youth Tutoring Youth spread rapidly. By the end of 1969 it was operating in over 60 cities; by 1972 it was operating in 450 cities, towns and rural areas. In 1968, the National Commission on Resources for Youth developed a research plan to formally evaluate the impact of Youth Tutoring Youth. Detailed research was carried out on specimen programmes in Washington, DC and Chicago. In brief, the findings were that tutors improved their language skills, achieved a more positive self-image, and developed an increased interest in going to school. The attendance of tutors at school also improved more than that of the non-tutors, although all were being paid. The Youth Tutoring Youth tutees achieved increased reading interest and skills, improved their self-confidence, and showed better behaviour in the classroom. The researchers comment that this finding about improved behaviour in tutees is perhaps one of the more important findings of the study. Having been helped by older children acting as tutors, the younger children started to adopt a helping relationship towards other people – a sort of transfer of tutor role to the tutees who extended this role to their peers. For example, tutees exceeded controls in: doing nice things for the class; helping quiet children to talk more; helping somebody to explain what he wants to say; stopping people from arguing in class; telling somebody that they think he has said something good; telling somebody who is whispering out loud to be quiet.

(b) The New York High School Homework Helper Programme

The High School Peer Tutoring (Homework Helper) Programme trained high-school and college students and employed them as tutors for high-school youths in the disadvantaged areas of New York City. The programme was developed by the New York City Board of Education and Mobilization for Youth Inc during the 1962/3 school year. Albert Deering, the programme co-ordinator reports, (Deering, 1975) that during the years 1963 to 1969 the Homework Helper programme was developed, on a decentralized district basis, in ten local school districts. Over 100 homework helper centers were developed in elementary and secondary schools throughout the city. In 1974/5, the programme employed approximately 1,000 college and high-school tutors who provided tutorial assistance to over 5,000 high-school students during the year. The aims of the programme were as follows:

1. To provide tutorial service to high-school youths in an effort to provide academic skill to participating students in the area of mathematics, reading, and English as a second language.
2. To provide tutorial service in order to improve the study skills and work habits of participating students so that participating students will be able to satisfactorily complete homework assignments.
3. To provide tutorial service in order to improve the attitude of participants towards school and school-related activities.
4. To provide academic models for participants in order to increase the educational aspirations of participating students.

Each homework helper centre consisted of a teacher-in-charge or Master Teacher, one adult para-professional, and a group of approximately 15 college- and high-school tutors. Tutoring took place on Monday, Tuesday, Wednesday and Thursday. Students generally attended two days a week

(Monday and Wednesday, or Tuesday and Thursday). Each tutoring session lasted two hours.

Tutors took part in an orientation programme before the start of tutoring activities. In addition, tutor-training sessions were held once a month on Friday afternoons and daily observations and meetings were held by the Master Teacher. Teachers and adult para-professionals took part in an orientation programme as well as in monthly staff conferences. Tutors were paid an hourly rate which varied with their academic credit-standing and experience in the programme.

Like Youth Tutoring Youth, the New York High School Homework Helper Programme was extensively evaluated: (See Cloward, 1967; Deering, 1975; Institute for Educational Development, 1973; Neckritz, 1971, 1972; Price, 1974; Teaching and Learning Research Corporation, 1970). Cloward (1967) was one of the first people to demonstrate systematically that *tutors* have as much to gain from tutoring as tutees (see Chapter 4).

The New York High School Homework Helper Programme is cited because it shows that, given adequate administration, tutoring can be operated on a very large scale indeed. The key to the success of the city-wide programme seemed to be an effective assignment of roles, (as between Master Teachers and tutors), and an adequate back-up programme of training sessions for tutors.

(c) The Tutorial Community Project, Pacoima School, California

The Tutorial Community Project at the Pacoima School, California differed from the Youth Tutoring Youth projects reported above and from the New York High School Homework Helper Programme in one important respect: it was an attempt to organize an *entire school* on the principle of tutoring. Most Youth Tutoring Youth projects were after-school activities; similarly, although it was one of the largest tutoring schemes, the High School Homework Helper Programme was also an after-school activity. By contrast, the idea of the Tutorial Community Project was to have each child in an elementary school involved in tutoring as part of the normal school instruction.

The Tutorial Community Project was, perhaps, one of the single biggest experiments in peer tutoring. Its initiators, R J Melaragno and C Newmark, have written extensively about their work: (See Melaragno, 1972, 1974, 1976a, 1976b; Melaragno and Newmark, 1969, 1971; Newmark, 1976; Newmark and Melaragno, 1969). Their study was conceived as a seven-year programme taking one grade-level at a time, introducing tutoring gradually, and letting the experience of one year modify the next. Kindergarten children were tutored by seven- and eight-year-olds (grades 2 and 3); primary-grade children were tutored by 8-, 9-, 10- and 11-year-old-children (grades 3, 4, 5 and 6); intermediate- and upper-grades were tutored from a nearby junior high school. The school was organized so that all classes were involved in tutoring and all classroom-teachers were paired for tutoring purposes. 'Sending' classes sent tutors; 'receiving' classes received tutors. Each teacher in the school was a member of a resource group, with seven groups each having seven to eight teachers. Each resource group in turn had a full-time resource teacher with primary responsibility for helping classroom teachers. Each resource teacher had school-wide responsibility for a given instructional area. In addition, 38 parent-aides were used, because one of the objectives of the project was to improve school-community relations. An elaborate scheme of evaluation was built into the programme.

Pacoima was selected for the project because it is a small community in the north east San Fernando Valley area, a 'pocket ghetto', a community made up mostly of blacks and Mexican-Americans surrounded by more affluent white suburbs. An important element of the Tutorial Community Project was, from the start, to involve local residents in planning the scheme. Without attention to this, the Tutorial Community Project staff might well have been perceived as just another group of 'experts' who were being paid enormous salaries, and who would leave the people of the community at the end of the study no better off than they were before. Second, without the attempt to involve the local community, staff would be thought to have no understanding of the needs and goals of black and brown people in general, and of black and brown Pacoima people in particular. Accordingly, the project involved an elaborate scheme of weekend encounter meetings, inter-racial encounters, and so on. The Pacoima experiment is particularly instructive to those planning tutoring schemes; in particular, it shows how critically important it is to attend to the logistics of tutoring.

No great logistic problems arose in the early stages of the project as individual classes were paired with others. Good results were obtained in improved reading scores of pupils involved as tutors or as tutees. However, as more and more classes became drawn into the tutorial scheme, the logistics became increasingly complicated to the point where even the Systems Development Corporation, who were responsible for the research on the project, could not cope with the timetabling problems involved. Added to this, staff changes in the school brought in people who were not fully aware of the original purposes of the Tutorial Community Project and who disliked the way in which the school organization had to revolve around the tutoring arrangements. Added to the strains of these complicated arrangements was inevitable 'battle fatigue' or 'experimental exhaustion'. Changes in curriculum and teaching methods imposed strains on all concerned and even modest changes in school procedure involved everybody concerned in extra work, particularly in the early stages. The Tutorial Community Project was an experiment spread over seven years. It is not surprising, therefore, that the tutoring at the Pacoima School is currently somewhat limited, and the tutorial community is by no means a reality. One of the obvious lessons to be learned from this scheme is to keep tutoring arrangements as simple as possible. Meanwhile, the experiment, apart from the useful experiences of tutoring and being tutored which it provided to pupils, has pointed up a number of important issues. Most important, from the point of view of the present study, is the suggestion that the training of tutors should be institutionalized.

> Given the necessity for tutors to be prepared for their new roles, tutor training needs to become a part of the school day. Students and teachers have to recognise that instruction through tutoring is a key aspect of a tutorial community, and have to make the training of tutors a part of the curriculum. Unless this is the case, tutoring will gradually become an appendage to the 'regular' routine instead of *becoming* the regular routine. (Newmark and Melaragno, 1969)

(d) Paired Reading schemes

Research into the efficacy of Paired Reading began in the mid-1970s with small numbers of case studies in clinical settings. Encouraging observations were reported and since then schemes making use of the technique have developed all over the United Kingdom, although predominantly in the north of England. In November 1983, a five-year project was set up in Kirklees, West Yorkshire, designed to help schools and other agencies develop Paired Reading programmes (Topping, 1987b).

Paired Reading is a strategy which emphasizes fluency in reading, use of context, and comprehension. It is based on a rationale incorporating six converging notions:

1. The involvement of 'significant others'.
2. The child's selection of interesting reading materials.
3. Modelling by the child of a competent reader.
4. The child's control of the feedback of information about the text from the tutor.
5. Positive reinforcement of the child's reading.
6. An increased 'time-on-task' by the well-motivated child.

The children to be tutored are paired with a helper. This could be a child from the same class, reading at a slightly higher level, older children or adults. The pairs then select a book of interest to the tutee (little emphasis is placed on the 'reading level' of the book, as by experience those organizing such schemes have found that children usually select books at an appropriate level). The tutor/tutee pair are then instructed in the Paired Reading techniques: they read aloud from the book together at the tutee's pace. If the tutee hesitates or makes a mistake, the tutor gives the correct word and asks the tutee to repeat it before continuing. If the tutee signals a wish to read alone, the tutor stops reading and follows the story. If the tutee hesitates or makes a mistake while reading alone, the tutor again corrects and then continues to read aloud with the tutee until the tutee again signals a wish to continue alone. The tutor is instructed to praise the tutee whenever the tutee reads a difficult word or sentence, corrects a mistake, or signals a wish to read alone.

Tutors usually need to be trained to use this style of reading, although it seems clear from project descriptions that the technique can be taught within one or two short sessions with children as young as 10 or 11 years of age (see, for example, Pumfrey, 1986; Topping, 1987b; Winter, 1986). Generally, tutors listen to a description of Paired Reading, watch a demonstration with a volunteer child acting the role of tutee, and then practise the technique with their own tutee while the teacher monitors the performance and offers constructive feedback.

Paired Reading has been used primarily with children reading at or below age-level, but who have attained some level of sight reading. These have been mainly junior-school students. One or two schemes involving infant children have been reported, but little work in this area seems to have been done with older children. Between 1984 and 1987, as a direct result of the Kirklees project, 83 junior schools had some involvement in Paired Reading; 2,759 schoolchildren were involved in 185 school-based projects. Tutoring usually occurs for approximately 15 minutes and the optimum length of an intervention seems to be about six weeks.

Reported results are encouraging: accelerated gains in reading accuracy and comprehension are commonly found for children of all reading levels, but particularly those with special needs (Pumfrey, 1986). Winter (1986) found that on post-tests 10- to 11-year-old children were able to read out loud faster, generally made fewer errors, and when a mistake was made, it was more probably self-corrected after involvement in a six-week Paired Reading project. In addition, anecdotal reports of teachers and parents claim that children become more confident and interested in reading as an activity after following this programme. Some teachers observe a change in classroom atmosphere away from competition and towards co-operation and helpfulness.

2.4 Tutoring schemes using adults other than students

Tutoring need not be limited to the use of people already inside the education system; enormous possibilities for enriching education exist if teachers are prepared to draw upon the help of other adults willing to offer their time and talents. Adults who participate in school activities become more aware of the positive functions of schools. Many adults derive much of their knowledge about schools from the mass media, which often offer only a negative image of schooling. By going into schools and working with teachers, older adults appreciate the good things which are happening. The schemes discussed below give examples of programmes involving adult tutors drawn from outside educational establishments.

(a) Project SEED (Special Elementary Education for the Disadvantaged), Berkeley, California

Project SEED used professional mathematicians and scientists from major universities and research corporations to teach abstract, conceptually-oriented mathematics to full-sized classes of disadvantaged schoolchildren. The volunteers usually taught one 40-minute period a day, four or five days a week. The mathematics was presented through the use of a Socratic group-discovery format. Project SEED also used peer teaching techniques (with children teaching entire classes of peers), but its unique feature is its use of very highly skilled mathematicians (PhD level and above) to help schoolteachers.

Project SEED was started in 1963 in Berkeley, California by William Johntz. Within ten years, it had reached approximately 12,000 pupils, most of whom were black children from poor urban backgrounds. Project SEED had three basic postulates:

1. Disadvantaged children do badly in school because they believe themselves to be inferior and because their teachers have low expectations of them.
2. The most effective way to mitigate this feeling of inferiority is to give the children a meaningful experience of success. Project SEED aimed to give children success in a high-status subject (mathematics) with the view of improving their overall interest in study.
3. Children will succeed with advanced algebra if it is taught by somebody highly trained in mathematics using the discovery method of asking questions in class.

Mathematics had particular attractions as the medium for this instruction. First, because it is not a linguistically-based subject, pupils from any background could participate on an equal footing. Secondly, as Johntz (1975) asserts, mathematics, as it is normally taught, has an almost 100 per cent casualty-rate for people from all socio-economic backgrounds because the people who teach mathematics at elementary level, due to no fault of their own, do not fully understand the mathematics they are teaching and consequently do not like it themselves.

Project SEED operated by a process of 'apprenticeship'. Volunteers were drawn from university mathematics departments, major corporations (such as IBM, Bell Telephone Laboratories, Prudential Life Insurance, etc) offering their services free of charge; other highly-trained mathematicians were retained on a part-time basis on a modest salary paid by Project SEED. In every case, schools were offered a free service by Project SEED. A new volunteer would sit in a class taught by a SEED specialist to observe the technique; when he or she felt ready to intervene he or she would do so informally and naturally. After a period of joint teaching of the class, the new volunteer would take over and the SEED specialist moved on to another class and another school. In every case, the regular teacher of the pupils' class was present in the room when the SEED mathematician was working with his or her class. Consequently, Project SEED provided an excellent on-going in-service programme for teachers in whose classes specialists were working. Regular teachers absorbed the mathematics, the Socratic methodology, and new expectations about their disadvantaged children without difficulty.

Project SEED was unusual not only in using highly trained mathematicians to help in schools, but also in using the volunteers to teach entire classes simultaneously – rather than give one-to-one tutoring as is more usual in tutoring schemes. The project has been described in many reports (see Boehm, 1970; IBM, 1970; Johntz 1967, 1973, 1975; Shafer, 1976; Waggoner, 1971). However, because the technique was spread by 'apprenticeship' it is more profitably observed than described. Project SEED is mentioned here because it illustrates an imaginative way in which university-level mathematicians can contribute their skills through volunteer tutoring. Just as the children in whose classes the mathematicians teach were stimulated by the experience, so too the mathematicians found the experience humanly rewarding and also intellectually stimulating.

(b) Senior citizens as tutors

Several schools and voluntary organizations have developed tutoring schemes involving schoolchildren and elderly people from within the community. These have generally been initiated by staff at primary and junior schools who view the older tutors as 'adopted grandparents' for the children (many of whom have little contact with members of the older generation). This type of project has been running in America for a number of years.

One excellent example is Project STEP – Senior Tutors for Educational Progress (Pica, 1976). In Redding, Connecticut, senior citizens were employed to work in schools with adolescents who were experiencing failure due to academic, physical, social or emotional difficulties. The adolescents were asked to join in a project to produce educational materials (learning games, puzzles, books, tape-recordings, maps, and equipment, etc) for elementary-school children. The senior citizens, trained by specialists in the programme, acted as their tutors and helpmates in this work.

The use of senior citizens in this project had many benefits. The senior citizens themselves made friends with young people and with each other, and had the rewarding experience of being part of a school, of being needed, and appreciated. Classroom teachers valued the help from the senior citizens, not least because, unlike parents, the senior citizens represented no threat to the traditional teaching role and, typically, were less critical both of schools and of teachers than parents would have been in the same context. Third, the adolescents valued these 'surrogate grandparents' who could give them more time and personal attention than an overworked teacher.

In Redding, project STEP operated five hours each schoolday, and the senior citizens were asked to commit themselves to the students and to the programme for three days a week. Senior citizens were recruited by advertisements, interviewed by the programme director, and subsequently trained. The interviewing and training were necessary so that the special interests and backgrounds of the senior citizens could be identified; so that any prejudices they might have against youthful tastes (in hair length etc) might be discussed; so that the special needs of the adolescents might be outlined; and so that the fears of the senior citizens about entering schools might be allayed. Pica (1976) reports that the senior citizens were apt to be fearful, anxious to please, unfamiliar with contemporary schools and curricula, and often in awe of teachers. For these reasons, they needed some orientation as to their role in the project.

Typically, on their days in the school, the senior citizens spent four 40-minute periods working with the adolescents; participated in one formal training period, also of 40 minutes; and had a lunch break. Senior citizens worked on a one-to-one basis with the adolescents with whom they were paired through a flexible system of mutual choice. They then helped the adolescents to produce material requested by elementary schoolteachers for helping specific children, or drew on the specific interests of the adolescent pupils with whom they were working. At all times, the regular teacher acting as programme director was available to assist the senior citizens in drawing out the needs, abilities, and interests of each pupil, and in supplying ideas for games, books, and other materials.

Another example is that of Bemidji Elementary School, Minnesota (Doggett, 1976) which set up a reciprocal tutoring project involving sixth-grade pupils and local senior citizens. In teams of four, 60 pupils visited a residential complex designed for elderly people, here they helped with chores, completed art and craft activities and spent time discussing a wide variety of topics with the old people. The elderly people received practical help, the young people received academic help.

Recently similar schemes have begun to emerge in the United Kingdom. For example, in 1988, Community Service Volunteers (CSV) launched the Open Doors Project in Newcastle-upon-Tyne (Parker and Davis, 1988). This scheme recruits and supports older people in voluntary work in primary schools. Model-making, history projects, country dancing, cooking and poetry, mathematics, language games, creative writing and drama are some of the activities older people have shared with children from reception classes to top juniors. The volunteers make a regular commitment to the school and through developing work within the curriculum become a natural part of the children's education. The project (funded by the Calouste Gulbenkian Foundation, the Health Education Authority and Newcastle Education Department) has been so successful in the schools concerned, that additional similar schemes are now being planned.

Staff at another school, Whitecross in Gloucester, have developed a scheme using the reminiscences of senior citizens as a basis for history projects (Rendall, 1987). Although the scheme was initially planned as a means of breaking down the generation gap and fostering mutual respect between the elderly and the young, it soon became apparent that a vast amount of historical and environmental education was taking place through the medium of conversation. Senior citizens are able to convey to children what life was like during the wartime period, what types of work were available when they were young and how the community has changed and developed. These exchanges have provided a springboard for interesting national and local history projects. The elderly people enjoy having a captive audience who show a real interest in their lifestyles, and enjoy sharing their memories. In addition, they get an opportunity to see how schooling has changed and what staff are aiming for in their teaching, this gives them a better appreciation of the ideals of the modern school system and a greater understanding of the young schoolchildren.

In 1985/6, the Institution of Electrical Engineers (IEE) initiated a pilot project, Project UNCLE, in Hampshire (Best and Winfield, 1986). In this scheme, retired engineers in the 55-70 age-group are linked with schools to help pupils with project work in Technology, Electronics, Physics and Craft Design Technology (CDT) lessons. The retired engineers, who can be flexible in the disposition of their time, have greatly helped the teachers. Education is changing rapidly towards open-ended approaches, based upon process skills rather than knowledge, the new examination syllabuses now allocate a great deal of time to project work. This, understandably, has caused problems for teachers inexperienced in setting and assessing projects, for example, in a class of 16 or 20 pupils all working on different projects. The retired engineers in Hampshire have helped with varied projects ranging from relatively simple third- and fourth-year projects to sophisticated competition projects. In this pilot scheme, which had the support of the Department of Trade and Industry, 54 engineers were involved in 38 schools. It is envisaged that Project UNCLE will be available nationally and will cover branches of engineering other than electrical engineering. Already, in the current academic year, 1987/8, 248 electrical engineers are working in 217 schools distributed over 12 geographic regions.

(c) Parents as tutors

Parents who help their children and who are not specialists in the subjects in which they give help may be thought of as peer tutors. They represent perhaps the most massive resource of all to supplement the work of professional teachers.

Many parents are already involved informally in the academic education of their children, but relatively few have much involvement in school-based learning programmes. In the past 20 years, following the Plowden Report (Central Advisory Council for Education, 1967), which made recommendations for action to promote partnership between home and school, there has been a wider acceptance of the principle of parental involvement. However, the practice of encouraging parents to participate in schools has not grown rapidly. Those schools which have encouraged parents to join in activities have often made limited use of the skills and experience which they bring to the classroom. Topping (1986b), in *Parents as Educators*, quotes a large-scale study of the extent of parental involvement in primary schools in the UK, conducted by Cyster *et al* in 1979. Questionnaire returns were received from 1,400 primary schools (83 per cent response rate). The schools were asked to describe any existing programmes involving parents of schoolchildren. It was found that when schools did employ such schemes:

- 78 per cent used parents to help on school visits and outings;
- 65 per cent used them to help with sewing and minor repairs;
- 54 per cent asked parents to help with providing transport;
- 45 per cent involved parents in imparting specialist knowledge and skills within the classroom, usually of a vocational type;
- 36 per cent asked parents to help with craft, cooking, music etc, under teacher-supervision;
- 29 per cent of schools had parents helping in the library;
- 26 per cent involved parents in helping in hearing children read under teacher supervision;
- 22 per cent asked parents to help with sports and school clubs; and
- 20 per cent involved parents helping to dress children after swimming or physical education.

The use of parents as tutors appears to be growing: a more recent study of 500 randomly-selected primary schools in England (Stierer, 1985) found that 53 per cent of the schools had unpaid people assisting with the teaching of reading on the school premises on a regular basis. Forty-five per cent of primary schools in the sample received reading help from parents, either exclusively or with other helpers. Most of the schools in Stierer's study had begun receiving help within the previous ten years, with well over half the schools having received such help only since 1979. Nearly half of the schools using 'other' helpers received help from nursery-nurse students, local sixth-form students considering teaching as a career, higher education students doing community-worked, and trainees on various Manpower Services Commission schemes. Among classes receiving help from parents, the average number of parents working regularly in the class was between two and three. Reading-helpers work for an average of two hours per week, helping five or six children per hour.

Where schools have applied themselves methodically to developing systematic parental involvement in academic learning programmes, they have concentrated mainly in the area of reading. Results of reading schemes involving parents in the UK which have been evaluated have been encouraging. Research has shown that whether parents hear their children read at home is a major factor in reading development, irrespective of other factors such as socio-economic status.

Work done by Tizard *et al*, (1982), on the effects of teacher and parent collaboration in assisting children with reading, did much to fuel the development of reading programmes in Britain. They conducted an experiment based on an earlier survey which showed that in working-class families, children whose parents said that they heard them read at home had markedly higher reading attainments at age seven and eight than children who did not receive this kind of help (Hewison and Tizard, 1980). The experiment in 1982 involved 1,867 children from six infant and junior schools in the London Borough of Haringey. The schools were of similar multiracial character, and occupations of fathers were almost without exception, in the Registrar General's Manual Working Class categories.

Every child in two randomly-chosen top infant classes at two of the schools (one class from each school), randomly allocated from the pool of six, was regularly heard reading at home from books sent by the class teacher. Parents, almost without exception, welcomed the project and agreed to hear their child read at home as requested and to complete the record card showing what had been read. They also agreed to allow a member of the project staff to visit them at home three times each term to hear the child reading to them.

The intervention continued for two years, ie until the pupils had reached the end of the first year in junior school. At the end of this time comparisons were made between the home-tutored children and control classes at the same schools, also with two randomly-chosen classes at two of the schools where children had been receiving extra tuition in reading from a schoolteacher. Results showed a highly significant improvement by children who received extra help at home when compared with control groups, but no comparable improvement by children who received extra help at school from the professional teacher. In addition, gains were made consistently by the tutored children at all ability levels. Parental help reduced the proportion of 'failing' readers (those operating at well below age-level), and improved the proportion of 'able' readers. Follow-up studies a year later indicated that 'parental involvement' children were continuing to perform at a higher level than the control children, even though no further intervention had taken place. Many schools are now also encouraging parental participation in Paired Reading programmes (as described above). Evidence from a multiplicity of schemes employing this technique suggests that parents of children between eight and eleven years of age, experiencing reading difficulties, could bring about considerable improvement in their children's reading abilities.

In a study conducted in Britain by Miller *et al*, (1986), parents of 33 failing readers in one local education authority were invited to participate in a Paired Reading controlled study. Their children were between eight and eleven years of age and had reading delays of at least 18 months. The parents were asked to read with their children using the Paired Reading technique for 20 minutes each night. If possible, for six nights a week. They also agreed to be visited by a project psychologist at fortnightly intervals to be observed in Paired Reading. In all, parents and children were involved in a mean time of 7.6 hours of reading. Although the children and parents were told that the schools would provide a range of books, the majority of materials subsequently chosen by children were books already at home. Some households, bought books specifically for the project or borrowed from local libraries.

After the six-week intervention programme those children taking part in the Paired Reading had made gains of 2.43 months in reading accuracy and a mean 4.63 months for reading comprehension, showing that parental participation in a Paired Reading project produced significant progress. Obviously, the success, or otherwise, of this approach depends on parents being given quite clear and specific advice by teachers on what they are to do, although indications seem to be that parents find the technique comprehensible, easy to learn and fairly easy to apply with their children.

Considering the uptake of reading projects which require parental cooperation, it is suprising that parents have not been included more in programmes to promote spelling, writing or mathematics, other basic skills in which children would benefit from receiving extra practice. Perhaps there is potential for a whole new area of work here. Topping (1986b) also reports a deficiency of programmes to support parents of gifted children who may not have the resources to stimulate them at home.

Other, more specific schemes have been established in schools. Topping describes a project by Molen et al (1983) which trained parents to train their children in safe road-crossing strategies. Hinze (1980) initiated a large-scale programme designed to help parents transmit health nutrition information to pre-school children. Distance-teaching by television associated with written material has also been found effective, and recent work developing problem-solving techniques with pre-school children (Shure and Spivak, 1980) also showed promise.

(d) Adult literacy programmes

The Adult Literacy and Basic Skills Unit (ALBSU) was established by the Department of Education and Science (DES) and the Welsh Education Department on 1 April 1980, to act as the central focus for adult literacy and related basic skills work in England and Wales (ALBSU, 1988). Following on the work of its predecessors, the Adult Literacy Unit (ALU) and the Adult Literacy Resource Agency (ALRA), established in 1975, it aims to:

> develop within the general education service in England and Wales provision designed to improve the standard of proficiency for adults whose first or second language is English, in the areas of literacy and numeracy and those related basic communication and copying skills without which people are impeded from applying or being considered for employment.

It is estimated that at least 13 per cent of adults in the UK have problems with reading, writing and/or basic maths – almost 6,000,000 people. In November 1986, just over 108,000 adults in England and Wales were receiving help with literacy, numeracy or a combination of both, (an increase of approximately 5 per cent on that of November 1985). Of the adults receiving tuition:

- 6 per cent were receiving help individually at home;
- 13 per cent were receiving help individually at a centre;
- 81 per cent were learning as part of a small group.

The Adult Literacy Campaign has attracted tens of thousands of adults volunteering to tutor other adults to read and write. In November 1986, just over 20,000 volunteers were involved in literacy and basic-skill tutoring programmes in England and Wales, servicing 1.7 per cent of the pool of adult students receiving tuition. Over 9,000 new tutors received initial tutor-training and a further 7,000 were given some form of in-service training.

In recent years, the demand for tutors for adults whose first language is not English has grown. In 1986, 37,000 adults were reported as receiving English-as-a-second-language (ESL) tuition, and some 2,500 volunteers were receiving initial training in the teaching of ESL students.

Other volunteer organizations are also implementing schemes to help adults of nationalities other than British who have difficulty with the language. The Home Tuition Scheme (HTS) has been running in Newcastle for 12 years. This programme organizes tutor/tutee meetings in the pupil's home and aims to help Asian women, who are traditionally tied to the home and, therefore, get little practice in using English. The tutor visits the student on her home territory where she is less likely to be overwhelmed, usually for one hour a week, and a regular one-to-one relationship is established. Some sixth-form students have been drawn into the Home Tuition Scheme and find the programme offers them a valuable insight into alternative ideas and practices of other cultures, while giving them the opportunity of helping someone to become more at ease in an equally bewildering culture.

2.5 Peer tutoring for special needs

(a) Peer tutoring involving the mentally and physically handicapped

In recent years there has been a growth in the number of tutoring projects involving handicapped students. These projects fall into three categories: projects in which non-handicapped students act as tutors of their handicapped peers; those in which handicapped students tutor younger similarly handicapped pupils; and reverse-role tutoring projects employing handicapped students as tutors of their non-handicapped peers.

Social rejection and academic deficiency are the two primary problems which face handicapped students. As more of these students are mainstreamed within secondary schools, evidence indicates that their problems are not being solved. Simply initiating contact between handicapped and non-handicapped students does not necessarily reduce the negative perceptions which other students have of their handicapped peers. Mainstreamed handicapped students continue to experience serious social rejection, and intervention strategies designed to improve social acceptance have met with mixed results.

Previous research, conducted primarily with non-handicapped students, has indicated that one of the potential benefits of peer tutoring is that tutors can interact with tutees in a socially structured setting (Osguthorpe, 1984). It is frequently difficult for non-handicapped students to interact with handicapped peers who may lack comparable social and linguistic skills. By initiating a tutoring scheme in which students are given a role in the teaching of handicapped pupils, they are given a natural and rewarding way of interacting with these students. They can quite easily be trained to tutor in reading or linguistics, areas which offer excellent opportunities for inter-personal communications.

In a study by Fenrick and Peterson (1984) designed to develop more positive attitudes towards moderately- and severely-handicapped students, attitudes of sixth-grade students who participated in a peer tutoring programme towards moderately- and severely-handicapped students were compared with those of a control group. Prior to the peer tutoring programme, tutors held more negative attitudes towards their handicapped peers than they did towards their own classmates. After seven weeks of tutoring attitudes of tutors towards handicapped students became more positive and not substantially different from attitudes towards their own classmates.

Much of the research on peer tutoring identifies social and academic benefits which the experience offers the tutor (see Chapter 4). As these are areas in which handicapped students frequently display deficiencies, those working with the handicapped have begun to implement schemes assigning the handicapped student the role of the tutor, either to handicapped or non-handicapped peers.

Shafer *et al* (1984) trained mildly-handicapped children aged five to eight years to facilitate changes in the social interaction skills of similarly aged autistic peers. The non-autistic children were taught how to initiate interaction with autistic pupils, resulting in immediate and substantial increases in the number of interactions between these students. The interactions were also of longer duration than those occurring before the tutoring intervention began. Their work demonstrated that, overall, the autistic students and their peer tutors became more mutually socially responsive as a result of the intervention. In a similar study, Strain (1977) showed that age-peers can be successfully trained to encourage positive social behaviour by classmates who are withdrawn and unsociable.

Projects have also been implemented assigning handicapped students the roles of tutors to their non-handicapped peers, so-called 'reverse-role' peer tutoring (see, for example, Eiserman *et al*, 1987, Osguthorpe, 1984a, 1985a, 1985b; Osguthorpe and Custer, 1982; Osguthorpe and Scruggs, 1986). An important aim of reverse-role tutoring (RRT) is to place handicapped students in a position where they will be viewed as competent teachers holding skills valued by their non-handicapped peers, thus increasing their social acceptance.

Cross-age tutoring offers great flexibility for handicapped students in the secondary school. With careful matching of tutor/tutee pairs, higher-grade mentally-handicapped students can tutor younger handicapped or non-handicapped students in reading, maths or some other content-area (Cook *et al*, 1986). One content-area which has been commonly employed in tutoring schemes with the handicapped is sign-language (Osguthorpe 1984). Osguthorpe, (a pioneer of reverse-role tutoring), points out:

> sign language offers several advantages as a reverse-role tutoring content; some handicapped children are already fluent in sign language, shortening the training time for tutors; it is an unknown topic to most non-handicapped children, allowing the handicapped children to master a cognitive task that is unfamiliar to their non-

handicapped peers; music can easily be introduced into the tutoring setting by allowing tutors to teach their learners to interpret a song and the content of sign language is a strong reinforcement for other language arts instruction for communication-impaired children.

Osguthorpe has conducted a series of research studies in which educable mentally-retarded, learning-disabled, and behaviourally-disordered children have functioned as tutors of sign language (Osguthorpe, 1984b, 1985 and 1986). All of these tutors showed academic gains whilst their tutees learned as well.

In a meta-analysis of available research documenting the effectiveness of handicapped students as tutors of other students, Cook et al (1986) conclude that tutoring is a viable and potentially powerful instructional intervention for special education, and that learning-disabled, behaviourally-disordered and intellectually-handicapped students can function effectively as tutors in academic areas.

(d) Peer tutoring involving the behaviourally disordered

Behaviourally disordered (BD) students typically exhibit deficiencies in both academic and social behaviours. They have poor attitudes towards school, display little interest in academic work, and they usually have poor 'self-concepts'. These attributes often make them a nuisance in class where they show little inclination for work and engage in disruptive behaviour in order to attract attention. The rationale for peer tutoring with such students is straightforward: employing tutors from higher up the school or from a nearby university or college for these children could be an answer to many of their problems, and the problems they pose for the teacher and other class members. A tutor is able to concentrate solely on the BD student and can, therefore, correct inappropriate gestures before they escalate into disruptive behaviour. Indeed, as much of the disruptive behaviour of these students seems to stem from a desire to be 'noticed', it may be that having the companionship of a tutor, they will no longer display such tendencies. In time, these pupils may come to see their tutors as role-models and 'imitate' their behaviour.

In addition BD students will be given the chance to make academic gains. (It is often academic deficiencies in the early years of school life which lead to behaviour problems at a later stage.) In a recent review study, Scruggs *et al*, (1985) examined the efficacy of tutoring programmes involving BD students. Seventeen studies were identified in which the tutees were considered to be exhibiting learning and/or behaviour problems. The subject area most chosen for tutoring was reading, but other content areas were employed including maths, spelling, and social skills. Of these studies, 13 examined the academic gains of the tutees as a result of the tutoring intervention. In all cases, tutees demonstrated measurable gains in the content area being tutored, (regardless of the degree of exceptionality). It seems that peer tutoring of behaviourally disordered students can exert positive effects on their academic functioning.

Peer tutoring can be employed in other ways which might be of even greater benefit to the BD students. Peer tutoring can produce gains in the areas of personal and social development, academic achievement, attitude to school, and self-concept (see Chapter 4 below). To offer to children classified as behaviourally-disordered the chance to gain in such areas, some recent peer tutoring schemes have assigned them the role of tutor.

Scruggs *et al* (1985 *op cit*) reviewing the social and academic benefits of peer tutoring with behaviourally-disordered students, conclude that if content-areas are carefully selected, and there is an appropriate difference in the level of functioning of the tutor and the tutee, then tutoring can have a positive effect on the academic functioning of the tutor.

Shisler *et al* (1986) conducted two studies involving BD students in tutoring schemes designed to increase their social acceptance and reading skills. In the first project ten upper-grade BD students in an elementary school were assigned the role of tutor to 12 younger, well-adapted tutees. Fifteen-minute tutoring sessions were held daily for 12 weeks; the tutors used instructional reading materials from a structured tutoring programme developed by Grant Von Harrison (1980), *Beginning Reading One*. At the end of the 12 weeks, there were significant gains for both tutors and tutees on reading achievement tests. While the statistical analyses of standardized self-esteem tests yielded no significant differences between tutors and non-tutors, parents and teachers reported improved self-esteem to be one of the main benefits of the programme. Both parents and teachers held positive perceptions of the programme and were keen that such programmes should continue and expand.

In the second study, ten BD students tutored a total of 30 gifted peers in sign language. The purpose of this study was to see if the social distance between the BD students and well-adapted peers would be reduced through a RRT programme and to see if the BD students would function in a socially acceptable way as tutors of gifted students. The BD students aged ten to twelve tutored sign language to 30 fourth-grade gifted students. The tutors were instructed in basic sign language for approximately eight weeks. They then began tutoring the gifted pupils for 15 minutes, three times a week (each pupil was tutored once a week), for a total of eight weeks. Following the programme, student attitude questionnaires indicated that the gifted tutees were less likely to respond negatively towards their BD peers than those who had not been tutored. In addition, teachers confirmed that the tutors were able to maintain socially acceptable behaviour. There were no instances when any of the students were removed from tutoring; in fact, tutors were motivated to complete their school assignments so that they would be allowed to tutor.

In a similar tutoring scheme, adolescents with conduct problems were used as cross-age tutors for elementary-school mentally-retarded students (Maher 1982). The tutors improved significantly on social science skills and language art grades and significantly reduced their rates of absenteeism and disciplinary referrals. Furthermore these changes were maintained during a follow-up period. The intervention involved only a small number of tutors (six), but certainly the suggestions arising from the work are encouraging. In another study by Scruggs *et al* (1985), in which 12 BD students acted as tutors to younger students, although anecdotal reports strongly favoured tutoring, all objective measures failed to indicate behaviour change. However, the experimenters point out that in the course of the investigation, 'project staff noted what appeared to be extraordinary behavioural progress in at least two cases, apparently due to the tutoring experience'. Possible reasons for this sort of disparity between psychometric study and direct observation are examined in Chapter 4.

Chapter 3

What Benefits are Expected From the Main Types of Peer Tutoring?

Summary

The organizer of a peer tutoring scheme has to balance the needs of the tutors against those of the tutees. Different educational theories underlie various forms of practice.

Role-model theory suggests that tutors' behaviour will be constrained by what tutees expect of a teacher and that the tutors will thereby come to sympathize with the teacher. Tutees are also more likely to learn from their peers than from their teachers who are perceived as coming from an alien world.

Behaviourist theory asserts that learning will be efficient if every correct response to a question by a pupil is rewarded, the reward acting as a stimulus to make another step in learning. Tutoring offers rapid reinforcement of learning.

Socio-linguistic theory stresses the effect of social upbringing on patterns of speech and therefore of perception. Tutoring offers pupils practice in speech codes with which they may be unfamiliar.

Gestalt theory asserts that learning will occur when the learner 'locates' an item in an intellectual structure. Tutors have to reflect on what they have learned to be able to represent it to their tutees and thereby master it better.

Tutors should benefit from peer tutoring by:

- developing their sense of personal adequacy (role-theory);
- finding a meaningful use of the subject-matter of their studies (Gestalt theory);
- reinforcing their knowledge of fundamentals (Gestalt theory);
- experiencing being productive (role theory);
- developing insight into the teaching/learning process (Gestalt theory).

Tutees should benefit from being tutored by:

- receiving individualized instruction (behaviourist theory);
- receiving *more* teaching (behaviourist theory);
- responding to their peers (role theory and Gestalt theory);
- receiving companionship from tutors (Gestalt theory).

Different types of tutoring seek to achieve these benefits in different ways:

- **same-age peer tutoring – interactive pairs;**
- **monitorial instruction;**
- **unstructured tutoring;**
- **structured tutoring;**
- **semi-structured tutoring.**

Teachers who arrange peer tutoring benefit because:

- **teaching becomes pleasanter;**
- **teachers are freed to do what their training best equips them to do – manage the conditions of learning.**

This chapter offers an analytic review of the major variations of peer tutoring, outlining the educational theories (social and psychological) upon which they are based, and lists the advantages to participants which are sought in each type of system. The sample of peer tutoring systems described in Chapter 2 indicates the range of social and educational goals held by those who organize the schemes. However, important differences of theory and practice may not be immediately apparent from these descriptions. Typically, the organizer of a peer tutoring scheme has to draw a balance between the benefits expected to accrue to the *tutors* and those expected to accrue to the *tutees*.

Youth Tutoring Youth Schemes characteristically emphasized the benefits accruing to both tutors and tutees, with the prime benefit being, perhaps, to the tutors. There are, however, many schemes where the focus is much more firmly on the tutees, with highly-structured programmes of tuition designed to ensure that recognizable cognitive gains accrue to the tutees regardless of the skill (or lack of it) of the tutors. In practice, tutoring schemes emphasizing benefits to the tutors are usually based on 'role-model' theories from sociology or social psychology. By contrast, schemes emphasizing benefits to tutees tend to be based upon the precepts of behaviourist psychology and learning theory, stressing the value of systematic feedback and reinforcement in the learning of the tutees. It is important for the planner of a tutoring project to decide for whom the scheme is primarily intended. Accordingly, this chapter classifies tutoring schemes in various ways to indicate options, referring briefly to the types of theory that apply. It is, in short, a menu of possible pedagogic aims.

3.1 Educational theories underlying the use of peer tutoring

(a) Role-model theory

The peer tutoring schemes and associated research carried out by Allen (1976) used a role-theory framework for the conceptual analysis of tutoring. Allen, who was a social psychologist, observes that social role is a concept used to designate a set of expectations that are associated with a particular position in the social structure, such as father or mother, teacher or student. These expectations always define the rights and duties of any person who occupies the given social position. Role expectations can be specified only in relation to complementary roles: thus, for example, the role of teacher consists of expectations relevant to the complementary role of student. That is to say, there exist certain behaviours appropriate to the social position that an individual occupies. According to role-theory, specific social behaviour adheres to the part and not to the actor. According to role-theory, individuals inhabiting specific roles will feel themselves constrained by the expectations of other people to behave in particular ways. For example, if a child is temporarily given the role of teacher, and put into interaction with younger children, the older child's behaviour will be constrained by the expectations of the younger children. The older child will, thereby, come to sympathize with the role of teacher and perhaps develop a deeper respect for learning.

Many reports of peer tutoring programmes draw upon this model of what happens. For example, Geiser (1969) describes a scheme in which troublesome ten-year-old pupils were given the job of tutoring. Despite the apprehensions of their teachers, the child tutors acted like teachers while they were tutoring, conducting themselves in a dignified manner in the classroom. For most of the tutors, Geiser reports, this led to improved behaviour in their own classrooms and a better attitude towards school work. When treated in an adult and respectful manner, the children responded by behaving in more adult ways. Through adopting the teacher's role, the children developed a sympathy with their teachers and began to co-operate with them.

The precepts of role theory likewise informed the arguments of James S Coleman and the Panel on Youth of the US President's Science Advisory Committee in their report, *Youth: Transition to Adulthood* (Coleman et al, 1974). Unless young people are put into responsible roles, they can never learn responsibility. Coleman and his colleagues recommended, therefore, a variety of expedients, including peer tutoring, by which young people can be given the experience of caring for others.

A second and equally important suggestion from role-model theory concerns the tutee. Communication is inhibited by differences in culture between teacher and learner; it is facilitated if pupils perceive their teachers as inhabiting a similar world to their own. There is abundant evidence from the study of youth subcultures and groupings in schools that many teenagers inhabit cultural worlds far removed from those of their teachers. (See for example Hall and Jefferson, 1976; Hargreaves, 1967; 1972; Murdock and Phelps, 1973; Willis, 1977). Role-model theory would suggest that pupils will learn better from tutors who are their peers, or who are similar in general culture and background, than from teachers who may be perceived as belonging to an alien world. Indeed, there are indications that small-group interactions free from the teacher's presence (even without the added dimension of tutoring) can produce beneficial results (see Barnes and Todd, 1977; Collier, 1983; Slavin, 1981).

(b) Behaviourist theory

A second group of peer tutoring schemes is informed by the theories of behaviourist psychology. In brief, they assert that learning will be efficient if every correct responseto a question by a pupil is rewarded, the reward acting as a stimulus to the pupil to make another step in learning. Programmed learning strategies, such as those of B F Skinner, follow these precepts. The emphasis of tutoring schemes based on these theories is on highly-structured systems of instruction through which the tutee is guided by a tutor who has merely to present materials in suitable order. Several centres have developed tutoring programmes along these lines. For example, D G Ellson and his colleagues at the Unversity of Indiana have produced and tested materials in a variety of schemes (see for example Ellson, 1969, 1971, 1974; Ellson, Barber and Harris, 1969: Ellson, Barber, Engle, and Kampwerth, 1965; Ellson and Harris, 1970; Ellson, Harris, and Barber, 1968; Ellson, Harris, Barber, and Adams, 1968). Similar work has been carried out in the South-West Regional Educational Laboratory by F C Niedermeyer and his colleagues (see Niedermeyer, 1969; 1970; Niedermeyer and Ellis, 1970, 1971, 1972). Another leading proponent of so-called 'structured tutoring', based on the precepts of behaviourist psychology, is G V Harrison of Brigham Young Univeristy, Utah, who has produced teaching materials which can be administered by people who are barely literate (see Harrison, 1969, 1971a, 1971b, 1972a, 1972b; Harrison and Brimley, 1971; Harrison and Cohen, 1969; Harrison and Wilkinson, 1973).

(c) Socio-linguistic theory

Bernstein (1964, 1965, 1970) has argued that the upbringing children receive equips them with different patterns of speech and, therefore, of perception and of ability to perform well in school. Broadly speaking, working class children, he claims, learn a 'restricted code' of speech which is weak in general concepts. By contrast, middle class children acquire an 'elaborated code' which is rich in concepts and which gives them, thereby, an advantage in school. For some time, it was thought that those brought up into a 'restricted code' were limited, unable to switch to an 'elaborated code', whereas those brought up in the 'elaborated code' could switch freely between codes. However, Lawton (1972) showed that working class children do have the potentiality to use the 'elaborated code', but they lack practice and therefore facility. Where they have an open choice in experimental studies (in written essays, sentence-completion tests, or in discussion groups), they tend to use the kind of language which is most familiar to them, and seem, thereby, only to be familiar with the 'restricted code'. However, if forced by a sympathetic interviewer to respond or remain silent, they are able to make some linguistic adjustment – to switch into an 'elaborated code'. Lawton suggests:

> If this is the case then we can be much more optimistic about the possibility of the future education – real education – of such working-class boys. It will clearly be possible, but special techniques will be necessary – perhaps involving more teacher-

individual pupil communication. This would provide yet another argument for moving away from the notion of the secondary school teacher's task being the simultaneous instruction of 30 pupils.

Peer tutoring may be the technique best suited to Lawton's purpose.

(d) Gestalt theory

Gestalt theories of psychology assert that learning will occur when the learner can 'locate' an item in an intellectual structure or field. Either party to a tutoring arrangement, tutor or tutee, can learn by perceiving the way an individual idea relates to a context. Drawing on the work of Bruner (1963), the main proponents of Youth Tutoring Youth argue that children who teach other children have to struggle to make the material meaningful to the learners and thereby have the opportunity of reflecting upon their own learning process. This opportunity may increase the tutors' awareness of the patterns of learning and consequently help them to develop their skill in seeing problems in new and different ways. For example:

> In the cognitive area, then, the child having taught another may himself learn as a result of a number of processes. He receives the material, he has to organise, prepare, illustrate the material to present it to his students: he may try to reshape or reformulate it so as to enable his pupils to learn it and thus himself see it in new ways; he may need to seek out the basic character of the subject, its structure, in order to teach it better, and may thereby himself understand it better. (Gartner, Kohler, and Reissman, 1971: 62)

The educational theories sketched thus briefly are not of course in conflict. They do, however, suggest different priorities and different types of activity in peer tutoring, favouring variously either the tutor or the tutee. It is, therefore, useful to catalogue some of the benefits which different types of tutoring are designed to produce.

3.2 General benefits sought for participants in peer tutoring schemes

Several writers upon peer tutoring have catalogued the benefits sought from the process (see for example Allen, 1976; Bloom, 1976; Cohen, 1986; Gartner, Kohler and Reissman, 1971; Klaus, 1973, 1975; McClellar, 1971; Thelen, 1969). Thelen, for example, was one of the first to indicate the immense potential of cross-age tutoring schemes in, for example, meeting individual needs particularly of pupils who might otherwise leave the school system too early to achieve useful qualifications.

Potential benefits to tutors and tutees can be classified as described below:

(a) Benefits to Tutors

1. Tutors develop their sense of personal adequacy (role theory)

Qualitative accounts of peer tutoring schemes frequently point out the serious and responsible way in which even previously troublesome children go about their tutoring duties (Maher, 1982; Scruggs et al, 1985; Shisler et al, 1986). Role theory would suggest that, by requiring tutors to live up to their responsibilities, peer tutoring is likely to develop in tutors an enhanced feeling of self-esteem. Many children experience nothing but failure in the school system, being, perhaps, backward in academic studies and inadequate in skills (such as sports or fighting) which their peers may value. Even children who are backward in academic terms are competent in skills which more junior pupils are struggling to acquire. Through tutoring, the older pupils can experience the respect and admiration of younger pupils and, provided that the tutoring tasks are properly planned, can enjoy the experience of success in social relationships. Osguthorpe and Scruggs (1986), for example, conclude from a major review and analysis that even special education students can function effectively as tutors if they are trained and supervised appropriately, and that these students experience academic and social benefits by functioning either as tutor or as tutee.

2. Tutors find a meaningful use of the subject-matter of their studies (Gestalt theory).

A problem at all levels of education is that students often do not see the significance of what they are studying because they have no immediate use for it. The relevance of particular subject-matter may not be immediately apparent. University students, no less than school pupils, may assimilate ideas and information simply to pass examinations – an object of limited appeal. Peer tutoring gives tutors a chance to make direct use of the knowledge they already possess and may, consequently, inspire them to seek more of it. Gestalt theory holds that as knowledge is progressively fitted into a structure or field which reflects students' immediate interests, it will be the better assimilated and students will become actively interested in acquiring more knowledge.

3. Tutors reinforce their knowledge of fundamentals (Gestalt theory)

Peer tutoring offers tutors the opportunity to review and restructure the knowledge they possess as they re-present it to students younger than themselves. Teachers often report that only when they begin teaching do they see how their subject area 'all fits together'. Peer tutoring can give anyone who acts in a tutorial role this rewarding revelation. Peer tutoring can also reinforce learning by requiring tutors to recapitulate elementary subject matter. Indeed, peer tutoring has given older children a face-saving way of studying material several years below their expected achievement level. It is deeply humiliating to a teenage child to be sent to, for example, a remedial reading class. However, the same teenager can study a reading primer with dignity, and with personal profit, by tutoring younger children.

4. Tutors, in the adult role and with the status of teacher, experience being part of a productive society (Role theory)

Modern educational practice keeps young people in school well past the point of physical maturity. A common consequence is that teenagers react against the feeling of dependence on adult society and envy those with adult status and those who are part of the productive society. University students, for example, are often dismayed by being merely passive receivers of other people's ministrations and find themselves diminished by being denied responsibility for anyone but themselves. Peer tutoring offers those who act as tutors the experience of being productive, a chance to develop part of themselves which might otherwise atrophy.

5. Tutors develop insight into the teaching/learning process and can co-operate better with their own teachers (Gestalt theory and Role theory)

Peer tutoring offers tutors the opportunity to reflect about the nature and purpose of educating institutions and, thereby, perhaps to articulate their points of agreement and disagreement with teachers. Gestalt theory maintains that, having perceived the overall purpose and shape of an educative process, tutors will be better able to 'locate' their own particular learning activities within it. Role theory stresses that the 'cultural migration' involved in peer tutoring, in which the taught become the teachers, will give the tutors insight into what their teachers are trying to do. Either way, by becoming more perceptive about the intellectual and social objectives of educating institutions, students, be they university students or elementary-school pupils, are more likely to be articulate about their points of agreement and disagreement with their teachers. It does not, of course, follow, that having seen what the teachers are trying to do, students will automatically approve! It is, however, likely that, having experienced the role of teacher, students will be better able to sympathize with and discuss rationally their teachers' aims.

(b) Benefits to tutees

1. Tutees receive individualized instruction (Behaviourist theory)

Behaviourist theory holds that learning increases if every response a learner makes receives instant feedback, and that learning is reinforced if correct responses are systematically rewarded. By giving every learner his or her own teacher, peer tutoring offers all the benefits of individualized instruction, whether or not programmed instructional materials are used.

2. Tutees receive more teaching (Behaviourist theory)

Just as peer tutoring individualizes instruction, so it provides more of that instruction. Because peer tutoring is designed to multiply the effect of the teacher, it can hugely increase the amount of personal instruction going on in a school or college. A single teacher coping with up to 30 pupils cannot hope to give much time to any individual pupil. Peer tutoring increases the number of personal contacts a pupil can have. Even at university level, students may need the chance to talk through problems they encounter in their learning, but do not always need to do so with a professor. A student only a year or two ahead can readily show a fellow-student the way through a problem, indeed, often re-formulating the problem with a student at a similar stage of the course can be sufficient to promote learning.

3. Tutees may respond better to their peers than to their teachers (Role theory, Gestalt theory)

Communication in educating institutions can be impeded by cultural differences between teachers and learners. For example, some young teenagers, immersed in the world of fashion and pop, are unwilling to take as role models older teachers whose cultural milieu differs from their own. These children may be 'reached' by other children a year or two older who, while sharing the same cultural tastes, have also acquired the knowledge and skills which formal schooling offers. Feldman and Allen (in Allen, 1976) found that children are more sensitive than adult teachers to non-verbal cues offered by other children to show that they do not understand something. It seems that the child tutor's cognitive structuring of the lesson is more akin to that of the tutee than is that of an adult teacher. In consequence, the child tutor may be better equipped than the adult teacher both to appreciate what the tutee is likely to have difficulty in understanding and to recognize when the tutee actually does not understand.

Gestalt theory, too, suggests that children will the more readily perceive relevant structures or patterns which make knowledge meaningful if they are invited to do so by people close to themselves in age and cultural outlook. The framework into which new knowledge has to be fitted may be more readily offered by peers than by others.

4. Tutees can receive companionship from tutors (Gestalt theory)

In many schools, it is the practice for new entrants to be 'looked' after by an older pupil who acts as a companion and guide during the first weeks when school customs and rules may be quite bewildering. At universities, too, special activities are arranged in which second and third year students show freshmen around and initiate them into the mysteries of the institution. ('Parrainage' has been used to describe these activities – see Goldschmid, 1988.) These forms of companionship can be adapted to the world of ideas. Just as a child feels more secure in the presence of an older person in a social situation, so the child may feel more secure when similarly guided in an intellectual one. Gestalt theory suggests that learning will be improved if the pattern or field, into which individual ideas and experiences must be placed, is simply, quickly, and painlessly communicated. Peer tutoring, by putting tutees in contact with tutors close to them in age, increases the likelihood of this happening.

3.3 Specific benefits sought from different types of peer tutoring

The teacher planning to use peer tutoring will need to balance the interests of tutors and tutees. Different strategies of peer tutoring are available which emphasize in greater or lesser degree the benefits listed above. Klaus (1973, 1975) has done signal service to our understanding of peer tutoring by highlighting various models. The following classification owes much to that of Klaus, though differing from it in several respects.

(a) Same-age peer tutoring: interactive pairs

Perhaps the simplest form of tutoring involves the arrangement of pupils in a classroom into interacting pairs. Many teachers already organize classes into small groups for various purposes, for example, to share scientific apparatus which may be in short supply. To turn this type of arrangement into tutoring requires only that teachers provide pupils with *tasks of mutual instruction*. For example, children can read aloud to each other. Able pupils can be paired with less able ones – an arrangement which can help less able pupils to keep up with the class, and which gives the more able pupils the chance to reinforce their knowledge as they go along. Again, pupils can be asked to read each other's written work. Those who write books know well that a fresh reader can pick up mistakes in the text which the author may have scanned carefully many times. Or, again, procedures which probably often occur informally can be formally built into the instructional process – one pupil or student being provided with a list of questions with which to test the other, roles being switched from time to time.

Peer tutoring of this sort does not, of course, draw on the benefits of extra knowledge which differences in age and achievement level may offer. It is, however, a useful way for the teacher to multiply his or her effect.

(b) The monitor system

Variations of the old Lancaster and Bell system offer many advantages. As Klaus (1973) has pointed out, the use of older students or pupils as monitors can counteract the frustration associated with unreasonably large classes. The teacher can divide the class into convenient-sized groups and assign monitors to lead the groups in drills or to supervise written exercises. By doing this, the teacher is freed to give full attention to the more manageable number of children in just one group. Similarly, the teacher can focus on each pupil in turn while the other pupils are occupied under the supervision of the monitors.

Schemes of monitorial instruction become increasingly attractive as schools move over to mixed-ability classes. In the United Kingdom, for example, the arguments in favour of the abolition of the ll-plus examination apply *con forte* to the abolition of streaming which divides pupils into ability tracks with almost as much rigidity as the 11-plus examination but without public visibility. In theory, pupils can move between streams in one school; in practice, however, this is not always easy to arrange. Mixed-ability groups offer the merits of fairness, but suffer from the disadvantages of convoys – having to proceed at the speed of the slowest. If, however, ability-groups can be identified within classes, and their work supervised by monitors from higher up the same school, from within the class, or from a nearby college or university, mixed-ability classes should become more manageable.

For many years, monitors have been used in schools to help the teaching staff keep discipline – peer tutoring extends their roles to helping in instruction. The danger, to which Klaus (1973) draws attention, is that teachers will under-use monitors, neglecting to give them teaching tasks for which they are quite fitted even without teacher training.

(c) Unstructured peer tutoring

In unstructured peer tutoring, older students or pupils help younger ones on a one-to-one or one-to-a-group basis with considerable freedom to choose the way in which they present the material to the younger children. The advocates of this method, such as Youth Tutoring Youth, emphasize the benefit to the tutors in having to organize their ideas in order to present them. Tutors who have responsibility for planning lessons in this way quickly find the gaps in their own knowledge and, given the responsibility for a young learner, have an incentive to repair those gaps. The bigger the difference in age and experience between tutor and tutee, the better unstructured peer tutoring is for the tutee. Conversely, the narrower the difference in age and experience, the better unstructured peer tutoring is for the tutor. Teachers planning peer tutoring schemes will need to strike a balance between the advantages to tutees of having well-informed tutors, (such as university students), and the manifold advantages to pupils who act as tutors of having tutees near to themselves in age and experience.

(d) Structured peer tutoring

Structured peer tutoring involves the use of closely-controlled procedures, sometimes even programmed texts. Those who advocate it stress the benefit to the tutees of the procedures. Tutors with even very limited education can be effectively trained to administer highly-structured material. For example, tutors are trained in specific procedures for teaching the recognition of letters and words, the use of phonic rules and context in word analysis, and the reading of words, sentences, and paragraphs with comprehension.

Ellson (1974) describes how a sequence of teaching is carefully planned to provide each child with a systematic coverage of the basic reading skills. High standards of performance are maintained so that the aquisition of each skill is mastered before instruction in the new skill is started. The procedures which the tutors follow are highly individualized so that each child progresses at the fastest rate of which he or she is capable. Through highly-structured material, each child progresses quickly through that which is easy and spends time only on those skills which he or she finds difficult.

By minutely detailed instructions, the tutors guide the tutees in their handling of the material. Characteristically, the tutors feed their tutees with it in small steps, reinforcing correct responses with praise and reinforcing material without comment after incorrect responses have been given.

Structured peer tutoring diminishes the responsibility of the tutor for organizing the material and is, consequently, tutee-orientated. Although there is little evidence systematically comparing the reactions of children to acting as tutors in structured and unstructured schemes, the advocates of structured schemes maintain that their tutors receive considerable satisfaction from seeing the progress of their tutees. There is evidence (see Chapter 4) that structured tutoring is more effective than unstructured in giving benefit to tutees. More importantly, teachers may more readily accept structured peer tutoring because the content of the teaching is more closely in their control. However, care is needed not to exploit tutors in structured schemes and to find ways in which the tutors can benefit from their experience. Accordingly, a further strategy of peer tutoring may commend itself.

(e) Semi-structured peer tutoring

Semi-structured peer tutoring tries to combine the advantages of unstructured peer tutoring with those of structured peer tutoring. In semi-structured peer tutoring, the tutors guide their tutees through a carefully-planned syllabus, but are free to amplify it and modify it in the light of their own interests and skills and those they discover in their tutees. For example, in the scheme known as 'The Pimlico Connection' (see Chapter 5), university students of science and engineering use worksheets prepared by the class teachers which guide the pupils step by step through a series of experiments. The students are able to present additional experiments and problems to pupils who move rapidly through the prescribed material, and to give additional help to those who find the worksheets difficult.

Tutors, be they university students or schoolchildren, are likely to feel insecure if given a completely free hand in presenting material to tutees. Likewise, tutees are likely to suffer from any incoherence or ignorance on the part of the tutor. For these reasons, some structuring of the material seems desirable. However, if the benefits to tutors outlined in Section 3.2 above are to be achieved, the tutors must have some part in the planning of the lessons and in discussing the overall teaching strategy.

3.4 Benefits to the teacher in using peer tutoring

Peer tutoring can help teachers in two major ways: first, by making the day-to-day business of teaching pleasanter; second, by freeing teachers to do what they are trained to do.

Peer tutoring makes the teacher's job pleasanter in several ways. First, pupils who are mobilized as tutors perceive their teachers as colleagues and an atmosphere of co-operation, rather than antagonism, can readily develop.

Second, peer tutoring makes it possible to reduce a large class into smaller groups with the consequent reduction in the strain of controlling large numbers of pupils simultaneously. Discipline problems are thereby reduced because it is a common experience of teachers that pupils often create trouble to get attention. Peer tutoring gives children a great deal of attention, whether as tutors or as tutees, and offers the possibility of reducing discipline problems.

Peer tutoring can also free teachers from routine tasks – giving them more time on the really difficult tasks for which teacher training is needed. The most important of these tasks is planning the curriculum and arranging conditions in which pupils can learn. These are tasks of such immense complexity that the role of the teacher is enhanced, rather than diminished, by the use of peer tutoring procedures. Far from replacing teachers, peer tutoring emphasizes their unique professional skills. Planning the overall strategy of a course of instruction requires understanding of the purposes and philosophy of education, knowledge of the intellectual and emotional needs of children, and training in a wide variety of techniques of adjusting what is to be learned to the interests and capabilities of learners. With tutors helping individuals in the class, teachers have the opportunity to give more thought to these wider concerns.

In addition, peer tutoring requires skills of management and organization. Indeed, in the early stages, it is likely that teachers will have to put more time and effort into their teaching than they would were they to teach classes by more conventional methods. It requires extra effort to reduce a complex curriculum to activities in which non-professional tutors can take part. The intellectual difficulties of doing this should not be underestimated. However, if the effort is made, the satisfaction of arranging peer tutoring can be immense.

Assessment is another task which requires the skills of a trained teacher. It is the responsibility of the teacher to define planning objectives so that the teacher, the pupil, and outside observers can all see whether pupils have achieved what is expected of them. Untrained personnel involved in peer tutoring may know specific facts; what they are unlikely to know is how to test, systematically and reliably, whether these facts have been understood and assimilated by learners.

Peer tutoring should been seen by the teacher as one of the many techniques available in education. Some teaching objectives may best be achieved by conventional chalk-and-talk methods; others by project methods based on pupils' use of the library etc. Peer tutoring is not intended to supplant other methods of teaching, but rather to complement them. It will always remain the teacher's responsibility and prerogative to decide which technique is desirable for given subject matter and a given group of pupils.

Chapter 4

How Effective is Peer Tutoring?

Summary

In recent years, there has been a movement in the evaluation of educational innovations away from psychometric study towards softer styles of evaluation. Psychometric (or 'agricultural-botany') methods are not wholly suitable for the evaluation of tutoring, not least because they involve a tension between the requirements of action and research. However, much of the American research on tutoring was carried out during a period when 'agricultural-botany research' was fashionable. Provided that they are treated with caution, the findings of such research are informative.

Studies are cited which show, for example, that:

- schoolchildren can improve their own reading skills by tutoring;
- tutoring appears to be more effective than an equal amount of normal classroom instruction;
- improved verbal skills from being tutored can persist in time;
- hour-for-hour, tutoring in mathematics seems to be as effective as teaching by trained teachers;
- tutors can improve their self-concepts by tutoring;
- pupils who are tutored in reading or mathematics improve more than control groups who are not tutored.

Factors that seem to affect the success of tutoring are reviewed. In particular:

- (not surprisingly) tutors who are trained are more effective than tutors who are not trained;
- tutees do better when learning materials are highly structured.

Non-professionals can be effective agents of instruction; through peer tutoring, they can also acquire skills themselves.

These are the two major findings of the research on peer tutoring.

While not setting out to be a comprehensive review of research on peer tutoring, this chapter reports some of the best-accredited findings about peer tutoring and points out their significance for those planning peer tutoring schemes. The chapter also examines some of the problems of planning evaluative research so that organizers of peer tutoring programmes who may wish to evaluate their schemes (as is recommended in Chapter 7) may the better judge what is possible and desirable.

For those seeking further information, Allen (1976), Kalfus (1984), and Klaus (1975) give critical reviews of research in the field. Feldman, Devin-Sheehan and Allen (1976) and Paolitto (1976) discuss some of the methodological problems involved. Wilkes (1975) has compiled a comprehensive, annotated bibliography on peer- and cross-aged tutoring and related topics for the period up to 1975. Cohen *et al*, (1982) offer a major meta-analysis (ie, statistical analysis of the large collection of results from individual studies for the purpose of integrating the findings).

4.1 Problems of conducting research on peer tutoring

In recent years, the evaluation of educational innovations has gone through what Kuhn (1962) would call a shift of 'paradigm' from 'hard-nosed' to 'softer' styles of evaluation. Parlett (in Tawney, 1976) and Hamilton (1977) have called the former 'the agricultural-botany paradigm'. Hamilton, for example, argues:

> The most common form of agricultural-botany type evaluation is presented as an assessment of the effectiveness of an innovation by examining whether or not it has reached required standards on pre-specified criteria. Students – rather like plant crops – are given pre-tests (the seedlings are weighed or measured) and then submitted to different experiences (treatment conditions). Subsequently, after a period of time, their attainment (growth or yield) is measured to indicate the relative efficiency of the methods (fertilisers used). Studies of this kind are designed to yield data of one particular type, ie, 'objective' numerical data that permit statistical analysis.

There are obvious deficiencies in this type of procedure when applied to real-life situations as opposed to 'laboratory situations'. One might, for example, wonder whether people's behaviour in social psychology laboratories has any resemblance to their behaviour elsewhere! For this reason, Cohen *et al*, (1982) included in their analysis only studies that had taken place in actual elementary or secondary school classrooms in reporting on quantitatively measured outcomes in both tutored groups and non-tutored control groups.

With peer tutoring, it is particularly hard to control all the variables which might affect the outcome of a tutoring experiment. For example, one might expect the effectiveness of a peer tutoring scheme to depend on, among other things: the duration of the scheme; the frequency of the peer tutoring sessions; the length of time spent by tutors and tutees in each lesson; the difference in age and educational experience of tutor and tutee; the amount of training in tutoring techniques received by the tutors; and possibly on differences in sex, socio-economic class, ethnic background etc, of tutors and tutees. Such factors, singly or in combination, make it extremely difficult to compile any definitive list of crucial variables affecting the outcome of peer tutoring.

Many reports on peer tutoring schemes are simply compilations of subjective, qualitative, observations which may be valuable for suggesting research hypotheses, but which cannot, however, be the sole basis for major administrative decisions affecting the education of young people. It was partly as a reaction against vague, intuitive, or simply ill-informed educational policies that the 'agricultural-botany' style of research became fashionable. Ralph Tyler, one of the leading proponents of the 'agricultural-botany' approach, was research adviser to the National Commission on Resources for Youth, one of the major proponents of peer tutoring in the United States. Indeed, much of the American research on peer tutoring (some of which is cited in this chapter), was carried out under the influence of Tyler and in a period when 'agricultural-botany' research was fashionable. Provided they are treated with caution, the findings can be informative.

A typical research design in this 'agricultural-botany' or psychometric paradigm compares an experimental group with a control group comparable in every respect to the experimental group. For example, the experimental group would be tutored; the control group would not be tutored but might be exposed to an equivalent amount of conventional teaching. Tests would be applied before the experiment to both groups and again after the experiment to both groups.

If all conditions are maintained the same, it is probable that any difference in the subsequent educational behaviour of the experimental group and control group could be attributed to the presence or absence of peer tutoring. Such would be a 'classical' experiment in social psychology. Statistical procedures are applied which indicate whether a given finding is likely to have occurred by chance or to be attributable to the experimental treatment. (For example, the studies which are quoted in Section 4.2 of the present chapter list findings where a 0.05 level of confidence, or better, was required by the researcher for one or more of the experimental outcomes. This indicates that the effect would have occurred less than five times in one hundred by chance.)

It is not surprising that the research resulting in findings at such high levels of statistical confidence was either very closely controlled in terms of the number of participants or, if the numbers were large, was extremely expensive to carry out. One might almost state as an axiom that the more complex a peer tutoring experiment is (in its responsiveness to social needs), the less amenable it is to psychometric research. To put this more starkly, one might say that the certainty with which a proposition about peer tutoring can be stated is inversely related to the complexity of the scheme. Educational decisions, like political decisions (if indeed one can disentangle them from each other) must be taken in situations with a high degree of uncertainty.

This uncertainty can be compounded from pressure for projects to 'succeed'. For example, Cohen et al (1982: 243) show that studies described in dissertations reported smaller effects than did studies described in general articles or published documents. In the research literature on peer tutoring, there may well be occurring a phenomenon which is attracting increasing (merited) attention, namely publication bias (Begg and Berlin, 1988). In brief, the phenomenon is that studies which do not produce statistically significant positive findings may not be written up. Of studies which *are* written up, it is possible that only those reporting positive treatment effects achieve publication – producing a bias in the published literature away from negative findings and in favour of the experimental treatments. The possibility of publication bias is yet another reason for treating findings with caution.

In this chapter, we have drawn upon unpublished theses with good experimental designs as well as on journal publications to attempt to give the most balanced possible picture of the effects of peer tutoring.

(a) Choosing an appropriate method of evaluation: tensions between action and research in evaluating peer tutoring.

Chapter 7 recommends that anyone organizing a peer tutoring scheme should provide for some sort of evaluation. It may be helpful, therefore, at this stage, to highlight some of the difficulties of combining effective action with effective research. The organizer of a peer tutoring scheme will no doubt wish to evaluate the scheme if only to iron out bugs, to help participants to see what they are achieving, and to make improvements for future years. This type of evaluation may be very different from academic research whose intention may be to test theories about human behaviour. It is important to keep this distinction in mind, because an inappropriate choice of evaluation methods can be frustrating and irritating to everybody. The research which is cited later in this chapter was mostly carried out with an academic rigour which may not be necessary, possible, or even desirable for the informal evaluation of a peer tutoring scheme. This is is not to say that academic evaluation should not be carried out; indeed, one of the attractions of having social science undergraduates acting as tutors is that they can carry out such evaluations as part of their college work. The following points indicate some of the contrasts of approach.

First, volunteers can be a nuisance in research! Lucas *et al* (1968) show that volunteers tend to be highly-motivated to succeed; their presence in a tutoring scheme may bias results unless precautions are taken to compare the achievements of volunteer tutors with those of a control group of volunteers who were not allowed to tutor. However, a co-ordinator of a peer tutoring programme may wish to make it voluntary (because experience suggests that reluctant tutors can be a curse), and may gratefully use any volunteers available.

Second, for purposes of research it may be necessary to hold time constant. Ideally, one should compare x hours of tutoring contact with x hours of another activity by a control group. However, the co-ordinator of a peer tutoring scheme may wish to do whatever possible to stimulate out-of-hours contact between tutors and tutees. One of the main attractions of peer tutoring is that it allows valuable human relationships to develop. It would be contrary to the spirit of the idea deliberately to prevent tutors and tutees from meeting each other as often as possible.

Third, in research one might wish to keep tutor groups and control groups apart so that the effects that one is trying to measure for the tutor group do not 'bleed' across control groups by the interaction of members of tutor group and control group outside the experimental framework. In practice, however, one might wish to *maximize* the interaction between those who have taken part in peer tutoring and those who have not so that any beneficial effects (on learning, social attitudes, etc) will spread throughout the educating institution.

Fourth, to determine the long-term effects of peer tutoring on participants, a research design might require that one keep tutors and tutees who have taken part in tutoring isolated from their peers for as long as possible, to avoid 'contamination' which might blur the measurable effects of the peer tutoring. In practice, this is impossible, even if desirable. Participants in educational experiments cannot go around in cocoons and, for the reasons given in the preceding paragraphs, one would not wish them to.

Fifth, a research design might require one to maintain peer tutoring conditions constant over a long period of time. For example, if one wished to check the effects of sex, age-difference, socio-economic class, ethnicity, etc, one might wish to have the same tutor/tutee pair in a peer tutoring scheme interacting over a long period of time. In practice, this is extremely difficult to achieve. It is necessary for a programme organizer to respond to emergencies – timetables, absences of tutors or tutees through illness, etc. In any case, the organizer of a peer tutoring scheme may wish to improve the scheme as it goes along, switching tutors and tutees as compatability of personality becomes apparent.

Finally, a comprehensive research design on peer tutoring might require one to vary systematically combinations of tutors and tutees to see which combination is most effective. Again, however, the organizer may wish to maximize the chances of all participants doing well and will probably vary conditions to maximize the benefits to tutees and to see that tutors are not exploited.

For these and other reasons, the best arrangement may be for the organizer of a peer tutoring scheme to invite in, if possible, independent evaluators whose task would be, by participant or illuminative or other means, to provide helpful information about how the scheme can be kept running smoothly or improved. It may, however, not be possible to combine this type of evaluation with that which would be suitable for advancing, for example, our theoretical understanding of how children learn.

(b) The particular problem of measuring attitude change

Role theory (see Chapter 3) suggests that the attitude and behaviour of children who act as tutors will be subtly modified: by living up to the role of teacher, they may come to accept a more positive attitude to learning, and, perhaps, develop enhanced self-esteem. One of the most striking features of the literature on peer tutoring is the overwhelming testimony to the efficacy of tutoring in this respect from subjective and qualitative studies, but the relative paucity of demonstrations of attitude change in psychometric studies. This apparent conflict of findings merits comment.

The qualitative literature is full of testimonies about the beneficial effects of being a tutor on the self-concept, attitude-towards-school, and general motivation of those who take part. Weiner *et al* (1974), for example, describe increased self-confidence and improved self-image among children who took part as tutors in a small-scale scheme. In particular, a 12-year-old girl with a history of traumatic rejection and regressive reactions, who had been a frequent client of social workers, tutored a younger child. In her tutorial sessions she showed none of the nervous, erratic behaviour which she displayed elsewhere and the new, more mature behaviour began to be transferred to other situations.

Dallas (1974) describes an experiment in which both 'high-risk' 13- and 14-year-old pupils (who were slow to learn, poorly-motivated, had poor self-concepts, or who were discipline problems) were given ten hours of training as tutors and then given the chance to take part in tutoring in an elementary school. Their teachers reported that these 'high risk' pupils performed remarkably well. Their classroom behaviour and their attitude to school improved; they responded dramatically to a situation which gave them status and which involved them in meaningful activity where their ideas were valued. They also produced remarkable results with younger children coming from similar backgrounds to theirs.

Balmer (1972) trained nine-, ten-, and eleven-year-olds as tutors for special-education-class pupils. Throughout the tutoring which ensued, the pupil-tutors were invited to express their feelings on tape. Balmer gives a composite of tutor feeling concerning the tutoring programme indicating that the tutors felt worthy; found they could do something good; felt needed; found they could be strong with their minds – not with their fists; experienced success.

Bean and Luke (1972) used under-achieving 14- to 17-year-olds in a tutoring scheme. These teenage pupils were used to help in reading classes in an elementary school. The teenagers were characterized by limited self-expectancy, school records of Ds and Fs, placement in low-ability class sections, social problems, record-folders filled with referral reports, disciplinary reports, and copies of letters to parents, and general disillusionment with remedial-reading programmes. Through careful planning of lessons, they came to enjoy the experience of tutoring, the one-to-one situation with a younger child providing a learning experience that was reassuring for older and younger pupil alike. By assuming the role of teacher, these teenagers assumed responsibility and thereby developed their self-esteem.

Geiser (1969), in an article called 'Some of our worst students teach!', describes the boost to the self-esteem which older pupils enjoyed when asked to tutor younger ones. A typical case was that of James, a 16-year-old known as a trouble maker. In class, he taunted the teacher, called out provocative remarks, cracked jokes, and played the clown. He was removed from his class and was asked to tutor a nine-year-old child in reading. He did this for an hour a day in one corner of the younger child's classroom during the regular reading period. The younger child was also a behaviour problem. James's behaviour in his regular classes did not change; but teachers, who saw how responsibly he behaved when tutoring the younger child, changed their attitude towards him. Teachers saw that, when treated in an adult and respectful way, James, like other children of his age, could respond by behaving in more adult ways.

In a similar tutoring scheme, Lane et al (1972) used disruptive 13- and 14-year-olds to teach reading to eight- and nine-year-olds. Both older and younger pupils made marked gains in their reading. However, more interesting was the change in behaviour of the older pupils. Reports submitted by guidance counsellors and teachers describe such behavioural changes as the following: greater motivation to achieve in class; less hostility towards authority figures; exhibition of more mature and goal-orientated behaviour; fewer anti-social acts in school.

Le Boeuf (1968) mobilized 13-year-old children to give science demonstrations to seven-year-old children. The effect on the older pupils was remarkable. Le Boeuf reports that they became so interested in learning their science well enough to teach it, that in a short time they were familiar with the whole unit of study and were able to divide it into parts for each member of the tutoring group. Not only did they learn the subject matter of their science, but they also became enthusiastic about the business of learning.

Other qualitative studies report how taking the role of tutor improves the self-concept, attitude-to-school, and general academic motivation of the tutors (see for example Barnett, 1973; Bell et al 1969; Fleming, 1969; Gabron and Lawler, 1971; Ramirez, 1971. Others (eg, Holcomb 1971) describe the beneficial effects of younger people coming into contact with older ones through peer tutoring.

In view of the accumulation of positive testimony as to the value of peer tutoring in improving the attitudes of tutors, it is remarkable how unsuccessful psychometric research has been in supporting this evidence. For example, Edler, (1967) studying the use of students as tutors in after-school study centres in Oakland, California, testified to the value of using students as tutors, but found no general change of psychological posture of the tutors. Olsen (1969), in a doctoral study, found no significant difference between tutored groups in most measures of attitude change, but did note significant improvements in language achievement and arithmetic achievement for the tutored groups and, as so often, reporting by teachers of positive changes in self-confidence and self-esteem of participating pupils. Foster (1972) used ten-year-old pupils to tutor seven-year-old ones with a view to studying the attitudinal effects on the older ones of taking part in tutoring. Her analyses of the structured data showed no statistically significant differences among experimental and control groups.

Bremmer (1972) used 12- and 13-year-olds to teach reading, mathematics, and language to six- to nine-year-olds. She was unable to detect any significant changes in attitudes as a result of the tutoring programme. However, almost half of the tutees showed greater academic progress with the tutors than without, and 60 per cent of the tutors improved their attendance records.

In another experiment, Swenson (1975) studied the effects of peer tutoring in regular elementary classrooms on sociometric status, self-concept, and arithmetic-achievements of slow-learning tutors and learners in a special-education resource programme. His measures showed no significant differences between experimental and control groups as a result of tutoring.

Freyberg (1967) studied the effect of participation in an elementary-school informal tutoring scheme (or Buddy system) on the self-concept, school-attitudes, and behaviours and achievements of ten-year-old negro children in Harlem. He was unable to show statistically any increase in positive self-concept or in school-attitude and behaviour of those who took part. Interestingly, an overwhelmingly large proportion of children who acted as elders in the scheme felt that the experience had been helpful to them and all of them substantiated their replies. Some of the replies, Freyberg notes, were most thoughtful and insightful:

> 'I learned how to help and understand others', 'I learned how to take care of little children and help them with their problems', and 'it helps me with some things I have forgotten from second grade', etc.

Although no measurable differences were found between the experimental group and the control group, the experimental group judged the 'Buddy scheme' to have been a success for them and felt that they had had a most favourable school experience. Commenting on the apparent non-appearance of an improved self-concept, Freyberg suggests that a non-projective measure of self-concept might be subject to conscious defensive control. One can never be sure that one is getting at children's real self-concepts as opposed to their ideal self-concepts.

In their meta-analysis, Cohen *et al* (1982: 246) too note that although the literature contains anecdotal reports of dramatic changes in self-concept brought about by tutoring programmes, quantitative studies do not support these reports. What can be the explanation for the disparity?

Nearly everybody who has observed peer tutoring in action is astonished by the responsible way in which even troublesome teenagers can settle into the role of tutor and apparently derive satisfaction from it. Perhaps one reason for the disjunction between the qualitative observations of what happens and subsequent psychometric attitudinal research is that attitudes and behaviour change only *while the tutoring is in action*. Perhaps, too, as Meyers (1972) suggests (also having failed to demonstrate significant attitude changes), attitudes are more resistant to change and require more time to modify than achievement. Similarly, Bar-Eli and Raviv (1982) attribute the relative lack of demonstrable attitude change in their scheme in Israel to the short duration of the project. Typically, peer tutoring occupies only a small part of a child's day. Only during the few hours or less a week set aside for tutoring does the child experience the positive feelings of being wanted, being respected as an adult, and taking part in a meaningful activity; the rest of the time, school goes on much as usual.

The remainder of this chapter reviews some of the findings concerning tutoring from conventional psychometric research; Chapter 5 offers additional evidence about one particular scheme.

4.2 Summary review of some 'classic' studies

The studies reviewed in this section are some of the 'classics' of the research literature on peer tutoring. They used control groups to assess the effectiveness of tutoring, and all report findings at the 0.05 level of significance or better.

(a) Cloward (1967) 16-year-old schoolchildren improve their reading skills by tutoring

Cloward evaluated the New York Homework Helper Programme (see Chapter 2). He assessed the effect on both tutors and tutees of taking part in a tutoring scheme designed to improve reading. Two hundred and forty 16-year-old children were paired with two hundred and forty nine- and ten-year-old children. The study was intended to analyse the effect of tutoring on both tutors and tutees in: (a) their reading achievement; (b) their school marks and behaviour; and (c) their attitudes and aspirations. The pupils were randomly assigned to experimental and control groups. The 16-year-old tutors were given about 16 hours of training to familiarize them with the programme. They also received two hours a week of training during the programme. The first few tutoring sessions were used to establish rapport; the tutors and tutees played games or talked. Thereafter, the tutees took homework to the sessions and asked for help. A typical tutoring session involved some 30 minutes of homework, 30 minutes of reading, 15-30 minutes of games and recreation, and 15 minutes of refreshments, role-taking, etc.

In the pupil experiment, experimental and control groups were tested at the beginning of the programme and five months later. The final sample for analysis included 356 experimental subjects and 157 control subjects. Some of the pupils attended the programme two afternoons a week (four-hour group) and others only one afternoon a week (two-hour group). Results were statistically significant only for the four-hour pupils, who showed an average of six months' reading improvement in five months' time and the control pupils showed only three-and-a-half months' growth during the same period. Cloward comments that the growth-rate of the controls (or, more precisely, their progressive retardation), approximates to the average rate for Puerto Rican elementary schoolchildren in the area. Thus, the four-hour experimental group not only arrested their retardation but began to catch up. Cloward concludes that tutorial assistance results in significant reading improvement providing that the assistance is given as often as four hours a week for a period of 26 weeks.

No significant differences were apparent in the measurement of pupils' attitudes and aspirations. Cloward suggests that this may be due to the insensitivity of his measuring instruments.

In the tutor experiment, 97 experimental subjects and 57 control subjects remained after attrition. Before and after data were obtained on reading skills, school achievement, attitudes, and aspirations. Tutors in the experimental group showed significantly more improvement than the tutors in the control groups on three sub-tests concerned with reading comprehension and study skills. The score difference was significant well beyond the 0.001 level of probability. Cloward comments that when the total standard-score means are translated into grade equivalences, in the seven months between pre- and post-study administrations, experimental subjects show a mean growth of 3.4 years as compared with 1.7 years for the control subjects. That is to say, 16-year-olds acting as tutors showed twice as much reading improvement as the controls. As with the pupil experiment, the tutor experiment failed to show any significant changes in attitude and aspirations.

Cloward's experiment was one of the earliest and remains one of the largest in scale. Its findings are remarkable. Cloward concludes that the average high-school student can learn to be an effective tutor. Contrary to expectation, high-school tutors proved effective with pupils who were severely retarded in reading. These are the youngsters who, because of their unsatisfactory progress in school, have come to expect ridicule, rejection, and continued failure. Teachers tend to regard these children as a burden and are reluctant to spend class-time in an attempt to teach them the basic skills that they failed to learn in earlier grades. In a tutorial situation, where emphasis is placed on individual attention and basic-skills training, these youngsters can make substantial progress in reading.

The major impact of the Homework Helper Programme was on the tutors themselves. Cloward suggests that the high reading-gains made by tutors, many of whom were reading far below grade-level at the beginning of the study, raised the intriguing question of whether high school drop-outs might successfully be employed as tutors, not just to help under-achieving elementary school pupils, but to improve their own academic skills.

(b) Klosterman (1970) Tutoring is more effective than an equal amount of normal classroom instruction

Klosterman carried out a tutoring experiment using students of education as tutors and nine-year-old pupils as tutees. Four elementary schools in a district of low socio-economic classes were selected to study. One school was randomly selected as the control, and the three remaining were the experimental schools.

In the three experimental schools, the pupils were (a) either tutored individually, (b) tutored in a small group, or (c) given normal classroom instruction. The tutors were students majoring in elementary education.

Reading tests were administered before and after the experiment which took place four days a week during a six month period. The tutoring sessions, half-an-hour in length, were part of the subjects' daily reading instruction.

The findings of this study are remarkably interesting and important. First, Klosterman showed that subjects receiving individual tuition made significantly greater gains than those having an equal amount of classroom instruction. Secondly, Klosterman showed that pupils tutored in *groups* also made significantly greater gains than pupils receiving an equal amount of classroom instruction, *and* that being tutored in groups was as effective as being tutored one-to-one.

The education students were not studied by systematic tests. However, they discussed their reactions to the experiment and claimed that it had helped them in many respects: for example, by increasing their awareness of children as individuals, by giving them experience with lesson plans, and actual teaching before going into the classroom, by having an opportunity to try out ideas presented in the teaching methods course with a small group before using them in a larger classroom.

(c) **Shaver and Nuhn (1971) Improved verbal skills from tutoring persist over two years**

Shaver and Nuhn studied the effects of tutoring on under-achieving 9-year-olds, 12-year-olds and 15-year-olds in Utah. One hundred and eighty-one pupils were tutored by women between the ages of 21 and 55 who had responded to advertisements in the local press and who had been found suitable by interview.

The aims of the study were to assess both the short- and long-term effects of tutoring on: (a) the STEP (Sequential Tests of Educational Progress) scores of the pupils; (b) their Grade Point Averages – a measure of achievements at school; and (c) to compare the effectiveness of one-to-one tutoring with one-to-three tutoring. Control students stayed in the regular classrooms and were known only to the project director. The results at the end of the first year were:

(a) the improvement of the tutored groups in reading and writing was significantly greater than that of the control group;
(b) the one-to-one tutoring ratio was not significantly better than the one-to-three ratio; and
(c) the tutored groups' Grade Point Average scores were significantly better than those of the control groups.

The tutoring was ended after one year, but post-tests were applied again two years afterwards. The results were:

(a) the tutored groups had significantly better STEP scores in reading and writing than the control groups; and

(b) the improvement did not differ significantly between the one-to-one and one-to-three tutoring groups.

The interest of this study is that, not only were non-professionals effective in tutoring pupils, but also that tutoring in groups was as effective as tutoring on a one-to-one basis. More importantly, the effects of being tutored persisted over time.

(d) Bausell, Moody, and Walzl (1972) Hour-for-hour, tutoring is as effective as teaching by trained teachers

Bausell *et al* carried out an experiment to compare tutoring and classroom instruction while controlling total instructional time and teacher differences. Mathematics instruction was substituted for reading to increase the generalizability of the results.

The tutees were 72 nine-year-old and 48 ten-year-old pupils drawn from 29 classrooms in three elementary public schools in a northern Delaware school district. The pre-test was administered three days prior to the experiment to all the students in the 20 classrooms. The tutors were two separate groups of teachers – ten second-year-level elementary education majors and ten fourth-year-level student teachers. The second-year student teachers had not received formal instruction in teaching methods or curricula, nor had they done any practice-teaching. The fourth-year-level student teachers had completed all required courses in teaching methods and curricula as well as the majority of the teaching experience given by the practice-teaching programme. The tutors were randomly assigned to the classrooms. Within each school, each student-teacher was randomly assigned two low-, two medium- and two high-ability tutees of the same grade-level. The two groups of teachers (second-year-level and fourth-year-level) were assigned the same number of tutees representing each grade-level in each school.

Under both tutoring and normal teaching conditions, pupils were taught 16 items by the same teacher and were subsequently tested. The results showed that tutoring produced significantly greater achievement than normal classroom instruction. Teacher experience and training did not, apparently, affect the overall achievement of the objectives.

As the authors comment, although absolute instructional time was kept constant for the two conditions, effective instructional time was probably not equivalent. In one-to-one instruction, a teacher can make instruction more relevant to an individual pupil's needs. This is precisely the strength and virtue of tutoring.

Russell and Ford (1983) report similar results from a study using reading as the subject of study.

4.3 Effects on tutors of taking part in tutoring

(a) Cognitive gains

As has already been indicated, schoolchildren taking part in tutoring as tutors have much to gain in doing so. Cloward (1967) showed how 16-year-olds could improve their reading by tutoring. Similar results have been obtained by, among others, Erickson and Cromack (1972); Hassinger and Via (1969); Kelly (1972); Kenemuth (1974); Mainiero et al (1971); Morgan and Toy (1970); and Strodtbeck and Granick (1972).

Allen and Feldman (1973) showed that ten-year-old children learned better by tutoring in science-related topics than by studying alone.

(b) Affective gains

As indicated in Section 4.1 above, affective gains have been more difficult to measure systematically than have cognitive ones. Improved self-concept has been particularly difficult to demonstrate. For example, several researchers found themselves unable to show statistically significant differences between tutors and control groups in terms of self-concept in experiments – see, for example, Dobbs (1975), Kenemuth (1974), and Mohan (1972). However, several important studies have shown that tutoring does improve self-concept. Haggerty (1970) compared the effects of being a tutor and being a counselee in a group on self-concept and achievement-level of under-achieving adolescent males. Reviewing literature which reports that low self-concept and under-achievement are related, he set out to improve both self-concept and scholastic success by having subjects tutor and participate in group counselling. Studying 68 under-achieving high-school children who were also behaviour problems, he placed the subjects in one of three treatment groups or in a control group. The control group received no treatment. The members of the counselling group participated in weekly group-counselling sessions. The members of the tutoring group tutored at a local elementary school twice a week. Finally, the members of the tutoring and counselling group participated in group counselling and tutored. The results of the study demonstrated that under-achievers have a lower self-concept and attitude towards school than do other pupils. The treatment effected some changes in the subjects. The subjects in the tutoring group and the tutoring and counselling group improved their self-concept and became more accepting of themselves. Their attitude to school, however, did not change. The pupils in the counselling-only group did not enjoy any improvement of self-concept, nor did their attitude to school change in a positive direction. Finally, the control group' self-concept and acceptance of self did not change and their attitude to school dropped significantly.

Robertson (1971) studied the effects of a tutoring experience on the self-concepts of 93 ten-year-old pupils who tutored 31 six-year-old pupils in the attainment of sight words. He used two experimental groups and one control group, holding tutoring sessions 30 minutes per day, three days per week, over a two-month period. Using a semantic-differential test to assess the self-concepts of the ten-year-olds, Robertson showed that the ten-year-old tutors developed significantly different and more positive self-concepts from those in the control group. Robertson suggests that factors contributing to this result were that the student tutors were thoroughly trained in tutoring behaviours and procedures, given a well-defined set of tasks to accomplish, given demonstrations on how to employ the programme materials, provided with opportunities to role-play the part of the six-year-olds and that the ten-year-olds were informed as to the purpose and expected outcomes of the programme, and directly involved in the evaluation process.

Mainiero et al (1971) report that the children who took part as tutors in the Ontario-Montclair tutoring scheme improved their self-concept. Likewise Strodtbeck and Granick (1972) report that the teenagers in the Youth Tutoring Youth Project also improved their self-concept. Yogev and Ronen (1982) demonstrated increases in empathy, altruism, and self-esteem among 16-year-old Israeli tutors.

Dobbs (1974) reports an improvement in attitude-to-school on the part of 13-year-olds who acted as tutors to elementary school pupils. Mohan (1972) reports that seven to ten-year-old pupils who took part in peer tutoring in mathematics increased their academic motivations.

Despite numerous subjective, qualitative reports of improvement in classroom behaviour, only Mainiero et al (1971) report systematic differences in classroom behaviour between tutors and control groups. However, several research studies show that being a tutor in a peer tutoring scheme improves the tutors' attitude to teacher and to school (see Hassinger and Via, 1969; Mohan, 1972; Strodtbeck and Granick, 1972).

Fenrick and Petersen (1984) found that peer tutoring is also an effective system for the development of more positive attitudes towards moderately and severely handicapped students. After interacting with handicapped students for three 30-minute sessions for each of seven weeks, sixth-graders found them to be more capable than did the control group, and expressed more willingness to be involved with the handicapped students in school and social settings.

4.4. Effects on tutees of being tutored
(a) Cognitive gains
That those tutored can benefit from taking part in tutoring schemes is one of the best-authenticated findings of all. Many studies have shown how reading skills of tutees can be significantly improved by contact with non-professional tutors. For example, Erickson and Cromack (1972) showed how eight-year-olds improved when taught by 12-year-olds; Hassinger and Via (1969) showed that teenagers and their nine-, ten-, and eleven-year-old tutees both improved their reading skills in a six-week experiment; likewise Mainiero et al (1971) showed that the reading skills of 13-year-old tutors and their nine-, ten- and eleven-year-old tutees improved in a similar scheme; Morgan and Toy

(1970) showed very strikingly (significant at the 0.01 level) reading gains of seven- to ten-year-olds who were tutored by 13 to 17-year-olds in a four-month programme working in 20 to 40 minute periods three times a week; Shaver and Nuhn (1968) showed that non-professional women, given minimal instruction, were able to improve the reading skills of 9-, 12-, and 15-year-old children; Snapp *et al* (1972) showed reading gains for six-, seven-, and eight-year-olds tutored by ten- and eleven-year-olds over eight 20-minute periods four times a week; and Strodtbeck and Granick (1972) showed reading gains for the children who were tutored in the Youth Tutoring Youth schemes.

Interestingly, the most consistent reporting of cognitive gains for tutees (particularly in reading) comes from the proponents of 'structured' tutoring. The rival merits of 'structured' and 'unstructured' tutoring are reviewed below. Meanwhile, suffice it to note that reading gains for tutees have been noted by, for example, Ellson *et al* (1968); Harris (1967); Klosterman (1970); McCleary (1971); Robertson and Sharp (1971); and Tannenbaum (1968). The meta-analysis by Cohen *et al* (1982: 246) also found that structured tutoring programmes produce especially strong effects.

Similarly, tutees have shown improvement in mathematics in tutoring schemes. For example, Horan *et al* (1974) show that 17-year-old tutors were successful in improving the mathematics achievement of adolescents through twice-weekly tutoring sessions over a period of six weeks. Likewise, Fitz-Gibbon (1975) showed how nine-year-olds improved their mathematics achievement when tutored by 14-year-olds daily for three weeks.

Mevarech (1985) showed that fifth-grade children achieved higher gains in mathematics when student teams were employed (using his Student-Team-Mastery-Learning, STML, strategies) than when taught in a more traditional style. Webb (1982), examining peer interaction and learning in co-operative small groups in mathematics, found that giving and receiving explanations was positively related to achievement.

(b) Affective gains

With tutees as with tutors, it has been difficult to show by psychometric research the way in which self-concept improves. However, Mainiero *et al* (1971) showed that the self-concept of nine-, ten-, and eleven-year-olds improved when they were taught by 13-year-olds. Strodtbeck and Granick (1972) showed that the self-concept of the tutees in the Youth Tutoring Youth Programme also improved. Scruggs and Osguthorpe (1986), studying tutoring interventions within special education settings, found, to their surprise, that the chief attitudinal gains were to the tutees. They suggest that this may be because the tutees feel more positive about themselves because of the attention they received from the tutors.

Mason (1975) showed that eight-, nine-, and ten-year-old high-achieving pupils who were tutored by university students improved their self-concept. However, the same tutors failed to produce an improvement in self-concept among low-achieving or average-achieving students.

Academic motivation can also apparently be improved through peer tutoring. Abidi *et al* (1976) report positive results from 13- and 14-year-old tutees who were given instruction in science from university engineering students. Interest in science increased for tutored groups compared with control groups and high-ability pupils showed preference for learning science by experiment after being tutored. In a similar study, Goodlad *et al* (1978) report that tutoring by university science and engineering students improved pupils' attitude to their science teachers and to their school.

Horan *et al* (1974) show that teacher-rated attitudes and classroom behaviour of tutees improved following maths tutoring by 17-year-olds. Mainiero *et al* (1971) and Strodtbeck and Granick (1972) describe how classroom behaviour of tutees improved after tutoring.

4.5 Factors which seem important in making peer tutoring effective

Feldman *et al* (1976) have given a comprehensive critical review of research concerning factors which seem important in making tutoring effective. We are able to confirm their findings from an independent study of literature and from visiting administrators, teachers, and researchers concerned with tutoring schemes in many parts of the United States.

(a) Pairing of tutors and tutees

Cloward (1967) found no significant effects of different sex pairings, nor did Mevarech (1985). Cicirelli (1972), studying the effect of sibling relationship on concept learning of young chldren taught by child-teachers, found that irrespective of the sex of the younger child: (a) sisters are more effective than brothers when teaching younger siblings; (b) sisters are more effective in teaching younger siblings than girls are in teaching younger unrelated children; (c) boys tend to be more effective in teaching unrelated younger children than in teaching younger siblings; and (d) boys and girls do not differ in effectiveness as teachers of unrelated younger children.

Drawing on extensive experience of running tutoring schemes, Mainiero *et al* (1971) recommend that an older boy should never be matched with a younger girl, but no research findings are offered in support of this suggestion. Topping and Whiteley (1988: 21), in a study of Paired Reading involving tutors and tutees of the same age, found that male-male tutorial combinations did particularly well all round. Female-female combinations were good for the tutees but poor for the tutors. Mixed-sex combinations were good for the tutors but poor for the tutees. Other previous findings were not confirmed in this study, and Topping and Whiteley comment that the common supposition that same-sex pairings are more effective than mixed-sex pairings is clearly a gross over-simplification, for the interactions between sex-combinations and outcomes for tutors and tutees are more complex than previous research has been able to show.

Following an experiment in peer tutoring with aggressive and withdrawn children, Lazerson (1980: 157) recommends that teachers should try to behaviourally mix and match. The hyperactive child should be paired with the withdrawn child; two aggressive or two hyperactive children should not be put together.

For all practical purposes, and within the limits of what can be achieved in classrooms, the preferences of children should, perhaps, be the best guide. Where this has been explicity studied, (see Szynal-Brown and Morgan, 1983), children seem to prefer to be paired with children of the same sex.

(b) Age and ability differences

The intellectual gains of tutors are, for obvious reasons, likely to be greatest when they tutor children as near to their own achievement-level as possible. The tutors benefit by systematically reviewing, for purposes of tutoring, subjects which they have recently studied.

Common sense would suggest that tutees would benefit most from having tutors somewhat advanced in age and achievement, who could bring a wider range of knowledge and experience to bear on the tutoring. Some research by Linton (1972) supports this notion. Linton studied the effects of grade-displacement between student-tutors and students tutored, and examined the effects of 13-year-old pupils being tutored by respectively other 13-year-old pupils, 15-year-old pupils, and 17-year-old pupils. His findings indicate that 17-year-old tutors were more effective for helping 13-year-old tutees who were making Ds and Fs in eighth-grade mathematics than 13- or 15-year-old tutors. However, the gains were evident whoever did the tutoring. In like manner, Sharpley et al (1983), in a study of peer tutoring in mathematics, found that the achievement-level of tutors had negligible effects on the general mathematics-achievement gains of the tutees. The matter is by no means clear-cut.

Fitz-Gibbon (1980: 18), offering conclusions from a study of peer tutoring in inner-city secondary schools suggests that cross-age tutoring is more promising than same-age tutoring. She suggests that age-differences between tutor and tutee from two to four years result in feelings of responsibility on the part of the tutors. Likewise, Bierman and Furman (1981), in a study of the effects on attitude of being assigned the role of tutor or tutee found that in same-age tutoring the positive effects of peer tutoring on the tutor were, to some extent, counterbalanced by less-desirable effects on the tutee. An emphasis on the competence of the tutor results in positive attitudes for the tutor, but the tutees tend to have more negative attitudes when assigned the role of tutee by chance. The problem is also highlighted by Cohen (1986).

One solution to the dilemma is to structure programmes so that students switch roles periodically. But Bierman and Furman (1981) suggest that cross-age tutoring arrangements may be seen as more equitable than same-age tutoring interactions and, hence, might produce more positive attitudes for the tutees.

Much depends upon what is being studied and at what level. For complex subjects, it seems likely that greater age and experience in tutors are useful – with the teaching of basic skills, this is less important. However, even with complex subjects, an age/experience gap of three years seems quite adequate. Anslow *et al* (1977), for example, were able to show that sixth-formers were as effective as university undergraduates in increasing the interest in science of 13- and 14-year-old-pupils. Likewise, in a study of tutoring in reading skills, Thomas (1972) found that there were no significant differences between the ability of sixth-grade tutors and college tutors to develop comprehension skills and improve oral reading performance on the part of second-grade tutees.

Where tutees are under-achievers and where basic skills are being taught, the age and achievement of the tutors is much less important. For example, Lombardo (1975) compared the effects on retarded tutees of adult non-retarded tutors, non-retarded pupil tutors, and retarded pupil tutors. His findings suggested that the retarded peers were no less effective than normal peers or adults as tutors of this population. Likewise, Kane (1977) showed that peer-tutor implementors, programmed and supervised by an instructional manager, were as effective as teachers of the learning-disabled in implementing a computational mathematics programme. Again, Levine (1975) showed that low-achieving ten-year-olds (fifth-graders) when placed in the role of student tutor could make a positive difference in the mathematics achievement of seven-year-old (second-grade low-achievers).

(c) Number and duration of tutoring sessions

Cloward (1967) suggests that tutoring sessions four hours a week for 26 weeks are more effective than two hours per week of tutoring for the same number of weeks. Tutoring schemes seem to have been effective over periods from two weeks to two years. There is some evidence that the longer the tutoring can go on (numbers of weeks in the year) the more visible the result. However, in a study designed to address this specific issue, Fresko and Eisenberg (1985) found that there did not appear to be an advantage of two years of tutoring over one year. Greatest gains of achievement tended to occur during the first year of tutoring. Osguthorpe (1985: 23) makes a similar observation suggesting that an effective tutoring programme will show positive results with as little as ten total hours of tutor-tutee contact. There is support for this figure from an early doctoral study by Harrison (1969) who found, with maths tutoring by college students, that there were statistically significant differences between tutored and control groups after ten hours of tutoring but not when the same groups were re-tested after 50 hours of tutoring.

There is little hard evidence about the optimal length of tutoring sessions. However, Fitz-Gibbon (1976) mentions that tutees found 20 minutes too short and 40 minutes too long; this accords with common practice which is to keep tutoring sessions to about 30 minutes' duration.

(d) Number of tutees per tutor

Klosterman (1970) found that one-to-a-group was as effective as one-to-one. Anslow *et al* (1977) confirm this. Similarly, Shaver and Nuhn (1968) found that one-to-three tutoring was as effective as one-to-one. These findings suggest that 'monitorial' instruction is likely to be as effective as the more expensive pairing of tutors and tutees. However, the technical efficiency of these arrangements must be balanced against the evident satisfaction both tutors and tutees get from developing personal relationships with each other.

(e) Training of tutors

Conrad (1975) found that the tutees of trained tutors did significantly better than the tutees of untrained tutors. What is at issue is not the presence or absence of full-scale teacher-training. As we have seen above, Shaver and Nuhn (1968) showed that training of this complexity had little influence on the effectiveness of tutoring. Rather, it seems highly desirable that tutors should be given some elementary instruction in how to proceed. Niedermeyer (1970) made the not unsurprising finding that behaviours of trained and untrained tutors differed with respect to basic instructional principles. Niedermeyer constructed an observation-scale to assess instructional behaviours related to the objectives of a structured tutor-training programme. Briefly, these behaviours were as follows:

(a) tutor engages pupil in non-instructional, friendly conversation;
(b) tutor verbally confirms correct pupil responses;
(c) tutor praises the pupil;
(d) tutor tells or shows the pupil the correct response when the pupil is incorrect;
(e) tutor, after displaying behaviour as in (d) then elicits correct response from pupil before going on;
(f) tutor following non-responses to his intitial question or direction, repeats it in different words; and
(g) tutor avoids attempting to elicit correct response by prompting.

In his study, he observed that tutors who had been trained in these techniques used them, whereas those who had not been trained in them did not use them.

Frager and Stern (1970) had 11-year-old children teach kindergarten-children pre-reading techniques. Some of the tutors were taught a procedure which consisted of five basic steps: defining goals, defining obstacles, specifying alternatives, identifying consequences of specific alternatives, and making selections among alternatives. The kindergarten children were divided into three treatment groups: children taught by tutors who had received a few simple suggestions about tutoring; children taught by tutors who had been given the training outlined above; and a third group used as a control. In each case, the sequence of lessons for the kindergarten children was carefully programmed. Both groups of children who received tutoring, whether by the first or the second method, were superior to the children who did not receive tutoring. The results were also marginally in favour of the children tutored by trained tutors.

Shafer *et al* (1984) trained mildly-handicapped peers to facilitate changes in the social interaction skills of autistic children. They found that implementing some simple training procedures resulted in immediate and substantial increases in the peer tutors' interactions with the autistic children. Similar findings are resported by Strain (1977).

Some form of induction is necessary if non-professionals are to assist professional teachers through peer tutoring. It is no part of the intention of tutoring to replace professional teachers, nor is it sensible to expect totally untrained people to be effective tutors without any training in the necessary skills. The training of tutors is one of the most interesting and rewarding tasks for professional teachers.

(f) Structured versus unstructured tutoring

As indicated in Section 4.4 above, there is a good deal of evidence that the interests of tutees are best served if the tutoring is structured. In structured tutoring, the instructional materials are closely-programmed so that the interaction between tutor and tutee is focused on specific, detailed tasks. Little discretion may be left to the tutor about how to present material to the tutee. Several studies have specifically compared structured and unstructured tutoring in terms of the achievement of tutees. For example, Harris (1967) carried out an experimental comparison of two methods of tutoring – programmed versus directed (corresponding to structured and unstructured). Harris studied the effect of the two types of tutoring among six-year-old pupils in 20 schools in Indianapolis. In a 13-week experiment, he compared tutoring with no tutoring, programmed tutoring with directed tutoring, and one session of programmed tutoring with two sessions of programmed tutoring. In brief, his findings were as follows:

(a) tutoring does facilitate reading achievement;
(b) programmed tutoring is more effective than directed tutoring (ie, structured more effective than unstructured); and
(c) two sessions of programmed tutoring are more effective than one session.

All these findings were significant beyond the 0.01 level.

In a similar study, Ellson *et al* (1968) carried out a field-test of programmed and directed tutoring. They, too, found that programmed tutoring was more effective than directed tutoring (structured than unstructured). They commented on the satisfaction of all participants, supervisors, tutors, and tutees, in unstructured schemes but say, rather tartly, 'but the favourable impression of directed tutoring as a teaching procedure was not supported by evidence that it improved reading achievement'.

The personal satisfaction to be derived from tutoring does not depend on a completely spontaneous relationship between tutor and tutee. It is more likely to develop when a personal relationship emerges from common involvement in a specific task. Robertson (1971) both trained his ten-year-old tutors and used structured materials. The ten-year-old tutors developed improved self-concepts, although they were using structured materials. Nor was it the training which improved their self-concepts, for, Robertson reports that subjects who were trained to tutor but were withheld from tutoring, and the control subjects did not develop significantly different and more positive self-concepts. Further support for the structuring of tutoring is offered by Medway and Lowe (1980).

Fitz-Gibbon (1977b: 22) suggests that the positive effects of tutoring may derive simply from the fact that tutors spend more time 'on task' than students in regular classes. Nevi (1983) makes a similar observation. Greenwood (1984), comparing teacher- versus peer-mediated instruction and noting the positive effects of tutoring, observes that peer tutoring produces a greater variety of academic responding (ie writing, reading aloud, academic talk) than normal teacher procedures. If this concentration and refinement of time-on-task is the essence of peer tutoring, then it is likely that structuring of the content will amplify the effects, if only in avoiding unprofitable chat between tutors and tutees. It seems clear that if both tutors and tutees are to benefit from peer tutoring, some structuring of the content by the co-ordinator of the programme is both necessary and desirable.

4.6 The cost-effectiveness of peer tutoring

Most research to date has concentrated on seeking to validate the effects of peer tutoring on tutors and tutees. Nowadays, however, it is becoming increasingly important to explore the cost-effectiveness of activities. In this regard, it is important to note that a recent study by Levin *et al* (1987) found peer tutoring to be more cost-effective than computer-assisted instruction (CAI) in improving the mathematics and reading performance of elementary schoolchildren, and both peer tutoring and CAI were more cost-effective than reducing class-size or increasing the length of the schoolday. Likewise, Ellson (1986) has provided powerful evidence that properly managed independent-study supplements to conventional teaching in general, and programmed peer tutoring in particular, can vastly improve the productivity of teaching.

Chapter 5

A Specimen Peer Tutoring Scheme: 'The Pimlico Connection'

Summary

In the scheme known as 'The Pimlico Connection', students from Imperial College of Science, Technology and Medicine, University of London, help to teach science, mathematics, and craft design technology (CDT) in local schools. At the time of writing (September, 1988), since the scheme began in 1975, some 750 tutors have given over 17,000 hours of instruction to over 8,600 pupils.

Research indicates that all parties to the arrangement benefit:

- pupils: 63 per cent find lessons easier to follow;
- teachers: 69 per cent find lessons more enjoyable with tutors present;
- tutors: 96 per cent get useful practice in communicating scientific ideas.

Some 52 per cent of the tutors are thinking of going into teaching. Of these, 64 per cent find tutoring useful in helping them to make up their minds whether or not to do so. Apart from offering tangible benefits to pupils, teachers, and students on a day-to-day basis, tutoring seems to attract into teaching more students than it deters.

The chapter describes the origin and evolution of 'The Pimlico Connection' project, highlighting factors which other people running inter-institutional projects may wish to adopt and adapt.

5.1 The origin of 'The Pimlico Connection' project

The focal object of 'The Pimlico Connection' is to make science, mathematics, and craft design technology (CDT) more enjoyable for the school pupils who act as tutees.

The secondary objects are, however, almost as important: namely, to offer university students realistic practice in communicating ideas, and to do something to take the strain off teachers in schools near to the university.

(a) Early experiments

In origin, 'The Pimlico Connection' was an experiment designed to examine the feasibility of students acting as tutors in comprehensive secondary schools. Funded by the Leverhulme Trust, and phased over three years, the original study was designed to discover whether peer tutoring involving undergraduate tutors would be more effective than ordinary classroom-teaching in increasing pupils' interest in science.

Phase 1, (Abidi *et al*, 1976) compared classes with tutors with classes without tutors at the Pimlico School, London, (from which the project derives its name).

Phase 2, (Anslow *et al*, 1977) examined the effect of varying the ratios of tutors to pupils and also sought to determine whether any beneficial effects of peer tutoring would be maintained a year after the Phase 1 tutoring had ended.

Phase 1 and Phase 2 were carried out as projects within the university studies of the undergraduates; they were conducted as classical social psychology experiments.

Phase 3, (Goodlad *et al*, 1978) continued the classical experiment at the Pimlico School, and extended the tutoring to the Stockwell Manor School and the Holland Park School. Phase 3 also reviewed the opinions of the participants in the tutoring – pupils, students, and teachers. Such surveying of opinions has been carried out on an annual basis in subsequent years.

As a form of Study Service, (see Chapter 6), 'The Pimlico Connection' was designed to provide students with practice in the simple communication of scientific ideas and to stimulate them to reflect about the meaning and purpose of their main disciplines. The Study Service of Phases 1 and 2 of the experiment was project work. At Imperial College of Science, Technology and Medicine, London University, third-year students of electrical engineering undertake group projects as part of their degree work. These projects represent 8 per cent of the degree-marks for the final year of the honours degree. As Socio-Technical Projects (see Goodlad, 1977), these group projects require students to study technical questions which are complicated by social, political, economic, moral, or other issues, or to study social problems to which engineers, or engineering students, can contribute remedies. Community Action Group Projects contain an element of direct practical service to some sector of the community; they are, in fact, a sub-variant of Study Service.

In the academic year 1975-6, 12 electrical engineering students visited the Pimlico School weekly for 15 weeks to help with the teaching of Combined Science to third-year classes. They carried out an evaluation of the peer tutoring as their group project (Abidi *et al*, 1976). In 1976-7, a second group of students carried out another group project to evaluate a more complex tutoring scheme involving 19 students deployed in various combinations. (Anslow *et al*, 1977). In 1977-8, 34 students acted as tutors in an extracurricular activity, (see Goodlad *et al*, 1978). In subsequent years, the tutoring has spread to other schools, including primary schools – largely in response to direct requests from teachers who have heard about the scheme on the network – and tutors now come from all departments of Imperial College. In 1980, 'The Pimlico Connection' was established as a society within the Imperial College student union: much of the administration (recruiting tutors, co-ordinating activities in the schools with the teachers, and collecting and sorting information for the annual report, etc,) is now undertaken by the students. Some tutors attend a course, 'The communication of scientific ideas', offered by the Humanities Programme at Imperial College, which gives an opportunity for academic reflection about the peer tutoring. (In December 1982, the course was accorded recognition under the Education for Capability scheme of the Royal Society of Arts.) Most tutors, however, are from departments/years in which this course is not available.

The Pimlico School, in which the project began, is within relatively easy reach of Imperial College. It is one of the 139 inner-London comprehensive schools which, together with the 286 comprehensive schools in outer-London, form about 13.7 per cent of the English comprehensive school system. It is a mixed school with approximately 1,250 pupils. The Stockwell Manor School and the Holland Park School, to which the tutoring was extended in 1977–8, are similar in size and composition, and are both likewise inner-London comprehensives.

(b) Type of work done by the tutors

When the services of the students were originally offered to Pimlico School, the teachers asked for the tutoring to be undertaken with third-year pupils for the following reasons:

1. Many third-year pupils had little interest in science, believing it to be a dry, specialized subject with little relevance to their daily lives. In large classes (up to 30 pupils per class), it was not possible for the teachers to give enough individual attention to pupils to break down this resistance.
2. The rate of truancy from third-year science classes was high.
3. The Combined Science syllabus (based largely on a Nuffield syllabus) which was used for the third-year science relied on learning by experiment. However, large classes with much noise and indiscipline made it impossible for pupils successfully to perform experiments and make deductions from them. Because supervision of large groups was difficult, some classes had been given only limited access to the experimental apparatus – which they tended to break or mishandle.
4. At the end of the third-year, pupils opt for fourth-year courses (academically-orientated or otherwise) which will determine their subsequent career options. Through unsatisfactory experience of science in the lower-school, some pupils might be deterred from taking science options in the fourth-year from which they might ultimately benefit.

Accordingly, in each of the three years of the initial experiment, students worked with third-year students at Pimlico. From 1977–8 onwards, tutoring spread to industrial workshop practice (metalwork and woodwork); science in the first two years; sixth-form classes; fourth-year options in electronics; and mathematics at all levels. The method of instruction of the third-year science classes in the initial phases of the project was a happy compromise between structured and unstructured tutoring (see Chapter 3). At the Pimlico School, the Combined Science teaching is based upon worksheets which the teaching staff have written to guide pupils through the experiments. These sheets provide a useful intermediate mode between totally unstructured tutoring (where the lack of tutoring experience of tutors can be a weakness) and totally structured tutoring (which can be somewhat inflexible and which can diminish the value of having university students as tutors).

In the initial tutoring sessions, (and, in the light of the experience, subsequently), the students, working with individuals or small groups, engaged the pupils in discussion about the experiments they were performing, answering questions, and posing supplementary questions which would guide the pupils more effectively through the subject-matter. Supervision of experiments was particularly useful when, as with the distillation of tar, the apparatus or techniques were potentially hazardous, and where one unaided teacher would be very hard-pressed to see that the whole classroom-full of pupils behaved properly. Teachers use the tutors in various ways; some ask them to work with one or two individuals who are disruptive in class, or with gifted pupils who will benefit from extension work; others ask tutors to work with a particular group of children on practical work – this may be the same group each week or a different one, whilst yet other teachers prefer tutors to wander around the classroom answering queries as they arise.

Figure 5.1 *'The Pimlico Connection'*: *Mathematics at Holland Park School*

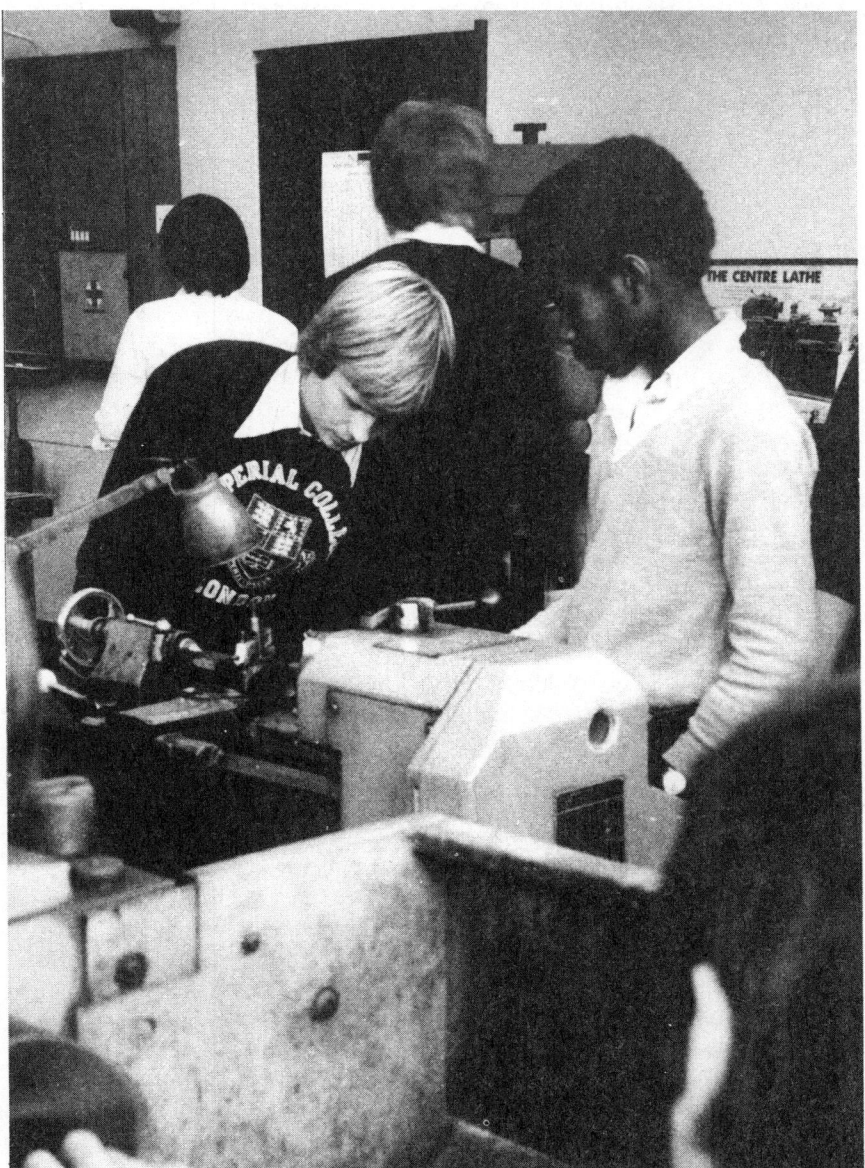

Figure 5.2 *'The Pimlico Connection': Metal work at Pimlico School*

(c) The training of the tutors

In each year of the tutoring, students have been given a one-day training session the Saturday before the university term began. The object of the session has been to focus the minds of the students on the task ahead of them, progressively moving from a qualitative evocation of the experience of being at school (which may, for some, be a few years distant), through a simulation of the learning experience of being a tutee, to specific advice on being a tutor.

Procedures described in various American tutoring manuals have been used, eg those recommended by Lippitt *et al* (1971), and by Mainiero *et al* (1971). For example, training has started with a brain-storming session on problems likely to be encountered in a large inner-London comprehensive school. Students are asked to suggest, in the brain-storming mode (no criticism, no discussion, 'blue sky', 'hitch-hike') what problems they think may be found in a large inner-city school. They have then viewed the BBC television film 'The Space Between Words: School' which illustrates some of the problems. When their predictions (which have been written on a blackboard) have been checked off, a further brain-storming session, followed by group discussion, has been held on how tutoring may address some of the problems. (In subsequent years, it is possible, even probable, that the film will not be used. Not only is it increasingly expensive to hire films, but it is also proving difficult to find an 'up-to-date' film depicting life in a typical comprehensive school. In addition, the setting up of a similar tutoring project based on University College London in October 1987 with a training session that had no associated film suggests that one can manage without it.)

A break for sandwiches has followed at this point – not only because the students have many matters to discuss, but also because the breaking of bread is an important way in which the secondary objective of a training session (that of letting tutors get to know each other) can be achieved.

The second part of the training is for tutors to take part in simulation exercises designed to illustrate the frustration of being a tutor or being tutored. For example, two students are seated back-to-back with a third acting as observer. One student has a complex geometric drawing which he/she has to describe to the other student whose task it is to reproduce it exactly. At first, this has to be done with the tutee not being allowed to ask any questions; then the tutee is allowed to ask for advice; and finally the tutor is allowed to look at what the tutee has drawn, but without revealing the drawing which is to be copied. Not only does this exercise vividly illustrate the frustration of being respectively either a tutee or a tutor, but it also dramatically illustrates the importance of feedback in a tutoring dyad and the need to establish where the tutee 'is at' before progressing.

Another simulation exercise is based on role-playing. After an initial warm-up (with a role-play based on an encounter between a student travelling on a bus without a ticket and a student acting as an inspector), one student (role-playing the tutor) is given instructions to teach Boyle's Law; another student (role-playing the pupil) is given instructions to try to disrupt the lesson by getting the tutor to talk about football. In this way, tutors begin to appreciate some of the difficulties and arguments which they may have to face in a classroom.

Teacher-representatives from the schools involved in the scheme have attended the training session to give brief descriptions of the teaching programmes used in their schools, usually bringing along a selection of materials which the pupils will be working with in class. This gives the tutors some opportunity to acquire a flavour of the workcards and exercises before the tutoring begins, and to get some appreciation of the teaching aims of the staff. These introductions usually have to be kept brief because of the wide variation in schools and age groups with which the Imperial College students work. It would be easier for tutors to study the materials and syllabus in more detail if only one school were used in the tutoring scheme; but tutors rapidly find their feet once the tutoring starts.

The final part of the training takes students through a list of tutoring techniques (a modified version of which is reproduced at Appendix A) which they have been asked to study during the long vacation. The rationale for the advice is explained in the light of the experiential activities in the first part of the training session.

The training concludes with a review of practicalities and logistics.

(d) Logistics of the scheme

In each of the years of the scheme, tutoring has been limited to 15 weeks – the Autumn term, and the first part of the Spring term – up to half term. This limitation on time has been designed to ensure continuity of service to the schools. From the second half of the Spring term onwards, final-year students become increasingly involved with job-interviews on Wednesday afternoons, and all students become increasingly preoccupied with examinations. It has been thought best to deliver a fixed number of weeks of tutoring upon which schools can rely, without the irritation of the scheme disintegrating under the pressures on the students. Some students choose to carry on tutoring beyond these 15 weeks, arranging this on an individual basis with the teachers of the classes they tutor. This strategy seems to have worked effectively.

During the 15 weeks of the tutoring, there have been sandwich-lunch meetings weekly for trouble-shooting purposes and general conviviality. As the scheme has developed, spreading to more subjects and more schools, for each subject area in each school, one tutor, (designated 'co-ordinator'), has taken responsibility for week-to-week administration, trying to secure meetings between teachers and tutors, re-assigning tutors if circumstances require it, and advising tutors in advance when possible of any pertubations of the tutoring likely to be brought about by arrangements in the schools. These co-ordinators are usually students who have already been involved in tutoring for one year and are familiar with the logistics of the scheme.

5.2 Methods of evaluation used

Because Phases 1 and 2 were undertaken as projects within the degree-work of the engineering students, it seemed best to move from the known to the unknown, exploring the strengths and weaknesses of the psychometric approach (which is most similar to engineering) and gradually feeling towards the complex reality of tutoring. Accordingly, evaluation in Phases 1 and 2 (Abidi *et al*, 1976; Anslow *et al*, 1977), followed the 'agricultural-botany paradigm'. For consistency, the same hypotheses, methods of measurement, and methods of statistical analysis were also used in Phase 3 (Goodlad *et al*, 1978).

The science attitude questionnaire published by the National Foundation for Educational Research (Nuttall, 1971) was used in the first three phases. A questionnaire was administered to tutor groups before and after the tutoring in each case, and statistical analysis was carried out on the results. In Phase 1, (Abidi *et al*, 1976), tutored pupils consisted of one top-stream class and one low-stream class. Similar classes were used as control groups. The results suggested the following:

1. Peer tutoring seemed to be effective in increasing interest in science for both tutored forms.
2. Peer tutoring seemed to be effective in increasing realization of the positive social implications of science only for the low-stream form.
3. Peer Tutoring seemed effective in increasing preference for learning science by experiment only for the high-stream form.
4. Peer tutoring seemed effective in increasing liking for science teachers in both tutored forms.

In Phase 2, tutored groups at Pimlico School consisted of five mixed-ability classes, and a withdrawal group of a variable number (two to eight) of pupils. Two additional mixed-ability classes served as control groups. In addition, the tutored and control groups from Phase 1 were re-tested with the science attitude questionnaire to see if the peer tutoring had had any lasting effect. Results similar to those of Phase 1 were achieved, and, in addition, pupils tutored in Phase 1 were found to have retained their interest (in comparison with the control group) a year after the tutoring of Phase 1 had ended.

In Phase 2 (Anslow *et al*, 1977), an additional feature was variation in the number of tutors to a class. One tutor to four pupils and two tutors to a class seemed to be as effective as 'saturation' tutoring (14 tutors to a class of 30 pupils); withdrawal groups seemed to alienate the pupils.

In Phase 3 (Goodlad *et al*, 1978), six mixed-ability classes at Pimlico constituted the tutored groups; five mixed-ability classes constituted the control groups. In Phase 3 the peer tutoring seemed to improve some pupils' attitude to school. Again, as in Phases 1 and 2 it was found that peer tutoring seemed to improve pupils' attitudes to their science teachers.

The psychometric experiment can obviously be criticized on the grounds that, as in the Hawthorne experiments (where people's behaviour changed in the hoped-for direction simply because they were favoured by being subjects of experiments), the statistically-significant findings are freaks which would not appear in the 'nth' year of a tutoring scheme. Against this, it can be argued that, with the turnover of personnel in educational institutions (teachers, students, pupils), each year brings to the peer tutoring a substantially new population. Perhaps it is best to 'Hitch-Hike on Hawthorne' as long as the positive effect can be made to last.

Considering that most children in the age-group tested spend some one thousand hours a year watching television (which often offers quite different values to those implied in the discipline of schooling), it would be surprising indeed if 15 hours of tutoring radically changed the pupils' outlooks. It is all the more interesting, therefore, that the psychometric research showed any statistically significant gains at all. In Phase 3 (Goodlad *et al*, 1978) the comparison of tutored and control groups which came nearest to a 'classical' experiment in social psychology – with the same teacher, the same syllabus, and the same number of hours of instruction, and only the presence of tutors being the variable – the most significant findings of all were recorded. (Improvement in attitude to science teachers was significant at the 0.025 level and improvement in attitudes to school at the 0.005 level.) Even though the 'improvements' in the tutored groups were in fact an arresting of the deterioration of attitudes found in the control groups, it is encouraging that tutoring seems to be effective in the most rigorous conditions (normal classroom work) and under the closest evaluative scrutiny (psychometric research).

The psychometric research carried out in the first three years of the Pimlico Connection Project produced findings which are necessarily tentative. As the scheme grew to different schools, and a wide variety of subjects, age-groups, teachers, physical conditions, etc, it became clear that it was no longer realistic to attempt to monitor the scheme by psychometric techniques. It is, nevertheless, extremely important to have some sort of systematic evaluation of what is happening – not only for purposes of accountability for those who pay for the scheme, but also so that everyone involved knows what has been going on. Accordingly, in each year of the scheme, information has been gathered from pupils, students, and teachers which has been written up in a series of reports (see Goodlad 1979, 1980, 1981, 1982b, 1983, 1984, 1985; Berry 1985, 1986, 1988). The annual reports have proved extremely useful documents. Not only do they offer a tangible record for students of what they have done, they also serve as documents to be used in schools coming into a scheme for the first time. Heads of departments do not need to give an elaborate explanation of the aims, objects, procedures, and so forth of the scheme each time a new teacher joins, they can pass on a copy of the most recent report.

The scheme has also been the subject of independent comment in print by a teacher (Page-Jones, 1976), a student (Adeney, 1988), a science journalist (Herman, 1983).

5.3 Opinions of the pupils about the peer tutoring

In each of the years of the tutoring scheme, from 1979-80 to the most recent year 1987-8, the same questionnaires have been used to solicit views from pupils and tutors. Teachers have completed the same questionnaires from 1980-81 to the current academic year 1987-8. The tables in the sections which follow give the cumulative information over these years. The quotations elicited by the open-ended questions show incredible similarity from year to year, and similar proportions of pupils respond in the various ways. For the sake of simplicity, a representative selection of quotations is given here.

The questionnaire to tutees read as follows:

> We would very much like to know what you thought about the visits of the Imperial College tutors last term and this term. Please write some comments by completing the sentences.

Space for comments was then left after each of the following sentence stubs:

1. The thing I liked best about having tutors was ...
2. The thing I liked least about having tutors was ...
3. The tutoring would be better if ...

Finally a fourth question asked simply:

> Have you any other comments?

(a) What the pupils liked best

Far and away the most popular feature of the peer tutoring in each year has been the *help* the pupils received, for example:

- 'You can ask them questions which means you don't have to wait so long to ask questions and you get attended to more quickly.'
- 'You get more work done due to extra help.'
- 'We didn't have to be calling our teacher all the time. There was always a tutor on our table to help.'
- 'They were very helpful and I got through more work than with only one teacher teaching the whole class.'
- 'They helped us a lot when we had our projects. They were very polite and helpful and I would like them to come next year.'
- 'When the teacher was with another person, they would come and give you a hand with whatever you were doing.'
- 'We had more attention and the work was explained in a simple way. This was when we were split into little groups.'
- 'Individual attention: There were enough students for six pupils to one student. It was a refreshing change to have someone different to talk to. They spoke to you and treated you like adults.'

The extra attention to pupils and the rapid reinforcement of their learning is one of the principal justifications of tutoring. Accordingly, it is gratifying to note that this has consistently been the most appreciated feature of the scheme.

Secondly, the *informality, friendliness, and kindness* of the students are regularly mentioned by the pupils. For example:

- 'Some of the tutors are nice and polite and helpful.'
- 'They didn't shout at you when you did something wrong.'
- 'Helpful and nice.'
- 'They were very friendly, and I think that when they were in the class they relaxed the atmosphere considerably. Also, we were on a first name basis. The formality of them being in the class was taken away and they were more like pupils than teachers, it seemed to me.'
- 'They were happy tutors and nice to have around.'

Figure 5.3 *'The Pimlico Connection': Science at Pimlico School*

Other factors liked vary greatly and have included the following:

- 'They made sure that we understood what we had to do.'
- 'They give you work.'
- 'You don't have the same teachers all the time.'
- 'To know them and show them what I can do.'
- 'I found out about what some of them were studying at Imperial College, biochemistry etc.'

- 'You could take out your feelings on them and they couldn't do anything in return.'

(b) What the pupils disliked

Most pupils report *no dislikes at all*. Others disliked aspects of the tutoring that were probably to their ultimate benefit. For example, some pupils thought tutors too strict:

- 'We couldn't mess about with them there.'
- 'They never let you muck about.'
- 'We had to do more work.'

However, a few pupils thought the tutors not strict enough:

- 'They were probably not stricked (*sic*) enough when the class got naughty.'

Each year, a few pupils have thought that the tutors interfered too much with the usual pattern of work:

- 'The way they watch you.'
- 'They are always looking over your shoulder.'

Or they objected when tutors went beyond their brief and did too much of the experimental work:

- 'They did too much to help us, did all the work, and we never had a chance to do the experiments.'

Fortunately, this has not been a common fault. There were even objections the other way:

- 'They did not do the dirty work for us and made us do it all (I mean the experiments).'

(c) How the pupils thought the peer tutoring could be improved

Many of the comments simply amplified what pupils said they disliked. For example, the few who felt that they had had too much help said the tutoring would be better if they got less. Those who felt they had not had enough help said they would have liked more. Similarly, some pupils wished the tutors were more 'stern' and that 'there was more strictness'; the tutoring would be better 'if the kids behaved themselves and took more attention of what the tutor is saying'.

The most frequent suggestions each year, however, have been (encouragingly) for more and/or longer tutoring sessions and more tutors. For example, pupils said that the tutoring would be better if:

- 'They stayed longer, discussing a few more subjects.'
- 'They came more often.'
- 'They spent more time with each pupil.'

- 'They came to all our science lessons.'
- 'We have them all the time.'

Other comments did not fit any distinct pattern. For example, tutoring would be better if: 'they were allowed to take some of their own lessons instead of just helping out the teacher all the time'; 'the tutors dressed neater'; 'tutors did not walk around the class'; 'they came round instead of just staying with one group'; 'there were more women tutors'; 'they were more experienced'; 'the experiments were better'.

(d) 'In every subject they should have some tutors'

Most of the remarks in the space for further comments have repeated points pupils had made elsewhere on the questionnaire. There were a few unfavourable comments, for example:

- 'They steal your comics and your pens' (unconfirmed!).
- 'I think tutors should wear uniforms.'

However, most comments have been favourable:

- 'They were very pleased with our work and they let us call them by their first names.'
- 'You could do more work when they are here because they are always there to help you.'
- 'I think they're sould (*sic*) be more tutors next year they are just what you need.'
- 'Good idea.'
- 'Having the tutors helped our teacher to observe his pupils' attitudes to learning.'
- 'The tutors being in the class enabled me to get more things done and learn more. I think this was accomplished because the one science teacher was not the only person in the class who was there to lend you a hand, so the tutors saw you quickly and you didn't have to hang around for the teacher, and you learned more.'
- 'I think that in every subject they should have some tudors (*sic*) to help you, not only in science.'

In addition to being asked for free responses, pupils were asked to check statements with which they agreed (in a multiple-choice section) to indicate whether, with tutors, lessons were:

(a) more interesting/less interesting/about the same as usual;
(b) easier to follow/harder to follow/about the same as usual;
(c) more enjoyable/less enjoyable/about the same as usual;

and whether with tutors they thought they

(d) learned more/learned less/learned about as much as usual.

Year-by-year, the findings have been strikingly similar (see the annual reports on the scheme – Goodlad, 1979, 1980, 1981, 1982b, 1983, 1984, 1985, Berry, 1985, 1986, 1988). The fact that the 'experiment' can be repeated suggests that the effects are due to the *system* of peer tutoring rather than to the personalities of the participants. To give a composite picture of the scheme, findings are aggregated in this chapter. Over all schools and classes, in the years 1979-80 to 1987-8 the percentages were as indicated in Table 5.1. (Percentages throughout are rounded to the nearest whole number: some figures do not add up to 100 per cent because some respondents did not answer all of the questions.)

Table 5.1 *Pupils' opinions. Percentages of pupils responding:*
n = 4,625 (Response rate 4,625/5,978 = 77.4 per cent)

	More	Less	About the same as usual
(a) Interest of lessons	55	4	40
(b) Ease of following	63	4	30
(c) Enjoyment of lessons	54	5	38
(d) Amount of learning	54	5	38

These overall percentages conceal some interesting sub-totals: peer tutoring at the primary schools, for example, seems to have been outstandingly successful. In 1987-8, for the first time, the details of the primary and secondary pupils were separately compiled and then integrated to give the cumulative findings as in previous years. Results from the questionnaires indicate that the 'interest' level was higher in the primary group by 17 per cent and the 'enjoyment' level higher by 20 per cent than those in the secondary schools. Both groups felt that they had about the same improvement in 'ease of following' their subjects with tutors (63 per cent primary and 62 per cent secondary), while more of the primary group felt that their learning had been improved with the presence of tutors (66 per cent primary compared with 56 per cent secondary). Science tutors can be particularly useful in the primary schools, where the class teachers may not be trained in a scientific discipline, not only in helping the children with their work, but in suggesting to the teacher new ideas for experiments.

5.4 Opinions of the students about the peer tutoring

All the tutors who have taken part in the scheme have received questionnaires which asked them to say, by ticking boxes, how they thought they had benefited by being tutors and to say whether the tutoring had interfered with their college studies (see Table 5.2). The remaining questions asked: 'What did you like best about the tutoring? What did you like least about the tutoring? How, on reflection, do you think the tutoring could be improved? Have you any other comments?'

Figure 5.4 *'The Pimlico Connection': Getting all steamed up at Fox Primary School*

Figure 5.5 *'The Pimlico Connection': Fox Primary School – when English is not your first language, it is good to have a tutor*

Completed questionnaires were received from 547 of the 752 tutors (72.7 per cent response).

Table 5.2 *Percentages of students indicating that they thought they had benefited from being a tutor in the ways listed: (n = 547) (response rate 547/752 = 72.7 per cent)*

	Greatly	Somewhat	Not at all	Not sure
1. By reinforcing your knowledge of some aspect of your subject?	2	38	56	4
2. By getting practice in the simple communication of scientific ideas?	55	41	2	1
3. By gaining insight into how other people perceive your subject?	35	52	10	3
4. By increasing your self-confidence?	15	59	19	7
5. By getting to know something about people with a different social background to your own?	39	43	13	4
6. By feeling that you were doing something useful with what you had already learned?	46	45	6	4
7. Did the tutoring interfere with your college studies?	1	30	61	8

(a) Benefits of being a tutor

1. Reinforcing knowledge of one's subject

If tutors and pupils are reasonably close in age and knowledge, it is likely that the process of thinking through material to teach it will help the tutor to master it. Reinforcement of learning has not, however, been a marked feature of 'The Pimlico Connection' tutoring scheme because: (a) the tutors were often tutoring subjects distant from their own disciplines (eg, a computing science student tutoring on microbes); or (b) the age/experience gap was considerable – seven years or more. Nevertheless, 40 per cent of tutors felt that tutoring had greatly (2 per cent) or somewhat (38 per cent) reinforced their knowledge of their subject.

One student who felt that tutoring had greatly reinforced his knowledge of his subject put it thus:

(I liked) the opportunity it provided in getting an appreciation of what science is really all about, both from the need to put it in perspective amongst other fields of human activity for (rather sceptical) tutees and from the process of setting up a controlled social (scientific) experiment.

Besides being fun at times, I learnt more electronics than I had learned at college. This was due to having to explain simple electronics but with more clarity and more explicity than I have been taught it.

Another tutor found that tutoring helped him to analyse how he approached problems:

The change in role was extremely stimulating, ie, the change from sitting in lectures and being fed the information required to 'survive' at the present, to actually having to make an active step and communicate some idea and make it plausible to somebody else – almost a role reversal. This makes one understand how ideas are presented and how the teacher in any situation is thinking and what he is trying to get over. Also very helpful in analysing how oneself approaches problems by comparing with the methods of the tutees – which are very different. Very useful in that it put my own problems with my studies into perspective, and also how important (or unimportant) they actually are.

One student urged that tutoring:

Should become a requirement for engineering students in the final year of their degree course as it is a means of 'grounding' conceptually high scientific material.

2. Practice in the simple communication of scientific ideas

Perhaps the principal value of tutoring in science and engineering for undergraduates is the practice it offers in the simple communication of scientific ideas. Accordingly, it was gratifying to note that 96 per cent of the tutors felt that they had benefited this way – greatly (55 per cent) or somewhat (41 per cent).

Many tutors obviously enjoyed explaining things, for example:

- 'I enjoyed explaining the various topics and then seeing the pupils learn something they did not know or understand before, ie, I enjoyed imparting knowledge (to put it grandly!)'

Again, another tutor enjoyed:

- 'Explaining to the children simple scientific facts they wanted to know. It gave me a chance to answer their questions and to tell them about university life that otherwise they might not know about.'

3. Gaining insight into how other people perceive one's subject

An important prerequisite for effective scientific communication in most jobs is for the scientist or engineer to understand how much (or little) other people regard the scientist's world of thought to be of any interest. An important part of tutoring is to put young scientists or engineers into close contact with people who perhaps do not think science to be very important.

Thirty-five per cent of the tutors thought they had greatly benefited by gaining insight into how other people perceive their subject: a further 52 per cent felt they had benefited somewhat in this way. Some students commented specifically on the lack of interest of the pupils, others were clearly surprised at how little the children knew, or wanted to know, eg:

- 'I was absolutely amazed at the ignorance of some of these kids of what were to me basic scientific principles, and their total lack of interest in finding out.'

4. Increasing self-confidence
Some studies of under-achievers who have acted as tutors have suggested that being a tutor can serve to increase a young person's self-confidence. Some of the tutors were surprised at the question, never having expected tutoring to develop their self-confidence. Nevertheless 15 per cent felt their self-confidence had been greatly increased, and 59 per cent that it had been somewhat increased.

5. Getting to know about people from different backgrounds
One of the least satisfactory aspects of education in the United Kingdom, especially through selective education and through the segregation of the children of the rich into public schools, is that people of different social backgrounds can remain largely ignorant of one another's way of life. In particular, many university students are grossly ignorant of comprehensive schools – a singular disability if they have any thought of going into teaching, but also unfortunate for their possible future roles as parents, politicians, or leaders of opinion. The schools in which the tutoring takes place also have a large proportion of black children; this may not have been the case in the schools which the undergraduate students attended. Accordingly, it was interesting to note that 82 per cent of tutors felt they had benefited by getting to know about people with different social backgrounds from their own – 39 per cent greatly, and 43 per cent somewhat. The setting in which teaching took place was also of interest to them, eg:

- 'I was fascinated by the difference from my own school experiences – no safe niches for belongings, battered buildings, noise, etc. Most teachers were relatively calm, though one did keep shouting to get quiet. I was surprised at my own ability to fit into their 'discipline' system. (I had been a proponent of strictness at my own school, believing that I should enforce the rules carefully.) Yet I did not feel alarmed at not being able to do this – nor did I feel frustrated. . . '

6. Feeling one was doing something useful with what one had learned
Being at university can be somewhat alienating for many students who become deracinated and cut off from the opportunities for productive work. For this reason, Study Service, which combines community service with study (either in an interwoven manner or in blocks), can give students a feeling of doing something useful with what they have already learned. This is perhaps

less urgent for students of science and engineering (many of whom are sponsored by industry and/or work in industry in their vacations) than for arts students. Nevertheless, 91 per cent of tutors felt that they had benefited by feeling they were doing something useful – greatly (46 per cent) or somewhat (45 per cent). A few who did not feel they had been useful had found the pupils so inattentive and undisciplined that they had wondered if their tutoring had really been useful. One student commented that it had never crossed his mind to feel that he was doing something useful, the experience gained was justification enough – and it was nice just to help.

Other types of benefit listed included:

- 'The chance to work with younger people.'
- 'Seeing inside the school from a teacher's point of view.'
- 'Increasing one's appreciation of the difficulties of teaching.'
- 'It was a new experience, and I like new experiences!'

7. Effect on tutors' college studies

The majority of tutors (61 per cent) felt that taking part in the tutoring (which occupied time normally set aside for games and athletics) had not interfered with their college studies. However, nearly a third felt that tutoring had interfered somewhat: students need to be warned of this possibility when recruitment is taking place.

8. Arousing an interest in teaching

Once the scheme had been running for a few years, it became clear that many tutors were using the opportunity to tutor as a 'test-bed' for a career in teaching. Since 1979 tutors have been asked at the end of the year if they have thought of going into teaching. Of those replying to the questionnaires, 52 per cent have thought of going into teaching; 64% of these find that peer tutoring helps them greatly (24 per cent) or somewhat (40 per cent) in deciding whether or not they would like to teach. Since 1981-2, the students have been asked to indicate whether their peer tutoring experiences have made them more or less keen to teach. The results are shown in Table 5.3: 25 per cent of the tutors are more keen to teach, 18 per cent less keen, and 55 per cent feel about the same. (These percentages do not total 100 per cent as some tutors failed to reply.) In addition, research conducted in the academic year 1986/7 showed that of the 18 tutors in that year who had *not* considered teaching as a career, six were more interested in teaching as a result of serving as tutors.

In view of the current government interest in trying to encourage more science and technology graduates to enter teaching, these findings are particularly interesting. Those students who have tried peer tutoring and are still keen (or more keen) to teach have a realistic idea of what teaching will involve before they commit themselves to Postgraduate Certificate of Education Courses. Those who are less keen as a result of peer tutoring are dissuaded from teacher-training while there is still time to think about some other career,

Table 5.3 *Tutors who had thought of going into teaching: n = 251 (52 per cent of respondents in questionnaire). Percentages of these indicating effect of tutoring on their interest in teaching*

Usefulness of tutoring in helping me to decide	Greatly %	Somewhat %	Not at all %	Not sure %	No answer %
Keener	11	9	0	0	5
Less keen	8	8	0	0	2
About the same	5	23	4	4	19

instead of finding out midway through their course that they are not suited to being teachers. Recognizing that the increased use by schools of higher education students as school tutors in science, engineering and mathematics offers the possibility of attracting more students in these shortage areas into teaching. The University Grants Committee (UGC) has provided funding (commencing 1987/8) to support peer tutoring schemes at three other universities – Cambridge, East Anglia, and Warwick. In addition, Imperial College has been awarded UGC funding from September 1987–September 1989 to build upon 'The Pimlico Connection' and to establish similar schemes linking schools with other higher education establishments.

(b) What the tutors liked best

Most frequently cited has been the sheer *satisfaction* of tutoring. For example:

- 'Satisfaction when a pupil understood a point I was trying to make.'
- 'The response of children who learned – especially their interest when stimulated by something we told them.'
- 'Tremendous satisfaction when a lesson went well and the pupils had responded with interest and enthusiasm.'

Similar was the pleasure of explaining things, for example:

- 'Showing some experiments to the pupils.'

These types of satisfaction were similar to that of being appreciated by the pupils, for example:

- 'That some of the pupils genuinely seemed to appreciate having tutors there and seemed to show increasing interest in the experiments.'
- 'Being able to build up a relationship with some of the tutees. Also, I was very pleased to see that different ethnic groups mixed freely without friction; I saw no evidence of any colour prejudice.'

Some students said they had enjoyed the social contact. The tutor teams seemed to have offered the collegiate type experience of energy directed towards a common goal which is sometimes lacking in a commuter university.

Some tutors specifically mentioned that they had liked gaining insight into a non-public school. Among other points mentioned were:

- 'That it took us out of college on what was nevertheless a college subject – not just education for its own sake.'
- 'The challenge of overcoming my difficulties in communicating with the children.'
- 'The total change from college.'
- 'The chance to help people who sometimes have not had the same opportunities as oneself.'

(c) What the tutors liked least

Most frequently cited each year has been the lack of interest of some of the pupils in the subjects they were studying. A typical dislike was:

- 'Meeting with a "brick wall" when trying to explain certain things – particularly with the brightest children who simply were not interested but totally capable of learning.'

The second most frequently cited dislike has been lack of discipline and noise. For example:

- 'Lack of discipline. This distracts and hinders those who would like to work.'
- 'Finding myself in a class in uproar with the teacher unable to control it.'

Apart from these two dislikes, most tutors seemed to have enjoyed the peer tutoring very much. Among dislikes mentioned once or twice each were: 'the limited time available'; 'trying to relate to 13-year-old girls'; 'the school system'; 'the feeling that what we were teaching the kids was totally irrelevant to their lives'; 'the rigidity of the syllabus'; 'the lack of textbooks'; 'the rush to get to Stockwell after lectures'; 'when not used in a class'; and 'being regularly "insulted" by some pupils (only a minority). This reduced my confidence and ability to help pupils.'

(d) How the tutors thought the peer tutoring could be improved

By far the most common suggestion each year has been 'more contact with the teachers'. Tutors visited the school before the peer tutoring began and had informal meetings with teachers after lessons; even so, tutors clearly thought more meetings would have been helpful. The time immediately after afternoon lessons is taken up by a multiplicity of staff meetings which reduce the opportunities for contact between the tutors and teachers. Such problems are likely to be common in tutoring contacts *between* institutions. They should be much less acute where tutoring occurs *within* a single institution – for example, with sixth-formers tutoring more junior pupils.

Other suggested improvements echoed tutors' dislikes, eg: 'more time per session'; 'better discipline'. There was also some support for a more informal, freer approach which could draw more fully on tutors' knowledge:

- 'By being more "different" from the everyday school routine than it was. I felt that we were seen as disguised teachers by the children, as such still on the far side of the fence – "them" and "us".'
- 'Let tutors take a class without the teacher at the end of the project.'
- 'More informal time with the tutees.'

Other suggestions included: 'better equipment'; 'more time on preparation of tutoring sessions'; 'same-sex tutoring'; 'more women tutors'; 'teach only interested pupils'; 'background information on pupils'; 'by extension to other subjects: more tutoring'.

(e) 'A phenomenal amount of untapped potential'

In the space for further comments, most tutors who had anything to say wrote enthusiastically about their experience. For example:

- 'I felt a genuine dread creep up on me as Wednesday afternoons approached and a relief when they were over. However, it usually happened that the days I dreaded most were the days that were most successful. Looking back, it was something I was glad I'd done.'
- 'I was fairly shocked by the grim reality of a large London comprehensive in comparison to my small country grammar school, but feel that tutoring, if given sufficient support and handled sufficiently well, offers some hope for alleviation, if not a solution, of some of the problems.'
- 'All in all I thought that the tutoring was worthwhile and I felt that many other students (and children) would benefit from a few months of such work. I wish you every success with the future tutoring schemes. I certainly would not have missed my time as a tutor for anything.'
- 'I enjoyed the tutoring very much although it finally put me off teaching.'
- '... there's a *phenomenal* amount of untapped potential in this sort of system.'

(f) Ex-tutors' views

In April 1987 questionnaires were sent to ex-Pimlico Connection tutors asking them about their current occupations. Some of those replying had gone on to become qualified teachers, others were involved in academic research, and many were working in industry. Despite this, their perceptions of the benefits of the peer tutoring experience were remarkably similar.

The ex-tutors were asked to respond to the following question: 'What are the principal benefits you think you personally derived from being a tutor?' A selection of the responses gives an indication of the views ex-tutors hold of their peer tutoring experience several years after leaving the scheme.

- 'Learning to look at my subject within a different framework ie, that of a non-technical person. This has given me a good insight into how to talk to people who are basically non-technical about my subject.'

- 'Experience in communicating scientific ideas in simple terms. Learning to pitch the explanations at the right level, relating them to familiar concepts.'
- 'It caused me to start thinking about the relevance of science and wider implications of science, through conversations with pupils asking 'Why are we doing this ?' Science became for me a wider activity than it had previously been.'
- 'I had, and still have, no intention of becoming a teacher, but it did help my skills of communication which have been beneficial during my employment as an engineer. I found that I missed the contact with children and have recently begun to help with a local Brownie pack which affords a similar satisfaction, although it is perhaps not as challenging.'
- 'Practice in explaining scientific ideas in a clear and simple way (I am now involved with an engineering project which my firm is running for a school in Guildford. The age group is different – 13- to 15-year-old boys – but the experience I gained at Fox Primary has been invaluable.)'
- 'Increased my confidence. (Keeping control of a group of ten-year-olds during an afternoon of experiments with water would do wonders for anyone's confidence!)'
- 'Communication of scientific ideas to others is very important: before doing the Pimlico Connection, I had forgotten how difficult it could be.'
- 'Two years later, I still consider this to be one of the most stimulating and useful exercises that I did within the framework of my degree. I am now in a highly technical job and have found the lessons learnt in the art of communication, instruction, and preparation very useful as was the insight into the teachers' side of the educational process.'
- 'Appreciation of the workings and atmosphere of an ILEA secondary school. The difficulties that teachers and pupils face in a mixed ability class, especially maintaining discipline and keeping every pupil interested.'
- 'A better understanding of an education system which I had never experienced personally.'
- 'Greatest benefit was realizing just "how the other half lived" – a real eye opener.'
- 'Realizing the "disenfranchizing" effect of an ignorance of science in a modern society.'
- 'I felt that it gave me a better understanding of how less able childen feel in the classroom. Even though I had wanted to teach, I had rather a "rose-coloured" view of the profession, I feel that tutoring at Pimlico gave me a much more realistic impression of what would be involved.'
- 'Contact with people full of life rather than overburdened with studies.'
- 'Simple enjoyment of kids themselves and science away from college pressures.'
- 'Maybe the real benefit was that it was fun !'

These quotations clearly reiterate the findings from the evaluation questionnaires given to tutors at the end of each year of tutoring. In these replies an appreciation of the opportunity to practise the communication of scientific ideas was highlighted again and again. However, one tutor did mention another personal benefit:

- 'I married a fellow tutor!'

5.5 Opinions of the teachers about the peer tutoring

Questionnaires have been circulated each year to teachers who had tutors in their classes.

The first part of the questionnaire to teachers was open-ended, inviting them to write comments on to sentence stubs:

1. My main problem in using the tutors is . . .
2. The best aspect of having tutors is . . .
3. The thing I like least about the way the scheme was introduced to us and set up was . . .
4. The following incident occurred . . . it suggested to me that . . .
5. The tutoring would be improved if . . .
6. Any other comments?

As there were relatively few teachers compared to the numbers of tutors and pupils, it is difficult to detect any clear pattern, other than of general satisfaction, in the responses.

Problems were mainly 'technical' ones of arranging the syllabus to make best use of the tutors, in particular engineering the timetable so that practical classes, rather than theory, took place when the tutors were available.

The best aspect of having tutors for the teachers was *having extra people about*. For example:

- 'It facilitates working in small groups, each with a tutor, which is particularly suited to the "electricity" topic.'
- 'Kids can progress much faster and at their own pace.'
- 'It has enabled the class to be taught in small groups which has been of great help in getting people to understand a difficult subject like genetics.'
- '. . . not having to have eyes in the back of my head! The room is fairly big, and I no longer have to keep rushing backwards and forwards.'

Like the tutors, the teachers thought that the peer tutoring would be improved if there was more opportunity for teachers and tutors to meet, in particular for the tutors to get to know more about the structure of the syllabus and the specific lesson plans.

The other comments received were favourable, with one exception:

- 'Perhaps male tutors should be warned of the possibility of their affecting third-year girls in unforeseen ways – which occasionally verge on hysteria!'

This comment underlines the suggestion (see Chapter 4), that same-sex tutor-tutee pairs are probably the most satisfactory.

Otherwise, the comments were favourable:

- 'The lessons which best succeed are those where a high degree of *understanding* is required, which discussion in small groups can bring out. Or those where the experimental instructions are unusually complicated and help is needed in getting it to work. As taught at present, this suggests physics and chemistry benefit more than biology.'
- 'Considering the tutors have no education training I feel that they have done very well indeed! Certainly no worse than many students from colleges of education that I have observed.'
- 'Their presence is greatly appreciated – I think it is a very good idea!'

Some teachers had tutors in more than one class. They were, therefore, given a separate questionnaire for each class. Table 5.4 lists *responses* not teachers, the response-rate being 162 over 267 = 60.7 per cent. Multiple-choice questions asked teachers to indicate whether, with tutors, lessons were:

(a) easier to handle/more difficult to handle/about the same as usual; and
(b) more enjoyable/less enjoyable/about the same as usual.

In addition, teachers were asked whether in their opinion pupils seemed to learn:

(c) more than usual/less than usual/about as much as usual with tutors present as without tutors.

Table 5.4 *Teacher responses (percentages):*
$n = 162$ *(Response rate 162/267 = 60.7 per cent)*

With tutors Lessons were	*Easier to handle* 62	*More difficult to handle* 6	*About the same as usual* 28
Teaching was	*More enjoyable* 69	*Less enjoyable* 2	*About the same as usual* 22
Pupils seemed to learn	*More than usual* 69	*Less than usual* 4	*About as much as usual* 25

As mentioned above, schemes similar to 'The Pimlico Connection' started up in the Autumn of 1987 at the universities of Cambridge, East Anglia, and Warwick. Within London, a scheme based at University College has also been started. In a collaborative exercise to see if the effects of 'The Pimlico Connection' can be replicated in other settings, the organizers of these schemes have used questionnaires for pupils, students, and teachers based upon those described above. First returns from these other schemes indicate remarkable similarity with 'The Pimlico Connection'; in particular, students highlight their appreciation of being given the opportunity to communicate scientific ideas. These initial findings suggest that it is probable that the positive effects of 'The Pimlico Connection' can be replicated in areas other than the inner-city, with students from campus universities and/or in more rural settings.

Figure 5.6 *'The Pimlico Connection': Pupil visitors see magnetic levitation at Imperial College*

Chapter 6

A Framework for Peer Tutoring

Summary

Peer tutoring has the potential to release huge amounts of hitherto untapped energy because it has many points of contact, both conceptual and administrative, with other activities which people find congenial. However, peer tutoring is characteristically more formal and more complex than other types of activity through which non-professionals instruct each other. As the degree of formality and complexity increases, it becomes necessary for the activity to be overseen by professional facilitators.

Within formal education, peer tutoring may be seen as a form of Study Service through which students or schoolchildren combine education with social action by doing work of direct practical social value as part of their studies – specifically *work which could not otherwise be done*.

Peer tutoring can contribute to most forms of higher education by introducing an element of reflection. This chapter examines the value of such reflection in Professional Education; in Teacher Training; and in Non-Vocational Education in the Arts, Pure Sciences, and Social Sciences, and examines teaching arrangements which can incorporate peer tutoring as Study Service.

In Secondary Education, the training which pupils need to undergo if they are to be effective can be the focus for a wide range of studies. Suggestions are offered on ways of building such training into schooling both as an adjunct to the curriculum and as part of specialist subjects, and of assessing the reflective element of work which involves peer tutoring as part of the studies of the tutors.

6.1 Types of framework: conceptual and administrative

Peer tutoring has the potential to release huge amounts of hitherto untapped energy. This is because peer tutoring has many points of contact, both conceptual and administrative, with other activities which people find congenial. *Mutatis mutandis*, many activities involving people in volunteer roles might be enhanced by attention to the principles of good practice which have nourished peer tutoring.

Conceptually, peer tutoring is similar to many activities, from the completely informal encounters of play to the most complex activities of co-operation in higher education, in which people help each other and learn by doing so. In natural history societies, sailing clubs, hill-walking and mountaineering clubs, archaeological societies, and a thousand and one leisure institutions, people teach one another knowledge and skills as a matter of course. No-one sees this as in any way strange or difficult, but the process is the very essence of peer tutoring.

At a more formal level, the beneficial effects on *amour propre* of advising or instructing others is already built into the practices and procedures of many organizations such as the Scout Movement, Alcoholics Anonymous, Synanon, and Gamblers Anonymous. The principle is precisely the same as that which is used in peer tutoring: namely, that the role-expectations built into the role of advisor constrain the individual to modify his or her behaviour, and the repeated presentation of ideas to others reinforces the advisor's own knowledge of and commitment to them.

The principal conceptual difference between peer tutoring and forms of recreational instruction is the degree of formality involved. Typically, peer tutoring involves elements of orderly procedure and precise detail often stemming from some form of professional input.

Another way of looking at types of framework is in terms of their administrative complexity. At the simplest level, and with the minimum administrative facilitation, people may be offered the opportunity to help each other. The parent who asks an eight-year-old to read a bedtime story to a three-year-old is, in fact, establishing an informal administrative framework for peer tutoring! Huge amounts of peer tutoring go on in after-school, and also pre-school, study centres organized by, among others, retired teachers, clergymen, community activists and students. Peer tutoring arranged in this way has two major logistic advantages over more formal in-school peer tutoring: time and space. School buildings can be used immediately after school with minimal inconvenience to everyone. Likewise, projects like SEED (Johntz, 1975), have used school buildings before the working day begins. In Project SEED, professional scientists and mathematicians have helped in schools in the early mornings, doing a stint of tutoring on their way to work. (It may be prudent to invite the school caretaker to join any committee of management of an after-school or pre-school study centre: the caretaker is the person whose working day is likely to suffer the most serious disturbance!) Likewise, timetabling problems disappear in pre- or after-school study centres. Typically, they are more relaxed than in-school work, particularly so if they are located in buildings other than schools (church halls, public libraries, club houses) where backward pupils can get away from the atmosphere of school. Figure 6.1 represents these ideas diagramatically.

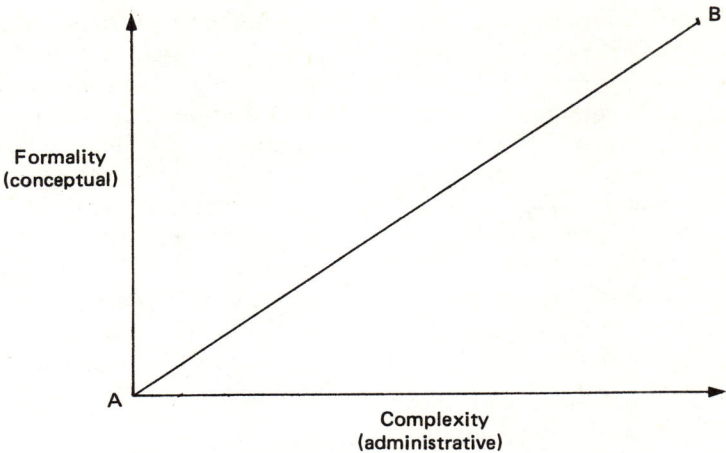

Figure 6.1 *A 'map' for analysing peer tutoring projects*

At the conceptual level, frameworks may be characterized by their degree of formality, and at the administrative level, by their degree of of complexity. It is neither profitable nor desirable to try to quantify these relationships: however, it is worth noting that the further one moves along the axis A to B, the more likely it is that a peer tutoring scheme will require the active efforts of a formal organizer. Readers contemplating starting peer tutoring schemes may wish to try to 'locate' what they plan on these axes. For example, Paired Reading is administratively less complex than cross-age peer tutoring; nevertheless, it may be undertaken with more or less formality. Again, learning cells (Slavin, 1981) require much less formal planning at the conceptual level (because university students can be expected to work out what they need to know more readily than can schoolchildren) but still require some basic administrative facilitation which may be quite complex.

On the assumption that most readers will readily see for themselves opportunities to develop peer tutoring opportunities at the lower levels of conceptual formality and administrative complexity, the remainder of this chapter will concentrate on administrative frameworks which are both formal and complex, but which, by that very fact, offer significant opportunities for enhanced learning, both in higher education and in secondary education.

6.2 Peer tutoring in higher education

(a) Study Service in higher education

Peer tutoring can and does take place in many ways in higher education. We have described in Chapter 2 how peer tutoring is one element of Keller-Plan Courses, and Slavin's work has illustrated many varieties of mutual instruction which go on within higher education. One form of peer tutoring which it is fruitful to consider is that involved in Study Service which is itself a subvariant of Experiential Learning in which students learn by doing.

Study Service is the term applied by UNESCO to work in which students combine study leading to the award of an academic qualification with some form of direct practical service to the community. Students in Study Service schemes do not compete with paid professionals, rather they do work *which could not otherwise have been done*. (Service-Learning is the term used in the USA for the same activity.) In a major examination of Study Service in the United Kingdom, (Whitley, 1980, 1982), Community Service Volunteers distinguished Study Service from staff consultancy/research on the one hand, and from purely voluntary extra-curricular student activities on the other. Four criteria distinguish Study Service from other work in which people in higher education serve society:

1. Students (not staff alone) should be involved.
2. The work should be an integral part of the curriculum and preferably assessed.
3. There should normally be direct contact, at some stage of the course, between students and intended beneficiaries.
4. The effect of the work should be detectable at individual or small-group level.

In the United Kingdom, for example, (see Goodlad, 1975, 1982a) law students have given free legal advice to people who cannot afford professional fees; town planning students have helped tenants to formulate and express their views about planning proposals which might affect them; engineering students have studied the needs of old and poor people for systems and devices (telephones, meals-on-wheels, sheltered employment) which neither government nor private industry had examined; theology and sociology students have worked within a very wide variety of community groups, statutory and voluntary, giving various sorts of practical service; students of languages have taught English to immigrants; and technical college students on day-release have built an adventure playground as part of their Liberal Studies. In every case, the involvement of the college staff has been designed to ensure that the service is *competent* – the basic requirement of all community service; the use of the community service as a focus for learning has also ensured *reciprocity* – both students and those whom they seek to serve benefiting in different ways from the activity – which diminishes thereby the likelihood of paternalism on the one hand, or exploitation on the other. The tutoring in 'The Pimlico Connection' (described in the previous chapter) is an example of Study Service of this type.

For more than 15 years, similar work has been undertaken in overseas countries (see Woods, 1975). University Development Services, Study Service schemes, and other forms of university-linked voluntary service have been undertaken in, among other places, Colombia, the Congo, Ethiopia, Ghana,

Guatemala, Honduras, India, Indonesia, Israel, Japan, Mexico, Nicaragua, Pakistan, Philippines, Singapore, Sri Lanka, and the United States of America.

Fussell and Quarmby (1974), who advised several governments in the early stages of their Study Service schemes, have categorized them as follows:

1. *Intervening* schemes involving a period of full-time service occurring between periods of academic study.
2. *Interwoven* schemes having service activities continuously integrated into or interwoven with the more traditional parts of the curriculum.
3. *Subsequent* schemes involving a period of service (usually full-time and long-term) following graduation.
4. *Parallel* schemes involving service activities undertaken on a part-time basis in the students' own time, or in part of their class-time that is not integrated or interwoven with their academic studies. (The lack of explicit integration of the study and service is a very important difference between parallel and interwoven schemes which they sometimes resemble.)
5. *Related* service schemes which are not organized in the context of formal education but which achieve some of the effects of Study Service schemes – for example, full-time long-term service following graduation as in the Peace Corps or Voluntary Service Overseas.

Peer tutoring can, and does, take place in any or all of these types of scheme. The important point to stress here is that tutoring is only *one* of a wide variety of forms of Study Service. It may usefully, in many contexts, be thought of as just one of a variety of activities to be undertaken by students, separately or in combination with other work, particularly when Study Service schemes involve long-term, full-time periods of work in remote places. The operational requirements of Study Service schemes in different countries determine the type of scheme that is used. In some Third World countries, for example, students live for long periods of time in rural areas where the cost and inconvenience of travel make interwoven schemes impossible to operate. Kann and Mokgethi (1981) describe how Botswana nationals on leaving secondary school are required to live and work for one year in remote villages of their country, teaching at primary school, giving health education, teaching literacy, and giving other non-formal education along with doing agricultural work and helping in community development.

In Third World countries, the emphasis of Study Service schemes is usually on economic development. Students have, among other things, taken part in pest-control campaigns; dug irrigation ditches and cleared new land; run model farms; developed co-operatives and crop-marketing schemes; drilled wells; laid pipelines; built hospitals and health centres; run campaigns to prevent cholera and dysentery; etc (see Fussell and Quarmby, 1974; Woods, 1975). Working as skilled workers or labourers, implementors of projects, builders of institutions, providers of information, originators or agents of social and technical change, university and other students have made massive contributions to economic development.

In Western countries, however, the problems needing attention are often different. There may be enough, indeed (tragically), more than enough, skilled people to carry out the basic economic functions of society. In the area of personal care, no amount of technical knowledge or physical resource can replace the value of the individual contact with another human being which volunteers can offer. For this reason, much volunteer activity in the West has concentrated on the old and the physically or mentally infirm, and, increasingly, on the needs of people who for one reason or another may need more personal attention than paid professionals can offer – prisoners, educationally-backward children, illiterate adults, and so on.

Whether they operate as specialists or generalists (in terms of their university studies), students can offer a multitude of services which could not otherwise be afforded. The value to the students is in terms of their education: Study Service, like other forms of experiential learning, forms a bridge between theory and practice.

Study Service requires specialized knowledge to be perceived in a context of co-operation with others and of practical application. As Fussell and Quarmby (1974) have written:

> Students are often encouraged to be passive listeners, with the most rewarded skill being the ability to remember the words of lecturers or textbooks at examination time. Initiative, self-confidence, self-reliance and the taking of responsibility, the seeking and acceptance of challenges, the questioning of opinions, and independent and original analysis of problems and the finding of solutions, are rarely encouraged and may even be discouraged, and students are often treated as children even when they are in their early twenties.
>
> Effective Study-Service Schemes, by placing students to work independently in remote rural areas, by challenging them to respond practically to real needs, treat students as adults, giving them responsibility, developing in them initiative, self-confidence, self-reliance, and the ability to analyse problems on their own and to come up with possible solutions.

It is not, of course, necessary for students to go to remote rural areas to experience the complexity of real life compared to the coherence often artificially imposed by textbooks: schemes like the MIT Undergraduate Research Opportunities Programme (see MacVicar and McGavern, 1984) encourage students to do this within the laboratories of their own institutions. Experiential learning, which is frequently on the interwoven model in Western countries, permits and encourages students to combine practical experience of work or social service with theoretical study by spending a few hours each week working in activities which are germane to their studies. Students of history act as museum guides; psychology students work in mental hospitals; politics students work in local or national government offices; science students in government or industrial laboratories, and so on.

The Carnegie Commission on Higher Education (1974) identified experiential learning as one of the most important growth areas in American higher education and recommended further work in this area:

Institutions of Higher Education should undertake those community service activities that revitalize its educational functions and constitute an integral part of its educational programme, are within the institutional capacity both in terms of personnel and resources, and are not duplicative of the services of other urban institutions.

In the USA, many organizations (such as the Council for Adult and Experiential Learning, the National Society for Internships and Experiential Education, and the Partnership for Service Learning) are now active in the field, producing publications to support initiatives locally (see eg, Kendall *et al*, 1986). Likewise, in the United Kingdom, the Advisory Service of Community Service Volunteers, the Education for Capability scheme run by the Royal Society of Arts, the Learning from Experience Trust, and others are actively promoting the idea.

Peer tutoring, as a sub-variant of Study Service, is attractive because it readily meets the Carnegie Commission criterion of being 'within institutional capacity in terms of personnel and resources'. It is also relatively simple to institute compared with other forms of Study Service (it may, in fact, be the means whereby students who do not see themselves as 'community action types' become interested in, and involved with, problems of people less fortunate than themselves). It is, therefore, useful to examine briefly some of the ways in which peer tutoring can fit into the frameworks of some specific types of higher education contributing to the fundamental purposes of education in those areas.

(b) The value of peer tutoring in higher education

Apart from increasing the social awareness of students, peer tutoring can contribute to most forms of higher education by introducing an element of reflection. One cannot teach a subject for long without pausing to reflect on the purpose of doing so. One also becomes more aware of the way in which a discipline holds together by trying to organize one's thoughts in preparation for teaching. In this regard, peer tutoring may be one agency whereby 'deep' rather than 'surface' approaches to learning may be inculcated (see, for example, Marton *et al*, 1984; Entwistle, 1987). The field is one ripe for substantial experimental investigation.

A reflexive element in study may be of particular value in the pure sciences and the arts where the primary purpose of study may be to deepen our understanding of the physical and social world, and thereby of ourselves. But it is important too in other forms of education for, without appropriate reflexivity, students may tend to perceive the provisional and tentative formulations of their disciplines as 'ultimate truths'. If 'authoritative uncertainty' is replaced as a primary academic value, (see Goodlad, 1976a), it is essential to offer students the opportunity to reflect about their disciplines.

1. Professional education

Whatever else education for the professions may be about, it is ultimately about the control and disposition of knowledge (see Goodlad, 1984). The fundamental work of professionals may be thought of as making clear to people less well informed than the professionals the areas of their choice in technical matters. For example, doctors explain to patients that this or that mode of treatment (or none at all) is possible; the patients then have to choose what they wish the doctors to do. Again, lawyers explain to their clients the ways in which the law affects their situation, and then wait for instructions. Likewise, architects ascertain their clients' general wishes and then explain the technical options (usually by drawings and models). The fact that professionals usually go on to execute the wishes of their clients should not obscure the fact that the primary task of professionals is that of indicating the grounds of choice.

In all professions, it is necessary for the professional person to communicate ideas simply and effectively to other people. In some professional schools (in engineering, for example), specific instruction in communication skills is included – through report-writing exercises and so on. Such work can be ineffably boring. Communication strictly defined means sharing; one cannot communicate unless one has something one wishes to share. It can be remarkably dispiriting to write reports for one's tutor when one knows that the tutor knows everything one could possibly say! Communication exercises are, however, transformed when they are done for 'real'. That is why Experiential Learning schemes in general, and Study Service in particular, are so attractive to students: the students may be working for real clients and have the interest and responsibility of writing reports which someone positively wants to read. Similarly, intending professionals can get tremendous stimulus from trying to explain technical ideas to other people in peer tutoring schemes. Many of the Imperial College students who take part in 'The Pimlico Connection' have no intention of becoming teachers, but (as the quotations in the previous chapter indicate), they greatly value and enjoy explaining ideas to other people.

Communication skills can be developed even through relatively low-level technical knowledge, indeed, it is sometimes more difficult to explain an idea at an elementary level than it is to explain it to people who already have a complex framework of ideas in which to 'locate' it. Responding to the needs of a specific audience; deciding the specific purpose of a communication; organizing ideas in some sort of structure; choosing the order of presentation; precise use of simple words; and so on – all these fundamental communication skills can readily be practised in peer tutoring.

The wider the range of intending professionals involved in peer tutoring (even in basic skills like reading and arithmetic) the better, for just as Study Service can give students a taste of different careers, so can peer tutoring expose the tutored pupils to a wide range of interests and ideas which might stimulate career interests. It may, for example, be particularly important for intending professionals to act as tutors because, in addition to passing on the basic skills, they can tell their tutees about work in their chosen professions.

The tutors do, of course, clear their own minds remarkably effectively by doing this! The career-exposure component of tutoring may be specially valuable for subjects which are not taught at school – law, town planning, architecture, food technology, social work, and so on.

2. Teacher training

Peer tutoring is, of course, uniquely valuable as a component in teacher training. By acting as a tutor, an intending teacher can participate in teaching without either the frustration of being a mere observer or the awesome responsibility of being in charge of a class (see Gray, 1983).

In the United Kingdom, peer tutoring is now doubly attractive in some institutions. In the Public Sector of Higher Education, intending teachers are increasingly taking parts of their studies alongside other students in 'diversified' institutions of higher education – following the closure of many mono-technic teacher training colleges, and the merger of others with universities, polytechnics, and other institutions of higher education. Students who might have felt 'trapped into teaching' by attending a mono-technic college of education can now, in theory, defer the decision to enter teaching until later on in their degree courses. However, students who have decided that they wish to teach may be frustrated by being required to study specific academic disciplines for two or more years without getting a sniff of a classroom in their nostrils. Peer tutoring, undertaken within the context of a traditional discipline, can give them a chance to become involved in schools early on in their higher education.

As indicated in Chapter 5, the experience of tutoring can also help students to decide whether or not they wish to go into teaching. For some students, exposure to the realities of teaching may dissuade them from undertaking PGCE work, and thereby prevent later disappointment and frustration. For other students, the perception of the immensely interesting and complicated task of the professional teacher (viewed through eyes other than those of a schoolchild) can show the challenge of the job.

3. Non-vocational education: arts and pure sciences

Discussing 'Summer projects for children with language difficulties', Hawkins and Derrick (1975) have argued that to link immigrant English-teaching schemes formally with the curriculum of the university students who act as tutors provides a unique opportunity for students to test their understanding of linguistic theories against practicalities. More importantly, they use a rock-climbing image to describe the desirable model of progress in education. In this model, each student would have two objectives: to make his or her own pitch, but then immediately to secure the rope and help some other learner up.

Peer tutoring in basic skills can, as in professional education, offer singular benefits to students who act as tutors and to their tutees. However, students can perhaps help themselves and their tutees more if they go beyond these skills. For example, it can be argued that the extreme cultivation of the few (in detailed, sophisticated, and sensitive appreciation of history, painting, music, literature, physics and so on) can only be socially justified if those who enjoy such education share their treasure with other people. The argument is the stronger the more people are supported by public funds. Less austerely perhaps, it can be asserted that one's enjoyment of the arts and sciences is enormously increased the more it is shared. The pleasure of a poem, novel, play, concerto, scientific discovery, is hugely enhanced when one can introduce someone else to it.

In all of these instances, students are constrained to reflect about the structure of their disciplines and to reflect on *why* they are worth studying. It is this element of reflection which is markedly lacking from much contemporary higher education. Engineering students often have 'liberal studies' which are designed to induce thought about the social, economic, political, philosophical purposes and meaning of their main subjects. But what is the equivalent in the humanities, arts, and pure sciences? Perhaps because many of the subjects are concerned with questions of value and purpose, the question is felt to be unnecessary. But how do individual students accommodate the organized knowledge of their disciplines into their personal knowledge? It is clear from Perry's work (1970, 1981), that not all students make this integration effectively, and certainly do not all do it at the same stage in their academic careers. Analytic reflection can, however, be effectively provoked by students' contact (through peer tutoring) with children who do not take for granted what may be of self-evident value to university students.

4. Non-vocational education: social sciences
The preceding arguments concerning reflection and the development of communication skills apply equally strongly to students of the social sciences. Such students can also help their tutees not only with specific skills in reading, arithmetic and so on, but can indicate career and study possibilities.

The field-experience involved in tutoring is, of course, bristling with possibilities for students of the social sciences. Some of the most interesting issues in the sociology of education can be explored with reference to peer tutoring. Similarly, anthropology students may find their study of cultures greatly enriched by close observation of teenage culture. Students of psychology and social psychology could do a signal service by carrying out research to try to determine whether specific tutoring projects have been successful or not and to add to our knowledge of the process. Students of social work would benefit by close contact with children of all backgrounds and interests; it may be difficult to comprehend social pathology without some experience of normality.

(c) Teaching arrangements which can incorporate peer tutoring
Students who take part in peer tutoring must be trained in some basic procedures. However, tutor-training is not necessarily the best focus for study in higher education. Students, unlike schoolchildren for whom detailed

training is advocated below, are usually pretty much at ease in their disciplines and can be trained in some standard tutoring procedures in a few hours. Teaching arrangements which can usefully accommodate tutoring will vary from discipline to discipline; one common technique, however, which is not discipline-specific, is project work.

The engineering students from Imperial College who tutored in the first years of 'The Pimlico Connection' (see Chapter 5) evaluated their tutoring as a final-year project for their degree (see Abidi *et al*, 1976; Anslow *et al*, 1977). Students currently tutoring who take a course on 'The communication of scientific ideas' also carry out projects related to their studies, such as an evaluation of the SMILE mathematics syllabus. Similar projects could readily be mounted in any of a variety of disciplines. Adderley *et al* (1975) offer some principles of good practice for project methods in higher education.

Experiential learning by individuals or groups of students can, of course, usually be supported by appropriate lecture courses and seminars. The study component of Study Service would be in the form of project work resulting in familiar academic products – reports, essays, dissertations, theses and so on. Such items, recounting students' practical experiences, interpreting them in the light of the theoretical preoccupations of their disciplines, and relating them to leading concepts can readily be assessed by the usual academic criteria – internal consistency, accuracy, evidence of familiarity with leading ideas, originality of observation, clarity, economy and so on.

Some teachers in higher education may (quite rightly) not wish to assess the peer tutoring itself, believing it to be beyond their competence to do so. A useful expedient, used in many American experiential learning schemes, is to separate out the action and reflection components of a course. Agency supervisors' reports (in peer tutoring, schoolteachers' reports) can be used to indicate whether or not students have done what was expected of them in the place of action (turning up regularly and on time etc). Academic supervisors' reports can be used to assess the students' competence in producing the academic work – report, essay, etc. In interwoven schemes, some universities require two separate courses to be taken simultaneously, satisfactory performance on one being a condition of achieving a grade on the other. The 'action' course can be graded pass/fail on the basis of the agency supervisor's report; the 'reflection' course can be graded 'A', 'B', 'C', or 'D' etc, on the basis of the academic supervisor's report. Commonly, students draw up 'contracts of expectation' at the beginning of a period of study which are signed by the students, their agency supervisors, and their academic supervisors – each signatory stating what is expected of the student.

6.3 Peer tutoring in secondary education

Many teachers in Secondary Education will be content to use peer tutoring either within their own schools, or in co-operation with their neighbouring primary school, as a beneficial adjunct to the curriculum. The following paragraphs are addressed to those who might wish to integrate peer tutoring in some way with the academic studies of pupils in secondary schools.

(a) Study Service in schools

For many years, large numbers of young people have been involved in community service, much of it centred on their schools, and some of it forming part of their studies. For example, the National Association of Secondary School Principals (NASSP, 1974) reported that 43 per cent of High School pupils in the USA were involved in some form of community service. Many more were working, most part-time and for pay. Pupils' interests had broadened beyond the classroom. The NASSP study reported that approximately 75 per cent of High School pupils believed that work and service opportunities should be offered during the schoolday for credit.

Likewise, in the United Kingdom, community service has for many years been part of schoolwork. The Schools Council Working Paper No 17 *Community Service and the Curriculum* (Schools Council, 1968) stressed that practical work in the local community could significantly reinforce and enrich the work of the classroom. The Department of Education and Science in *Community Service in Education* (DES, 1974) added that much of the educational value of community service derives from the pupil's discussion and recording, and the interpretation of the pupil's experience by sensitive adults. This follow-up, it was suggested, must be regarded as an essential part of any scheme which was to be given a place within the curriculum. Study Service was seen as crucially important in developing in pupils a sense of responsibility: 'the educational principle that an individual will learn more about a situation in which he himself is involved remains as true in this setting as in other settings, as does the adage that one cannot teach responsibility, one can only give it'.

Just as the Carnegie Commission urged that Study Service in Higher Education should recognize the capacities of given institutions, so the DES document urged that it is essential that Community Service Work undertaken as Study Service should be within the capacity of the pupils. This is why peer tutoring is so attractive as a form of Study Service: there are few pupils in secondary schools who do not have something to offer to children younger than themselves.

(b) The training of tutors as a focus for study

Research indicates (see Chapter 4) that children who are to act as tutors must be trained in certain basic skills if they are to be effective. For example, children will need to be told how to recognize when a younger child has a learning difficulty; how to maintain good relationships with the younger child;

how to make young children feel liked and important; how to co-operate with teachers; and so on. Typically, a peer tutoring scheme will require that the tutors attend a short induction course followed by regular (often weekly) briefing sessions. Providing the necessary training may be a considerable strain on an extra-curricular peer tutoring scheme; however, if the training is built into the curriculum of the tutors, the training, quite apart from the tutoring itself, can be of immense educative potential.

Teachers who adopt peer tutoring will no doubt be best able to judge precisely what curriculum would best suit the pupils who are to act as tutors, and where this would lock into existing studies.

Klaus (1975) has sketched a ten-lesson training-plan synthesized from what is practised in many United States schools:

Lesson 1. Orientation to the Programme; the tutor's responsibilities in terms of extra effort, attendance and deportment; discussion of why students have volunteered for the programme and their expectations; presentation of what the programme is trying to accomplish.

Lesson 2. Description of the Learners; who they are and what kinds of learning problems they may have; how tutors and learners will be paired; introduction to the receiving teachers; discussion of how the younger children will view the tutors and what tutoring experiences would be pleasant and unpleasant for them.

Lesson 3. Meeting the Children; how to act in the learners' classroom; where to hold the session; how to introduce yourself to the learner, what to say and do; role-play practice on getting acquainted with the learners and showing interest in them.

Lesson 4. Visit with the Learners; a get-acquainted session in the learners' classroom, preferably organized as an 'informal' party-occasion followed by brief individual meetings between the tutors and several children including the intended tutoring partner.

Lesson 5. Resolving Tutor Concerns; discussion of visit with the learners and how the tutors feel towards the children; what the tutors have discovered about the children, and what questions they have; role-play practice on establishing rapport with their partner.

Lesson 6. Interaction with Partners: Another visit to the learners' classroom; getting acquainted with the agreed-upon tutoring partner; inspection of the learners' materials and observation of their current performance; making name tags for each other.

Lesson 7. Analysis of the Tutoring Process; description of typical tutoring activities; inspection of materials to be used; using praise and avoiding criticism; how to deal with the learners' errors; role-play demonstration of tutoring session with praise-only critique.

Lesson 8. Practice in Tutoring; multiple role-play practice on the tutoring process with emphasis on giving praise and withholding criticism; dealing with learner errors, adapting the instruction to the learner, and meeting instructional objectives.

Lesson 9. Coping with Problems; how to detect and handle loss of interest; apparent rejection of the tutor by the learner; misbehaviour and disturbances and how to deal with them; discussing their school and personal problems with the learners.

Lesson 10. Planning the Sessions; how each day's session will be planned; collecting or developing materials; making a log or record of the learners' progress; what to do when absent; how to co-operate with other tutors when help is needed; the role of school personnel.

Such a scheme should, of course, be adapted to the educational level and sophistication of the putative tutors.

Another example of a course, (described in *High School Courses with Volunteer Components* (NSVP, nd)), offers tutoring in a lower-school as part of a high-school social studies course on child development. In this course, the high-school pupils tutor for three consecutive hours once a week and have an additional two hours of classroom work. The course provides the necessary practical instruction to help the pupils be effective as tutors; in addition, it helps them to interpret their experience through an intellectual framework.

The first section of the course on child development, requires the tutors to take detailed observations of their charges: body-movements, language, responses to people and parents, attention-spans, reactions to authority. The second section deals with educational methods and structures, examining alternative types of education such as traditional, Montessori and Summerhill approaches. This material stimulates the pupils' thinking about their own education. A third section examines socio-economic factors which affect education, dealing with the education of the poor, urban education, and the effects of social unrest and social change in the schools. Finally, pupils are encouraged to initiate, plan, and execute projects which will directly benefit the lower school or a particular group of its pupils.

Courses such as these not only make schoolchildren into effective tutors; they also enrich the children's education by encouraging introspection, observation, and reflection.

(c) Making space in specialist subjects for experience in peer tutoring

In principle, there is no problem at all in constructing a special course, like those described above, as an adjunct to a GCSE subject, as an element in existing GCSE courses such as child care or social studies, or as an element in advanced general studies. Peer tutoring could, of course, constitute one form of work experience. A more significant challenge, however, will be to make space in specialist subjects for students to undertake peer tutoring and to reflect upon their experience. Just as the association of community service activities only with less able pupils will diminish the importance attached to Study Service by all pupils, so too will the association of Study Service with minority time. The whole concept of Study Service becomes devalued if service is only undertaken when the pressure of other work permits.

The arguments rehearsed in Section 6.2 for building peer tutoring into the various disciplines of higher education apply with equal force to doing so in secondary education. As *Community Service in Education* (DES, 1974), points out, clear communication is essential in most community service situations and the incentive to improve spoken and written English is limitless. In addition, pupils reporting on peer tutoring work can be encouraged to reflect on the organization of ideas in the disciplines which they are studying and in which they are tutoring. For example, pupils studying English and tutoring in it could discuss the literary value (or lack of it) of the books and magazines enjoyed by their tutees and thereby come to enhance their own literary discrimination. Similarly, pupils studying history could conduct visits to sites, organize pageants, prepare presentations around slides or documentary films of contemporary history, and so on. Pupils studying geography could assist with the education of younger pupils by helping them to make maps, carry out meteorological observations, conduct surveys about aspects of town and country planning, collect materials (maps, photographs, local artefacts, raw materials) from foreign countries. Pupils studying art could prepare short lectures based on slides of important paintings or buildings or, better still, take younger pupils on guided visits to art galleries and museums. Pupils studying science can help in laboratory classes and help with visits to science museums or local industries. Indeed, in some cases, (such as the San Francisco Exploratorium), college students and high-school pupils are employed in museums of science and technology as hosts or explainers. As 'interactive science centres' grow in popularity, so will grow the need for peer tutoring of this kind.

Activities such as these give older pupils the chance to inspect their existing knowledge, organize it for the benefit of younger children, and get new knowledge, all with a view to communicating the essence of their disciplines. Where peer tutoring in routine skills (reading, writing, arithmetic, basic techniques of scientific measurement, etc) is involved, it is likely that the older pupils will reinforce their knowledge of fundamentals. If they give formal attention to justifying their actions, as part of their advanced studies, they will benefit all the more.

(d) The assessment of Study Service in schools

A statement of intent (or more grandly 'contract of expectation') can itself be a document suitable for assessment in the curriculum. In *High School Courses with Volunteer Components* (NSVP, nd), the National Student Volunteer Programme suggests that a study-course proposal might address such questions as 'What is the proposed project?'; 'What are the students' goals?'; 'How will it benefit their community?'; 'How will it benefit the students?'; 'Where and with whom will the students be working?'; 'What will the students specifically be doing?'; 'How will the students know if they are succeeding in their goals?'; 'What preliminary planning and information will the students need to prepare themselves for the project?'; 'How will the students share their experiences with others at their school?' To these might be added: 'How does the proposed project involve questions which the students' main discipline may help to handle?' This would invite the students to make an explicit link with the central theoretical questions of the discipline – an extremely complex and demanding task which is rarely adequately accomplished even at postgraduate level in universities!

Second, students can be required to keep log books on their peer tutoring work (or indeed on any form of Study Service). Like a scientist's log book, those of pupils can be asked to state session-by-session what the pupils intend to do, how it is to be done, what actually happened during the tutoring sessions, and what was concluded from this. 'Significant incident reports' can be particularly valuable in this context. Pupils note things which happen which they think somehow important in the overall activity and explain why. In *Learning from Service*, Conrad and Hedin (1976) suggest that pupils can relate an incident to the more comprehensive picture by recording their own careful observations, interviewing the 'natives' (in peer tutoring schemes, teachers and pupils who may have been involved in a row) to learn the meaning *they* place on their actions; finding special informants who may be specially sensitive to what is going on, either through 'ringleader status' or perhaps by being 'malcontents'; consulting outsiders who have special knowledge of the target group – supervisors, experts, etc; comparing findings with information available elsewhere – written materials on the subject, experience of classmates, own previous experience. A well-kept log book could provide an external examiner or moderator with excellent material for assessing a pupil's powers of observation, analysis, synthesis, and so on.

Third, pupils can write essays or reports evaluating their experience in peer tutoring. An essay can test (or assay) some proposition or other relevant to the pupils' main discipline, or more specifically relevant to a proper understanding of the peer tutoring activity, and the relationships involved, intellectual procedures adopted and so on. Similarly, reports can consolidate pupils' experience of their work.

A particularly valuable form of report is one aimed at the next incumbent of a pupil's Study Service role. Reports can be designed to communicate as much as possible of the pupils' experience for the benefit of their successors in peer tutoring, explaining what strategy was adopted and why, which tactics seemed effective (such as which books the tutees liked), what results were of any importance, evaluation procedures adopted, and so on. Not only can such reports be useful assessable documents, they can also serve a very valuable purpose in preparing subsequent students, and for that reason are the more interesting for pupils to write. Passing on the baton, as it were, can save huge amounts of administrators' time in Study Service. One Study Service student's report can tell the next student how the school/hospital/nursing home or whatever is organized; who must be consulted about what; what organizational or administrative difficulties can occur; and so on – all things which hard-pressed teachers/doctors/chief nursing officers would otherwise have to explain to each succeeding student or group of students.

6.4 The need for structure

Peer tutoring offers the possibility of social integration within an institution between pupils of different ages and between pupils who act as tutors and the teachers with whom they co-operate. Peer tutoring also offers possibilities of work which integrates the concerns of different types of educating institution – universities/secondary schools, secondary schools/primary schools, and so on. More importantly, peer tutoring (and this is true of many forms of Study Service) can form a focus of intellectual attention, integrating several levels of concern. However, it must be said that the more formal a scheme (conceptually) and the more complex (administratively), the more difficult it is to operate. It is possible, even probable, that peer tutoring may develop most rapidly and easily either as an after-school (extra-curricular activity) or within individual classrooms through such expedients as Paired Reading. However, even the simplest activity may need some loose facilitation: even children looking after younger siblings find it easier to do so if they are given some adult guidance about things to do to keep the younger child occupied! The more formal the scheme, and the more complex it is administratively, the greater the need for structure. The chapter which follows offers some suggestions for starting a tutoring scheme, identifying the minimal range of issues to be considered. It is written anticipating a complex scheme: the ideas put forward should obviously be adapted for any simpler scheme that is adopted.

Chapter 7

How to Start a Peer Tutoring Scheme

Summary

Anyone planning to start a peer tutoring scheme will need to consider a number of administrative issues. This chapter reviews some which have been found to be important.

- Define aims. Who is to teach what to whom for what purpose? Objectives should be simple and readily achievable. A written statement of objectives can point out possible problems.
- Evaluate the tutoring. Perception of suitable objectives is sharpened if one tries to decide how one will know if the objectives have been achieved. Also, people like to know how things are going.
- Structure the content. Tutees learn best, and tutors can cope most readily, when teaching materials are structured. The material must: be readily intelligible to the tutees; give something for tutors to do; ensure appropriate reinforcement of tutees' learning; offer some choice to participants.
- Ensure proper consultation and define roles. Failures in communication and loss of impetus can be avoided if *one* person is given overall responsibility for co-ordinating a tutoring scheme.
- Train the tutors. Whatever form the tutoring may take, tutors need to be shown how to start tutoring; how the syllabus is organized; how to reinforce tutees' learning: what to do if things go badly; how to end a session. Techniques are described which are useful for training tutors, such as interviewing, role-playing, and brain-storming.
- Support the tutors. Regular de-briefing sessions are needed for the organizer and/or professional teachers to keep in touch with the tutors. Tutors need to be given clear instructions about what to do. Lists of tutoring techniques are offered.
- Logistics. Tutoring schemes should be kept as simple as possible. Particular attention needs to be given to: suitable times and places for tutoring to take place, and for the introductory and de-briefing meetings; selection of tutors and tutees; documentation (so that tutors, tutees, and organizers know how everyone is getting on); finance. Appendix B offers a check-list of factors to consider.

Who is to teach *what* to *whom* for what *purpose, when, where,* and *how? Who* will co-ordinate activities? How will *success* be assessed? These are some of the questions which must be answered by anyone planning to set up a peer tutoring scheme. The purpose of this chapter is to review some of these issues. Much detailed advice is available in reviews of tutoring schemes and in manuals and resource packets specifically designed for supervisors of projects (see note in references on training materials and resource packets). Some of these publications contain minutely detailed instructions, specimen letters, specimen materials, etc for those planning schemes where children teach children (eg, Lippitt *et al*, 1971; Mainiero *et al*, 1971; Melaragno, 1976a). Others review factors which seem to determine the success or otherwise of tutoring (eg, Allen, 1976; Bohning, 1980; Fitz-Gibbon, 1977, 1978a, 1985; Ross, 1982). For an admirably practical guide concentrating on same-age peer tutoring (with special references to Paired Reading), see Topping (1987a). The details of any tutoring scheme will, of course, be determined by its purposes – and the personnel to be involved. The present chapter does not, therefore, offer a formula; rather, it identifies factors which must be considered. Appendix B offers a checklist which may be used in conjunction with this chapter.

7.1 Define aims

Who is to teach *what* to *whom* for what *purpose*?

Although the advantages of tutoring may seem self-evident to all concerned, it is none the less important for the planner of the peer tutoring scheme to be clear in mind about the specific objectives of the scheme. For example, are the benefits sought primarily academic or social? If a compromise has to be made between benefits accruing to tutors and those accruing to tutees, in whose favour will the scheme operate? (see Fitz-Gibbon, 1978b).

The organization of a peer tutoring scheme, the selection of participants, the choice of tutoring materials, etc, all depend on the scheme's objectives. By writing down a precise statement of objectives, it is possible to see where potential conflicts exist and where problems may arise. Klaus (1975) stresses that it is important not to attempt too much. Likewise, Jenkins and Jenkins (1985) urge planners to start small. To maintain the morale of all concerned, objectives of a peer tutoring scheme should be simple and readily achievable so that everyone may see how the scheme is working.

The clarity of intention and thrust of a peer tutoring scheme is best served if its objectives can be stated simply in a single sentence. For example:

- to give six-year-old children increased reading practice at their own level by providing eight-year-old tutors; or
- to permit ten-year-old pupils who are backward in reading skills to review basic skills by tutoring seven-year-olds; or

- to provide 14-year-old pupils with the opportunity to develop their own self-esteem through tutoring elementary schoolchildren.

Simple statements such as these indicate to all concerned what a peer tutoring scheme is all about. An added sophistication is, of course, to state the objectives of a scheme in terms of precise behavioural outcomes. This is particularly important if the scheme is to be the subject of academic research. There is, however, a danger that undue stress is created by statements of, for example, academic goals to be achieved when the purpose of the peer tutoring is to provide a humanly enriching experience for all. A simple expedient is for the planner of the tutoring scheme to write down *focal* and *subsidiary* objectives. The focal objective may be the guiding statement for the programme (for example 'to give six-year-olds increased reading practice at their own level'). The subsidiary objective could be in terms of the questions to which research will be directed (for example, six-year-olds who receive help from ten-year-old tutors will achieve X points better in test Y than pupils from a matched control group who do not receive tutoring but who spend an equal amount of time in normal classroom instruction). Whether the tutoring scheme be part of the regular teaching arrangement of the school or part of a research project, it is valuable to plan some form of evaluative research to measure the progress of the scheme.

7.2 Evaluate the tutoring (see also 4.1(a))

Quite apart from any value it may have in deepening our understanding of peer tutoring, evaluative research offers two important benefits to the planner of a scheme:

First, one's perception of suitable objects for a scheme is sharpened if one tries to determine how one will know when those objects have been achieved.

Second, everyone involved in the scheme (tutors and tutees, as well as administrators) will feel satisfaction if there is 'something to show for it all'.

At the crudest level, evaluation can consist of anecdotal observation by teachers of both tutors and tutees recorded before, during, and after a peer tutoring scheme. For example, teachers can be asked to give subjective impressions as to whether the pupils taking part in the tutoring are showing greater participation in class; have better ideas on how to study; show less tension in class and are less likely to fool around; are better able to express themselves; are better groomed and better behaved, etc.

Subjective observations can be more thoroughly exploited by the use of rating scales which invite specific attention to different types of behaviour. Statistical analysis of the effects of tutoring becomes possible when numerical values can be assigned to before and after performance in specific areas. If evaluation and research are to be combined (and, as Chapter 4 has argued, it is important to note the distinction) it may be useful to evaluate a peer tutoring scheme with standardized tests of, for example, vocabulary, mathematics, spelling, etc. Again, it is useful to keep numerical records of objectively-observable behaviours which might be relevant such as number of absences of tutors or tutees, number of late arrivals of tutors or tutees, etc. Criterion-referenced teaching materials (that is to say ones that show the performance of each *individual* learner) have built-in facilities of evaluation. Structured tutoring schemes, based on closely-planned materials are attractive in that, typically, they make use of these types of materials. The principal advantage of this procedure is that participants in the peer tutoring scheme can see how they are getting on as they go along, rather than waiting for a once-only test at the end of the proceedings. Allen (1976) offers advice to those planning research associated with a peer tutoring programme. For example, testing procedures can upset teachers very much. The tests themselves can be perceived as spying and the testing sessions can be very disruptive of class-time and also time-consuming for all concerned. Allen recommends that test materials should be made available to all teachers before the scheme is instituted. Researchers should avoid springing things on people, should avoid scheduling tests at busy times of the school year, and should give teachers the results as soon as possible after the testing. If the test results are to be used for psychometric research, various other factors must be considered: the completion of tests should be adequately supervised; the test instruments should be clear and unambiguous; the number of open-ended questions should be minimized, etc.

7.3 Structure the content

The major decision for anyone running a tutoring scheme is the degree of control to exercise over the content of the teaching. The extreme conditions are:

(a) when tutors are given complete responsibility for choosing teaching materials; and
(b) when tutors operate with programmed texts in which the steps are laid down very precisely.

For most purposes, some compromise seems suitable. Bloom (1976) has suggested useful criteria for the planner of tutoring to bear in mind in choosing materials.

First, she suggests that material should be selected which makes learning-cues more meaningful and salient to the tutees. Feedback and correction for the tutees' individual responses, and appropriate reinforcement of correct responses, combine to convince the tutees that they really can learn what they may have thought of as being hopeless. When material develops in step-by-step progression and success is certain, a tutee can give full attention to a limited cue with a greater expectation of success. For materials in reading and language arts, Bloom suggests three minimum requirements to satisfy a principle of making cues salient and meaningful:

1. It must be based on specific skill-needs of tutees for which they perceive the need.
2. It must be systematically organized in a sequence of planned tasks with the essential oral component built in.
3. It must provide clear models of correct responses, desired behaviours, and appropriate procedures that tutors can use to develop independence in tutees.

Second, Bloom suggests selection of material to ensure maximum participation. She stresses that it is almost impossible for tutors spontaneously to invent many examples to cover the variety of instances necessary for practice. These examples must be built into the material. Above all, the example must involve human interaction – for it is the human relationship in tutoring which keeps both tutor and tutee at a given learning task for sufficient time.

Third, Bloom stresses that the material must ensure appropriate reinforcement. Much of the value of having live tutors is in their capacity to offer reinforcement in a humanly rewarding manner. However, tutors do not do this automatically; they must be trained in the necessary procedures. Even with training, tutors will be better able to give necessary reinforcement if the reinforcement is built into the teaching materials. The first reinforcement by success is particularly important and depends entirely on the appropriate material. Material which is too difficult will frustrate the tutee and will probably prevent trust between tutor and tutee from developing. Reinforcement is aided if the teaching materials include a simple checklist providing instant information for both tutor and tutee about the result of their work. Criterion-referenced systems (as suggested in Section 7.2) aid evaluative research as well as offering personal reinforcement to tutors and tutees.

Fourth, teaching materials should offer some choice to participants in tutoring. Much of the satisfaction to tutors is in making a unique, personal contribution to the education of their tutees. A peer tutoring scheme which allows no opportunity for originality is likely to hold little appeal for tutors. Accordingly, some mixture of structure and freedom is necessary.

Whatever the content of a peer tutoring scheme – mathematics, reading, science – it is important to keep a balance between these considerations. Experience suggests that both tutors and tutees will feel at ease if there is some readily apparent structure to the tutoring; similarly, human contact can most readily develop around material which is the unique contribution of the tutor. The responsibility of the planner of peer tutoring rests in selecting appropriate teaching materials and also in providing time for unstructured interaction based on those materials. Tutors can use the unstructured time to build upon, amplify, and embellish the structured material.

Non-specialist organizers of peer tutoring schemes (parents, clergymen, community activists and others) may wish to seek the help of professional teachers (for example, reading specialists) when deciding the content of tutoring.

7.4 Ensure proper consultation and define roles

When peer tutoring schemes have failed, two major factors have often been present:

1. There was a lack of communication – people who should have known what was going on did not.
2. There was a loss of initiative and impetus – nobody seemed to know who was responsible for what.

Most of these difficulties can be circumvented if *one* single person is given overall responsibility for the project.

Communication is without doubt the most difficult single aspect of peer tutoring. Education has become so specialized, so fragmented, that frequently teachers in schools and colleges do not know what other teachers are doing. Indeed, conventional classroom-teaching is a very lonely and private activity. By contrast, peer tutoring, which frequently involves interaction between at least two groups of people, requires movement across many boundaries – some of which are defended with fierce intellectual territoriality.

There is no formula to achieve effective communication (although for those who like a systems approach, Melaragno (1976a), offers a step-by-step procedure for those wishing to introduce peer tutoring). Communication is, however, facilitated if the co-ordinator of a tutoring scheme produces a brief 'statement of intent', a document defining the aims of the peer tutoring scheme and describing briefly the procedures of administration and evaluation involved. Such a statement can be used not only in the planning phase of a peer tutoring scheme (in obtaining necessary permission, finance, etc) but also as a public relations document to be distributed to all people whose interests (real or imagined) may be infringed/involved by the scheme. Likewise, an annual report on a peer tutoring scheme can be very useful not only as a permanent record for participants (tutors in particular value this), but as material to offer to people coming into the scheme for the first time.

Definition of roles is, in fact, an element of the communication process. Communication means sharing, and sharing of responsibility is the essence of effective administration. Accordingly, the planner of a peer tutoring scheme may find it useful to write down (for example, in the 'statement of intent') a list of the expected responsibilities of each party to the operation.

Lippitt *et al* (1971) suggest some possible ascriptions of task. For example, *heads of schools* (principals) may be responsible for: sanctioning the programme; designing some orientation activity for all the teaching staff of the school; interpreting the programme to parents and to school administrators; making time in the school timetable for co-ordinating activities between teachers, seminars for staff, and periodic team meetings.

Sending teachers (those from whose classes tutors are drawn) may be responsible for: recruiting older pupils to act as tutors and interpreting the programme to them; adjusting detailed class schedules; evaluating the significance of the tutoring to older pupils; using the experience of tutoring for the education of the older pupils; matching the tutors to the tutees in collaboration with the teacher of the younger children; keeping in touch with the tutors and keeping a schedule of their tutoring assignments, etc.

Receiving teachers (those to whose classes the tutors go) may be responsible for: the diagnostic work of selecting the younger pupil-tutees; briefing the older pupils (tutors) on the objectives of the syllabus and on the detailed content for use with the younger people (tutees); ensuring feedback to the older pupil-tutors about the progress of their tutees; helping in the matching of tutors and tutees; supporting the older pupil-tutors in their work with the younger pupil-tutees; reporting episodes of helpful behaviour to the sending teacher, etc.

The co-ordinator of the programme can be responsible for: liaison between members of the team; co-ordination of research (if any); the operational requirements of the tutoring; trouble-shooting; the provision of information about the programme to any interested parties; keeping a master-schedule of activities; sharing meetings of participating staff, etc.

All people we met who have been, and are, concerned with peer tutoring schemes are agreed that if initiative is to be maintained, and if the scheme is to be coherent, ultimate responsiblity must rest with one single person. This point cannot be over-emphasized. Who the co-ordinator is to be will, however, depend on the precise nature of the scheme. Allen (1976) discusses the relative merits of the co-ordinator being a teacher, a para-professional, or a researcher. If, for example, the tutors come from a university or from another school, there is some merit in the co-ordinator being a teacher in the school to which the tutors go. In these circumstances, a co-ordinator will be familiar with the details of the school's ways of operating and can handle, on the spot, difficulties and grievances as they arise. Allen gives as an example the introduction of control groups (in a tutoring scheme which was the subject of an experiment) which angered and dismayed teachers who thought that all pupils needing tutoring would get it.

If tutoring is being offered to people of a distinctive neighbourhood or ethnic background, there is merit in the co-ordinator being a para-professional – perhaps a resident of the neighbourhood, or member of the minority group, who has the same background as the participants. Such a person can more readily interpret elements of the programme to those for whom it is designed and has a better appreciation of their needs.

Research staff can be effective as co-ordinators particularly where their expertise is necessary. Allen points out that research staff can often be particularly helpful in planning careful evaluations, in getting support from outside agencies (such as computer services), and giving intellectual coherence to the programme.

Some schemes, (particularly after-school study centres) have been co-ordinated by energetic para-professionals. Many women, with independent means and a high level of education, find the co-ordination of a tutoring programme immensely rewarding. Inevitably, a scheme involving collaboration between institutions and/or activity scattered through a variety of centres (such as Homework Helper Centres) involves much detailed administration. It can be very useful to have the services of a dynamic person with a car and a telephone who, freed from the routine task of teaching, can provide impetus and initiative and can trouble-shoot if problems arise.

There are obvious resource implications for institutions if university, polytechnic, or college lecturers or schoolteachers are to act as co-ordinators. 'The Pimlico Connection' scheme (described in Chapter 5) requires some 12 person-days of administration for each yearly cycle. Peer tutoring schemes will be the more stable (and effective) if properly resourced from the outset.

7.5 Train the tutors

To date, research has provided no very clear guidance as to what is the best form of training for a given situation. Feldman *et al* (1976: 375), for example, suggest that research does not show unequivocally that any one particular method of training is superior to others. Suffice it to say that *some* form of preparation for the tutors is needed. Even trained teachers are unlikely, without proper instruction, to be able to operate effectively. Training tutors is, perhaps, one of the most important and rewarding tasks of the professional teacher in a peer tutoring scheme. Just as tutoring can help tutors to organize their thoughts, so the planning of tutoring can help teachers to organize theirs.

Chapter 6 has stressed the immense educative potential of tutor-training in the education of the tutors. However, because not all tutoring schemes will be interlocked with a curriculum, it is therefore necessary to identify the minimal skills in which untrained persons will have to be coached if they are to act as tutors. Various lists have been drawn up eg Bloom (1976); Klaus (1973, 1975); Melaragno (1976a). Special techniques, such as role-playing and brain-storming, have been found useful in giving tutors direct experience of exercising the skills they will need to use.

The following tutor-skills require special attention:

1. *How to start a tutoring session by establishing a friendly atmosphere.* Tutors will need to get practice in establishing a relaxed atmosphere by smiling, calling the tutees by their first names, acting in a friendly manner, sitting next to the tutees rather than opposite them, etc.
2. *Familiarity with the content of the syllabus.* Tutors will need to be familiar with the overall structure of the syllabus, the teacher's objectives, and the mode of assessment, and will need to learn any step-by-step procedure by which the tutees are expected to learn and gain practice in the application

of the skill. If programmed or highly-structured texts are used, the tutors will need time to read the material and to have the chance to discuss it with a trained teacher.
3. *What to do when the tutee gives a correct answer.* Tutors will need to learn how to properly praise their tutees to provide the necessary reinforcement in their learning.
4. *What to do when the answer is wrong.* Without training, it has been found that young tutors sometimes punish their tutees, sneer, speak sarcastically, etc. Tutors need to be trained in helping their tutees to achieve the right answer but without doing the work for them. Tutors may need practice in repeating the question in different words, modelling the correct answer, judging the correct amount of time to leave before giving the correct answer, avoiding punishment of the tutees, etc.
5. *What to do if a tutoring session goes badly.* Child-tutors are often apprehensive about what to do if their younger charges misbehave. Most peer tutoring schemes require the tutors to refer all discipline problems to the teacher. However, the tutors can prevent discipline problems arising by being sensitive to the needs of the tutees. Tutors will need practice in the personal relations necessary: how to show interest in tutees without being patronising, being firm without being repressive, assuming a dominant role without being domineering, etc. It may be necessary to role-play incidents of boredom, non-co-operation, 'trying-it-on', etc so that the tutors may achieve the necessary confidence.
6. *How to vary the content of peer tutoring sessions.* Tutors will need practice in interweaving difficult and easy material, structured and unstructured material, and different activities (writing, reading, oral response, etc) in tutoring sessions.
7. *How to end a peer tutoring session.* Tutors must be made vividly aware of the importance of recapitulating material at the end of the tutoring sessions to reinforce the tutees' learning and to see that mastery has been achieved. Tutors must also get practice in ending sessions on a positive, pleasant note so that the tutees will look forward to the next session.
8. *Record keeping.* Given the importance of evaluation, not only for monitoring the progress of an entire peer tutoring programme, but also for stimulating individual tutors and tutees, it is necessary to instruct the tutors in whatever procedures of record keeping are devised. If a pro-forma is used, the tutors will need to have practice in filling it in. Alternatively, if 'significant incident' reports are required, the tutors may need guidance about what to include.

The way of training tutors in these skills, and the amount of time to be given to each of them, will, of course, vary depending upon the background and qualifications of those engaged in the peer tutoring scheme. What should be apparent is that most of the skills are ones which must be acquired by practice rather than by private study. If no slot is available in the curriculum of the tutors, some sort of training workshop will need to be arranged. Such a workshop can not only provide the occasion for training tutors in the necessary skills, but also an overall orientation towards the whole programme. Most commentators suggest that, in addition to any such workshop, regular debriefing sessions will be needed in which the co-ordinator can sort out with tutors any problems which have arisen.

Three techniques have been found particularly useful in the training of tutors: interviewing, role-playing, and brainstorming.

(a) Interviewing

Tutors and tutees of whatever age taking part in a tutoring scheme may feel awkward and embarrassed in the unfamiliar situation. Some semi-structured device to put them into interaction has been found useful for ice-breaking. A common procedure is to have the tutors interview the tutees. Older children can, for example, ask younger ones how many brothers and sisters they have; what are their favourite television programmes; what the children enjoy at school, and what they hate at school; what football teams they support; what jobs they might wish to do when they have finished school; and so on, as a prelude to discussing the children's feelings about, and interest in, the particular studies which form the focus of the peer tutoring. Similarly, tutees can be offered the chance to interview their tutors. Older people taking part in tutoring who may be at ease in conversation, may not need any such resource. However, it may be worthwhile for the co-ordinator to build some such practice into the tutor-training so that the tutors have the skill available 'just in case they need it'.

(b) Role-playing

Role-playing can be used not only to simulate tutoring encounters, but also to stimulate discussion among tutors in training sessions. One of the principal problems experienced by untrained teachers is to identify with the lack of knowledge, and consequently frustrations, of their tutees. Role-playing can not only equip tutors with the skills necessary to handle the tutoring, but also can give them the profoundly disturbing experience of being in the tutees' shoes.

As used by Lippitt *et al* (1971), Melaragno (1976a), Mainiero *et al* (1971), and by Youth Tutoring Youth (NCRY, 1968a), role-playing involves the following procedure. The tutor-trainer describes in general terms the situation which is to be enacted; chooses the actors from among those taking part in the tutor-training; briefs the actors as to their actions; assigns tasks to the audience and observers; sets up the scene, describing what each actor should do; starts the action when everybody is ready; cuts the interaction after the point-to-be discussed has been illustrated; thanks the actors (using their real names to give them back their identities); and discusses with all present what was observed. The discussion concentrates on determining what happened in the transaction; investigating how the actors felt in their roles; exploring what caused the situation to develop as it did; and focusing on what could be done differently.

Most people find role-playing a congenial and informative activity. Children, perhaps more than others, used to 'let's pretend' games readily invent their way into situations. For people not familiar with the technique, it may be useful to start by role-playing some familiar situation, such as one person acting the part of the passenger on a bus found by the inspector (acted by the other person) to be without a ticket, or two people arguing over the choice of a television channel.

Once the technique has been accepted, it is valuable to use role-playing to explore actual fears which tutors may have of the tutoring situation itself. One tutor can voice these fears while the other tutor, taking the part of the trainer, can suggest reasons for not having the fears. The Youth Tutoring Youth Trainers Manual (NCRY, 1970) gives detailed suggestions about how to keep a role-playing session going – making the problem specific so that people find it easier to fit into roles; beginning with simple problems, not explosive or overly exciting ones; having the entire audience form into role-playing groups, all acting-out the same situation and discussing it afterwards; having somebody direct role-playing at all times; not letting role-players break out of their roles to comment on what they are doing; discouraging over-eager 'actors'; gently encouraging inhibited people to take part, etc.

Suffice it to note here that role-playing has been found a highly effective way of encouraging tutors to think about the tutoring. The technique can be used not only to introduce tutors to the ideas of tutoring, but also in review sessions when actual problems brought to de-briefing seminars by tutors can be simulated and then discussed.

(c) Brain-storming

This is a technique for the rapid generation of ideas and for putting tutors into discussion with each other. As described, for example, by Melaragno (1976a), a brain-storming session would be conducted as follows. First, the leader would identify a topic about which ideas would be generated and write it at the top of the blackboard. This might include, for example, listing all the excuses a tutee might have for being absent from a tutoring session; how to help a child to feel important and successful; why children have problems learning in school; why teachers need the help of tutors; how to help a tutor to feel successful. Second, the leader would ask for ideas. Third, the leader would write these ideas, in abbreviated form, on the blackboard: taking each contribution one at a time, repeating the essence of a contribution as far as possible in the contributor's own words, checking that everyone has understood what the contributor meant, etc. (In our experience with 'The Pimlico Connection', it has been necessary to have *two students* writing on the blackboard – suggestions flow so quickly.) In this way, an immense number of ideas can be generated quickly. The essence of the technique is that ideas are listed without discussion or evaluation. Quantity is crucial.

Rules commonly applied to brain-storming are as follows: No criticism. No discussion. Hitch-hike (that is to say, build on a previous contributor's ideas).

Blue sky (that is to say any idea however fantastic is accepted). After ideas have been generated, they may be organized and reviewed, with the best ideas being discussed, acted out, or permanently recorded. However, the main task of a brain-storming session is to give everyone a chance to contribute ideas. Anecdotes are discouraged (because they hold up the flow of ideas); silences are allowed (because people may be thinking of new ideas and connections between ideas); and the leader can judiciously insert ideas of his or her own (but without dominating the proceedings). Lippitt *et al* (1971) argue that brain-storming makes everyone's ideas available as resources for a group; maximizes individual participation; pools the thinking of a group to develop a list of the most creative solutions to problems; uses one person's thinking to spark off another person's thinking; warms up a group to focus on a subject or on a specific task; and helps the group to look at a situation or problem from as many viewpoints as possible.

The particular value of brain-storming as a technique for training tutors is that, like role-playing, it provides the opportunity for tutors to think their way into a peer tutoring situation, and to discover the resources which they can bring to it.

Brain-storming sessions seem to work best when they are kept short (maximum 10 to 15 minutes). They can, of course, be combined with evaluation and discussion. If they are used in de-briefing seminars, held at intervals throughout the tutoring, they can be used to get a discussion between tutors going, for example on how to resolve a particular difficulty which one of them may have encountered.

7.6 Support the tutors

In peer tutoring, the professional teacher passes to non-professionals responsibility for tactics while maintaining tight control on strategy. The professional teacher, using tutoring, can ensure a proper inter-relationship between strategy and tactics, not only in the ways already specified (defining aims, planning evaluative research, structuring content, ensuring proper consultation and defining roles, training tutors), but also in providing detailed support for the tutors. Ideally, this support will include regular de-briefing sessions. If these can be made part of the curriculum of tutors, so much the better. If that is not possible, it may be necessary for the professional teacher leading a tutoring scheme to enunciate a series of rules for tutors to follow and then to sample tutoring sessions (perhaps by use of a video-tape-recorder) and review with tutors how they are getting on.

Well-structured materials will, of course, have built-in instructions to keep the tutors on the right lines. Whether or not such instructions are available, it may be useful for the tutor to have a quick-reference list of instructions to review (on the bus on the way to tutoring sessions and at other times between tutoring sessions). Such a list of instructions must obviously reflect the sophistication and responsibility of the tutors. However, two examples may be useful. The first is that of Klausmeier *et al* (1972):

> Be on time to the tutoring session: be prepared with the materials you will use; sit beside, rather than in front of, the tutee; speak to the tutee pleasantly *throughout* the session and talk about something that will be of interest; discuss with the tutee what will be studied or practised that day; look at the tutee when either of you speaks; when you ask a question or give an instruction to the tutee, speak slowly and clearly; wait for the tutee to answer each question you ask or to complete each exercise given; for each correct and complete answer, tell the tutee that the answer is correct; praise the tutee for trying; correct the tutee's wrong or incorrect answers; set a good example for the tutee by paying attention to the work and indicating that you like the subject matter; be pleasant and try to be helpful throughout the session, especially when the tutee may not seem to learn or understand; near the end of the session, review what was learned during the session and praise the tutee for having worked hard and learned; tell the tutee when and where you will meet for the next session.

De Rosier, in a handbook for High School tutors (1971) offers a similar list:

> 1) Be friendly. 2) Be yourself. 3) Know yourself. 4) Remember how you felt when you were the age of the tutee . . . how you reacted to a loud voice, to commands, to praise, to offers of help, to planning. 5) Be as professional a tutor as you can be . . 6) Keep confidences. 7) Be positive. 8) Know what you are doing. Practise before you try something new. 9) Remember that all activities you plan may not be successful. Take courage. If you fail, try something else. What works with one may not work with another one. 10) Use your imagination . . . 11) Keep a sense of humour . . . 12) Admit that you have made a mistake, that you don't know something, but do make an effort to find the answer together. 13) Sometimes teachers are reluctant to give you responsibilities to help their children because they really do not know what you are like. Surprise them. Use the form which shows what you did, how you did it and when. Ask them if they would go over the work with you and make suggestions . . . 14) Keep track of what you do – *daily*: evaluate it – what was good about the activity? What was not good about the activity? How can you teach something better? Would you use this activity at all again? How did your tutee react? 15) Help your tutees to feel good about themselves. Praise them for the things they *do*. Find another way to get them to do the things they *won't* do . . . 16) Provide alternatives or choices so that the children do not feel as if they being 'sand-bagged' into doing an activity. 17) Show the children *you* are interested in *them* as individuals who are worthwhile.

A list of tutoring techniques based on those supplied to undergraduate students of the Imperial College of Science, Technology and Medicine who act as tutors in inner London schools can be found in Appendix A.

7.7 Logistics: keep the scheme as simple as possible

The logistics of peer tutoring are so important that, rather than being discussed in this seventh section, they might well have been put in the first. Even schemes based on impeccable theory, with enthusiastic supervisors, keen

(a) Time

When, in a school day, is peer tutoring to occur? How often is it to occur? How long is it to go on in the school year? How much time must be allowed for tutors to travel? What is the most efficient length of time in terms of pupils' attention? Must time be built into the scheme for tutors to prepare their materials? Although many tutoring schemes are run as after-school activities, commentators agree that it is best to schedule peer tutoring sessions in class-time if possible. To do this avoids depriving children of play time and involves fewer problems with school security personnel. Bohning (1980) wisely suggests that if sessions have to take place in lunch-times, they should be scheduled *after* tutors and tutees have eaten lunch!

Timetables can be unbelievably rigid. Indeed, the willingness of a school head or principal to adjust a timetable to accommodate peer tutoring is some measure of the institutional acceptance of the idea! In a survey of 82 peer tutoring projects, Fitz-Gibbon (1978b: 29) found that scheduling problems occurred in 52 per cent of them!

So complex is the problem of scheduling a multiplicity of classes involving the simultaneous availability of other pupils (who will act as tutors) and younger pupils (who will act as tutees), that many ambitious schemes, have, after a few years of operation, imploded to involve, say, only one teacher and a handful of tutors. There is really no simple answer to this problem. The moral is: start small. A common expedient is to pair classes for tutoring – so that timetabling frees one class of tutors and one class of tutees simultaneously. The problem, of course, disappears when tutor-tutee pairs are from the same class – as in Paired Reading schemes.

(b) Space

The expedient of pairing classes makes it possible for half of the class of elders to go to the classroom of the youngers, while half of the youngers go to the classroom of the elders. If this is not possible, the co-ordinator may need to seek additional space in which peer tutoring can take place. If a school is well-provided with space (a very unusual circumstance!) a special room can be set aside for tutoring in which tutor-pairs can meet. This has the advantage that the co-ordinator can supervise the tutoring and render assistance where necessary. Alternatively, out-of-the-way places must be found (such as locker rooms, dining rooms, corridors, corners of the library, etc); such places can increase the informality of tutor-tutee contacts. However, they not only expose the tutor-pairs to many interruptions, but also make supervision extremely difficult. These elementary points about time and place may seem self-evident truths; but they have all too often been neglected by planners of peer tutoring schemes with catastrophic results.

(c) Meetings

A drawback or a delight of peer tutoring (depending on how one looks at it) is the need for regular contact between different teachers within an educating institution or between different educating institutions. Peer tutoring undoubtedly involves more time and intellectual effort from teachers than other types of teaching. The pay-off is that the teaching itself can be infinitely more rewarding than conventional teaching. However, unless the co-ordinator takes note of the need for meetings, trouble and chaos will follow.

Ideally, teachers involved in peer tutoring should have time for planning and co-ordinating meetings built into their schedules. Once the greater efficiency of tutoring (in maximizing the amount of instruction going on in the educating institution) is realized, such meetings may become regular timetabled phenomena. Meanwhile, it is inevitable that time and patience will be required of all those who join forces to set up a peer tutoring programme. The peer tutoring co-ordinator must decide when and where such meetings will take place.

(d) Selection and training of tutors

One of the principal jobs to be carried out in the meetings of teachers is the selection and pairing of tutors and tutees. Often, there are very many constraints on the system and one has to put up with less than perfect arrangements. However, some commentators suggest guidelines for the matching of older and younger pupils in a children-teach-children peer tutoring scheme. For example, Mainiero *et al* (1971) recommend that the achievement-span between the younger and the older should be two years or more. They also recommend that an older boy never be matched with a younger girl. They recommend other matching factors (which have often proved successful) as follows: a quiet introverted older with a quiet younger who does not seem introverted and does not need drawing out; a sensitive out-going older with a quiet introverted younger; a strong self-assured older with a younger who is a discipline problem, ie, hyper-active, short-interest span, etc; similar interests such as art, or athletics, etc, especially in the case of quiet youngers. Although this selection and matching is a logistic problem, it may well precede the defining of aims.

When and how are the tutors to be trained? Is it possible to build the training into their curriculum (in the manner suggested in Chapter 6)? Or must it take place outside school hours? In either case, when and where is the preliminary orientation to take place?

An important minor consideration, relevant where a class is being divided for purposes of tutoring or being tutored, is what work will be done by the pupils not involved in the tutoring? Parents, for example, on the rare occasions when they have objected to tutoring schemes, have asked what work their children will be missing when they act as tutors. The co-ordinator of a peer tutoring scheme must have an answer to this question.

(e) Documentation

People will not fill in complicated forms; or if they do fill them in, no-one will have time to sort out the information in them! Accordingly, record-keeping should be kept as simple as possible. Ideally, the co-ordinator will supply each tutor with a list of items which the tutee has to learn, the tutor can then tick off each item as mastery is achieved. Structured tutoring programmes usually provide for this as a matter of course. Co-ordinators planning less-structured schemes may need to make a list of items to be covered in tutoring sessions so that everyone – co-ordinator, tutors, tutees – can see at a glance what is going on. A useful expedient is for each tutee to be provided with a folder in which all materials, including record-keeping documentation, are kept. If tutors rotate, it should be possible for a new tutor to take over where the previous one left off without the intervention of the regular classroom teacher.

(f) Finance

The most economical tutoring schemes are those which take place within a single educating institution. However, if full benefit is to be derived from the more elaborate schemes, such as those involving university students visiting secondary schools, it will be necessary to meet travel costs from somewhere. How much will it cost? Who will pay? There may also be additional expenses in duplicating record-keeping materials: has adequate provision been made for this in departmental budgets? And of course the co-ordinator's time represents a real cost which must be accounted for properly.

It would be tedious to elaborate this list of logistic factors at length. The main point is that logistics are extremely important. Peer tutoring, for all its many merits, is structurally more complicated than conventional chalk-and-talk teaching with one teacher to a classroom-full of pupils. It behoves the co-ordinator of a peer tutoring scheme to put much more on paper than would be expected of a teacher doing conventional teaching. The absence of a co-ordinator (through illness or accident) can be quite catastrophic if logistics are neglected.

Appendix B offers a check-list of factors which the planner of a peer tutoring scheme may wish to consider.

Chapter 8

Concluding Observations

The preceding chapters have concentrated on hinting at what *could* be done by describing what *has* been done – by whom, when, where, why, how, and with what effect. We hope that we have offered a balanced account of the process and possibilities of peer tutoring, in particular, by highlighting the amount of planning and attention to logistics needed if it is to be effective.

In these last few paragraphs, we offer some more speculative observations.

8.1. Peer tutoring as a model for professional practice.

As a method by which professional teachers can multiply their effects, peer tutoring can be regarded as a model for many other forms of contemporary professional practice. Unless knowledge is to be regarded as the personal property of professional persons, to be deployed selectively for personal profit, it can be argued that technical knowledge is common property which professional people help non-professionals to use. This view of the role of professional people does not imply that there should be fewer professionals, rather, it has implications for the nature of their work.

In many societies, there is a persistent, chronic shortage of knowledge where it is needed. There is, for example, no economically feasible way in which fully-trained doctors can be made available to serve the needs of all sick people; para-professionals can, and should, carry out much routine health work and health-education work. Similarly, many legal problems are fairly routine. Clients do not necessarily need the expensive services of fully-trained lawyers when many of their interests can readily be served by students acting under the supervision and guidance of qualified lawyers. The commanding officer does not need to shout every order on the parade ground. This military metaphor was, significantly, used by Andrew Bell, the pioneer of peer tutoring. Professional teachers, like other professionals, through their detailed and lengthy training, are best equipped to deal with strategy; many of the detailed tactics can be delegated to non-professionals.

It is an appalling paradox that hospital beds lie empty while people wait years for medical attention, or that thousands of people are illiterate while teachers are unemployed. Likewise, it is incredible that there should ever be talk of 'the problem of leisure' when thousands of old or sick people are withering from lack of human contact. What is obvious is that paid work must ultimately be rationed by some sort of social process. There is, as Fred Hirsch has convincingly demonstrated (in *Social Limits to Growth*, 1977) an obvious social limit to the distribution of physical resources and goods. There is, however, no such inevitable limit on *services*, provided that no-one expects them to be exchanged for physical goods. The service to others becomes its own reward, and the multiplication of services thus available becomes the 'good' that society exists to promote.

Many people gain immense satisfaction from sharing in the basic processes of civilized existence through various forms of volunteering – including peer tutoring. Leisure only becomes a 'problem' when professionals put up barriers, suggesting that people should have licences to be allowed to care for each other.

8.2. The urgent need to stimulate 'volunteering'

There is a further reason why 'volunteering' should be further stimulated both within education (through peer tutoring and other forms of Study Service) and more widely. Many Western societies are currently experiencing two significant demographic phenomena: first, a drop in the 18- to 22-year-old age cohort (which, in the United Kingdom, will 'bottom out' in 1995), and second a growth in the number of elderly people. The consequence of the drop in the number of young people is that there will be, unless drastic steps are taken, grave shortages of qualified people in many occupations. The consequence of the growth in the number of retired people (partly, of course, due to improvements in health-care) is that there will be many able-bodied people around who might (wrongly) become perceived as a burden on the economy. One obvious approach to this two-headed problem is to foster developments in professional practice which will make room for retired people to assist as volunteers.

Peer tutoring points the way forward.

Most of the procedures for effective peer tutoring examined in this book can be readily adapted to other situations. For example, the suggestions in Chapter 7 above about starting a peer tutoring scheme could just as well apply to, for example, a volunteer programme to assist old people who have returned home from hospital after an operation. 'Peer tutors', drawn from other old people who have had the same experience, could be invited to assist healthcare professionals by visiting daily, taking the 'tutee' through an exercise regime (building from walks of a few yards to visits to shops) or helping in the kitchen until the 'tutee' gets back the capacity and desire to cook appropriate meals.

The 'tutor' in such a situation could be trained by being invited to be present (in, say, the physiotherapy department) for the last few sessions before the 'tutee' is discharged from hospital to become acquainted with the detailed regimes needed. The principal modification of professional practice indicated is, as with peer tutoring in or as an adjunct to education, that professionals pay more attention to their *facilitative* role than to their *executive* role. This in turn may involve putting more on to paper than people have hitherto been used to so that volunteers may see where and how they can contribute. The comparative cheapness of word-processors makes this an increasingly feasible option. A volunteer can readily be supplied with a set of 'Notes of guidance' incorporating the broad aims of the volunteer policy; a statement of the anticipated benefits of a specific treatment regime; a list of basic instructions; names and telephone numbers of support persons; and a copy of the detailed instructions given to the 'tutee' about what they should do when they go home from hospital.

In short, the emphasis that current demographic trends require is that professional work should move firmly away from the tactical towards the strategic, and from the executive towards the facilitative.

All the indications from the studies that have been made of peer tutoring in education are that the 'tutors' will not only gain immense satisfaction from their roles but will also learn by teaching.

Appendix A

Tutoring techniques: a list for tutors

Notes on tutoring based on those supplied to tutors in 'The Pimlico Connection' (see Chapter 5)

At each tutoring session:

1. Get started with your tutees as quickly and quietly as possible:

    (a) Greet the tutees by their first names – and let them call you by your first name.

    (b) Ask about anyone who is missing; find out, in a friendly manner, what happened to anyone who is present at this session but was missing the previous week; give tutees a chance to tell you about any personal events which have happened since the previous week – accidents, punishments, birthdays, football matches, etc.

    (c) As soon as possible after establishing personal contact and rapport, ask them to describe their previous lesson – good practice for them as well as a source of information for you.

2. Orient the tutees to the task for the day:

    (a) Tell the tutees precisely what they are to do.

    (b) Explain the general and specific purpose of the day's lesson, linking it to the structure of the course as a whole and to the outside world.

3. Always try to proceed by asking questions, rather than making statements. Do not prompt your tutees with subtle clues or cues. Do not tell them the answers to the questions, but rather lead them to answers by supplementary questions (breaking major points down into simpler ones). Try to evaluate your tutees' responses. You can learn from their mistakes. If you have an appreciation of their misconceptions, it is easier to direct them along the right path.

4. Praise your tutees when they are doing well or give correct answers.

5. Do not punish your tutees. If they give incorrect answers, just go on asking questions until they give the right answer, then repeat the right answer with them. Try to quieten them by interesting them in some aspect of the work, even if it means broadening the context.

6. If your tutees are restless or undisciplined, ask them what is the matter: do not shout at them or order them about. In case of serious indiscipline, call the teacher.

7. Do not expect too much from your tutees. Try to get the feel of an appropriate rate of learning. Try to be aware of individuals who may not be keeping up with the rest of the group and give them some individual attention. If you join a lab group, it is best to observe for a few minutes first to get a feel for the roles of individuals in the group.

8. Reinforce the tutees' learning:

    (a) Tell them when they have got an answer right, and praise them.

    (b) Do not punish them when they have given wrong answers; simply state the correct answer (if your supplementary questions do not elicit it) and ask them to repeat it.

    In general – praise in public; correct persistent faults privately.

9. Be prepared to be flexible; there is no point in pressing on to some lesson-target if pupils have not grasped the earlier steps. Try to assess how much of the earlier work needs to be reinforced before progressing further. Show your interest both in the tutees and in the subject-matter of the lessons.

10. Try to use illustrative examples which draw on your tutees' interests – eg sport, TV programmes, pop, etc and/or examples with which they will be familiar such as incidents in the kitchen.

11. Know the subject-matter and the lesson plan. Being one step ahead will make you feel confident. However, do not be afraid to admit that you do not know an answer: pupils will respect this. Learn together.

12. Do not discriminate or show favouritism. And be aware of your tutees' sensitivities – ethnic or social class background, sex, religious beliefs (eg with Muslim pupils). For example, do not correct them for what you may consider to be bad language; they may resent you for judging them. Teach by example in this respect, otherwise your relationship with them may be damaged.

13. Evaluate the tutees' knowledge frequently by asking questions. For example, if you are not being called over to help tutees, try to join a laboratory group to observe it, and ask tutees what they are doing and what they have found out.

14. Do not assume that the tutees' secondary behaviour (such as shifting on the stools, drumming fingers, unwillingness to make eye-contact, tendency to giggle and gossip) is an indication that they dislike you; they may just be

shy or somewhat embarrassed by their lack of proficiency in the subject. (Some children, for example, may have difficulty in reading.)

15. Towards the end of the lesson, go over the points learned.

At the first session:

1. Tell your tutees your name, and show them it in writing.

2. Ask their names, including first names.

3. Explain who you are and why you are there – eg, by telling them about Imperial College (where it is, and that it is a part of London University, how many students and staff there are); saying what you are studying and what job you think you might do; what the tutoring is all about (how often you will be coming – 15 weeks – and on what day). In addition, say where you live (home and college).

4. Ask the tutees about themselves – eg, where in London they live; how many brothers and sisters they have; whether any of them have been at this school; what they like best about their school; what subject they most enjoy; what they like doing best out of school; whether they have any part-time jobs (paper-rounds, supermarket work, etc); what they think they might do when they leave school.

5. Having 'broken the ice', ask about their interests in science. If they say it is all boring, try sympathetically to unearth the source(s) of their dislike. In all sessions, but more importantly in the first one, try to understand any difficulties the tutees may have and encourage the tutees to be frank with you. For example, girls may think science 'is boys' stuff!' Or boys may think science is 'just learning facts'. Gradually, and without pushing too hard, stress the interest, excitement, and importance of systematic enquiry as the basis of science.

6. Try to overcome (or disguise) any apprehension that you may have about tutoring as this will quickly be communicated to the pupils. Once you get started, you will be too involved to worry about your role in the class!

7. Smile – the fastest ice-breaker!

At all sesssions:

1. The teacher is in charge of the class, legally as well as morally. Always consult the teacher before going off on a new track or departing in any significant way from the syllabus.

2. Try to build around the teacher's demonstrations, worksheets, etc. The teacher has to continue with the class long after the tutoring has ended: it is essential to maintain and reinforce the tutees' confidence in the teacher.

3. Do not be afraid to ask the teacher's advice on how to approach a problem with a particular child. The teacher will probably have a better appreciation of the child's abilities and where extra help may be needed.

4. Take things into lessons (games/books/photos/objects) which illustrate the work being covered. Such items could be used as a focus to reinforce a specific topic.

Sinclair Goodlad

Appendix B

Check-list for planning tutoring schemes

1. Organizer : who will be in overall charge of the scheme:

Tutors	*Tutees*
2. Sending teacher(s):	3. Receiving teacher(s):
4. Who will tutor:	5. Who will be tutored:
6. Number needed:	7. Number to be tutored:
8. Aim for tutors:	9. Aim for tutees:
10. Tutoring materials needed:	11. Syllabus of tutees:
12. What written instructions will be given to tutors (append):	13. What orientation will be given to tutees:
14. When and where will tutors be trained: When: Where:	15. When and where will the tutoring take place: When: Where:
16. When and where will review meetings between organizer and tutors take place: When: Where:	17. When and where will review meetings between tutors and tutees' teachers be held: When: Where:
18. Evaluation: tutors' attitudes	19. Evaluation: tutees' attitudes
20. Evaluation: tutors' knowledge	21. Evaluation: tutees' knowledge
22. Academic problems expected:	23. Academic problems expected:

156   PEER TUTORING

Tutors	*Tutees*
24. Administrative problems expected:	25. Administrative problems expected:
26. Expenses likely: Travel: Duplicating:	27. Source of funds:
28. Additional factors to be seen to:	29. Scheme authorized by:

A separate copy of the checksheet could be used for each component of a complex scheme, eg, where several different classes are to be tutored, with different syllabus materials and so on.

References

Abidi, A.A. *et al* (1976) *The Pimlico Connection*, London: Department of Electrical Engineering, Imperial College of Science & Technology.

Ackerman, A P (1969) *The Effect of Pupil Tutors on Arithmetic Achievement of Third-grade Students*, University Microfilms 70-15, 307, PhD University of Oregon.

Adderley, K *et al* (1975) *Project Methods in Higher Education*, Guildford, Surrey: Society for Research into Higher Education

Adult Literacy Resources Agency (1976) *Adult Literacy: Progress in 1975/76*, Department of Education and Science and Scottish Education Department London: HMSO

ALBSU (1988) *Annual Report 1986-87*, London: Adult Literacy and Basic Skills Unit (ALBSU)

Allen, A (1967) Children as Teachers *Childhood Education*, **43**, (6), 345-50

Allen, V L (ed) (1976) *Children as Teachers* London: Academic Press

Allen, V L & Feldman, R S (1973) Learning through tutoring: low achieving children as tutors, *Journal of Experimental Education*, **41**, 1, 1-5.

Allen, V L *et al* (1976) Research on Children Tutoring Children: A Critical Review, *Review of Educational Research*, **46**, 3, 355-85.

Anslow, P *et al* (1977) *The Pimlico Connection: Phase 2*, London: Department of Electrical Engineering, Imperial College of Science and Technology.

Armstrong S B (1979) *The Cost Effectiveness of Peer and Cross Age Tutoring*, paper presented at the annual International Convention Council for Exceptional Children.

Aspira-Mace (nd) 1. Bilingual Tutorial Reading Manual; 2. Bilingual Education in the United States – a brief historico-critical analysis.

Bailey, D J (1972) *The effects of tutoring first, second, and third grade tutees on the academic achievement, academic potential, and self-concepts of the seventh grade tutors*, University Microfilm 72-33,350, PhD University of Virginia.

Ball, M (1976) *Young People as Volunteers*, Berkhamsted: The Volunteer Centre.

Balmer, J (1972) Project tutor: Look! I can do something good, *Teaching Exceptional Children*, **4**, 116-115

Bar-Eli, N & Raviv, A (1982) Underachievers as Tutors, *Journal of Educational Research*, **75**, 3, 139-143.

Barnes, D & Todd, F (1977) *Communication and Learning in Small Groups*, London: Routledge & Kegan Paul.

Barnett, H (1973) Peer Teaching, *Hispania*, **56**, (3), 635-638.

Barnett B and Long C (1986) Peer assisted leadership: principals learning from each other, *Phi Delta Kappan*, **67**, 9, 672–5.

Bausell, R B, Moody, W B and Walzl, F N (1972) A factorial study of tutoring versus classroom instruction, *American Educational Research Journal*, **9**, 592–7.

Bean, R and Luke, C (1972) As a teacher I've been learning *Journal of Reading*, **16**, 128–32.

Begg C B and Berlin J A (1988) Publication bias: a problem in interpreting medical data, *Journal of the Royal Statistical Society*, **51**, 3, 1–27.

Bell, A (1808) *The Madras School, or Elements of Tuition: comprising the Analysis of an Experiment in Education made in the Male Asylum, Madras; with its facts, proofs, and illustrations; to which are added, Extracts of Sermons preached at Lambeth; a Sketch of a National Institution for training up the Children of the Poor; and a Specimen of the mode of Religious Instruction at the Royal Military Asylum, Chelsea*, 4th edition, London. (*See* Salmon *below*)

Bell, E S (1981) *'Training the Tutor': A Comparison of Attitudes toward Writing*, paper presented at the South Carolina Council of Teachers of English Spring Conference.

Bell, S, Garlock, N, and Colella, S L (1969) Students as tutors: High schoolers aid elementary pupils, *The Clearinghouse*, **44**, 242–4.

Bender, K R (1967) Using brighter students in a tutorial approach to individualization, *Peabody Journal of Education*, **45**, 156–7.

Bernstein, B (1964) Social Class and Psychotherapy, *British Journal of Sociology*, **15**, 54–64.

Bernstein, B (1965) A socio-linguistic approach to social learning, in J Gould (ed) *Penguin Survey of the Social Sciences*, Harmondsworth: Penguin.

Bernstein, B (1970) A socio-linguistic approach to socialisation, in J Gumpers and D Hymes (eds), *Directions in Socio-Linguistics*, New York: Holt, Rinehart & Winston.

Berry, D J (1985) *Hard Work – But Fun! Report on the tenth year of 'The Pimlico Connection' tutoring scheme*, London: Department of Electrical Engineering, Imperial College of Science and Technology.

Berry, D J (1986) *Many Hands Make Light Work. A report on the eleventh year of 'The Pimlico Connection' tutoring scheme*, London: Department of Electrical Engineering, Imperial College of Science and Technology.

Berry, D J (1988) *Enthusiasm, Expertise, Explanation: A report on the thirteenth year of 'The Pimlico Connection' tutoring scheme*, London: Department of Electrical Engineering, Imperial College of Science and Technology.

Best, R and Winfield, D (1986) *Project UNCLE: Report on the Hampshire Pilot Scheme 1985/86*, London: The Institution of Electrical Engineers.

Bierman, K L and Furman, W (1981) Effects of role and assignment rationale on attitudes formed during peer tutoring, *Journal of Educational Psychology*, **73**, 1, 33–40.

Bligh, D (ed) (1986) *Teaching Thinking by Discussion*, Guildford: Society for Research into Higher Education and NFER-Nelson.

Bloom, B S et al (1956) *Taxonomy of Educational Objectives*, London: Longmans.

Bloom, S (1976) *Peer and Cross-Age Tutoring in the Schools*, Chicago Board of Education, District 10, Chicago, Illinois.

Boehm, G A W (1970) How to teach the esoteric mathematical principle of infinite convergence – and make sixth-graders eat it up, *Think*, September–October, 10–14.

Bohning, G (1980) *Peer Tutoring: Two are Better Than One*, Paper presented at Florida State Reading Council Annual Conference held October 1980.

Bohning, G (1982) *A Resource Guide for Planning, Implementing and Evaluating, Reading Improvement,* **19**, 4, 274-8.
Boraks, N (1977) *Recent Research in Reading as Reflected in Peer Tutoring Research,* Paper presented at the Annual Meeting of the Conference of English Education, 1977, Knoxville, Tennessee.
Boud, D (ed) (1988) *Developing Student Autonomy in Learning* (2nd edn), London: Kogan Page.
Boutwell, R C and Mondfrans, A van (1972) A comparison of the structured tutoring model with criteria from idealized instructional models, *Improving Human Performance,* **1**, 4, 8–14.
Bowman, R P (1983) Special Focus on Peer Helpers, *Elementary School Guidance Counselling,* **18**, 2, 111–46.
Boyd G S (1970) Reading achievement and personal adjustment: a study of the effects of participation as a tutor and as a pupil in an elementary school tutorial reading program, *Dissertation Abstracts,* **30**, 11A University Microfilms No 70–9329, PhD University of Alabama.
Bradshaw, C I (1971) *Remedial reading instruction by student tutors in inner-city schools,* paper presented at the Annual Meeting of the California Educational Research Association, April 1971, ERIC No ED 052 230.
Bremmer, B L (1972) *Students helping students program,* Seattle Public Schools, Planning and Evaluation Department, August, ERIC No ED 074 473.
Bridge, W (1975) *HELP Evaluation Report,* University of Surrey: Higher Education Learning Project in Physics, Institute of Educational Technology.
Briggs, D. (1974) Juniors in charge: children teach children, and cross-age teaching *Times Educational Supplement,* 1 November 1974, No 3101 24.
Bright, R L (1972) Tutors in the Vanguard System, *Improving Human Performance,* **1** (4), 27–38.
Brown, A (1985) *Starting The High School Writing Center,* Illinois: USA.
Brown, J C (1972) Effects of token reinforcement administered by peer tutors on pupil reading achievement and tutor collateral behavior, *Dissertation Abstracts,* **32** (7A), 3775, University Microfilms No 72-3020, PhD, Emory University.
Brown, S and Davies, T (1973) The development of an 'Attitude to Science' Scale for 12-14 yr olds, *Scottish Educational Studies,* **5**, Nov, 85–94.
Bruner, J S (1963) *The Process of Education,* New York: Vintage Books.
Bruffee, K (1978) The Brooklyn Plan: attaining intellectual growth through peer-group influence, *Liberal Education,* **64**, 4, Dec, 447–68.
Burke, E and Lewis, D G (1975) Standards of Reading: A critical review of some recent studies, *Educational Research,* **17**, 3, 163–74.
Byrne, K (1972) A Cross-Age Study in Elementary School Science, *Dissertation Abstracts,* **33**, 4A.
Cairns, G F, Barnes, J and Letson, J W (1971) *Evaluation of the Youth-Tutor-Youth Project Summer,* Atlantic Public Schools, Research and Development, ERIC No ED 064 455.
Callender, J, Port, A and Dykstra, G (1973) Peer tutoring: A rationale, *Educational Perspectives,* **12**, 8–11.
Campbell, D T (1969) Reforms as experiments, *American Psychologist,* **24**, 409–29.
Carlson, R T (1973) *An Investigation into the Effects Student Tutoring has on Self-concept and Arithmetic Computation Achievement of Tutors and Tutees,* University Microfilms No 73–27, 585, PhD Northern Illinois University,
Carnegie Commission on Higher Education (1974) *A Digest of Reports of the Carnegie*

Commission on Higher Education, London: McGraw Hill.
Carsrud, A.L. (1984) Graduate student supervision of undergraduate research: increasing research opportunities, *Teaching of Psychology*, **11**, 4, 203–5.
Cass, H, Grant, K, Lassman, M and Stone, S (1978) *Take Six Children, Account of an imaginative project undertaken by a small team of volunteers, designed to help severley handicapped children in a subnormality hospital*, London: National Society for Mentally Handicapped Children.
Central Advisory Council for Education (1967) The Plowden Report, London: HMSO.
Chesler, M A (1965) Tutors for disadvantaged youth, *Educational Leadership*, **22**, 559–63, 605, 607.
Chickering, A W (1977) *Experience and Learning: An introduction to Experiential Learning*. New Rochelle, New York: Change Magazine Press.
Christine, R O (1971) Pupil-pupil teaching and learning team, *Education*, **91**, 258–60.
Cicirelli, V G (1972) The effect of sibling relationship on concept learning of young children taught by child-teachers, *Child Development*, **43**, 282–7.
Clark, B D (1973) An experiment with early school-leavers, *Journal of Moral Education*, **2**, 3, 243–53.
Cloward, R A (1967) Studies in tutoring, *Journal of Experimental Education*, **36** (1), 14–25.
Cohen, D (1978) *A Training Program for Student Mathematics Tutors*, State University of New York, Cobleskill Agricultural and Technical College.
Cohen, J (1986) Theoretical considerations of peer tutoring, *Psychology in the Schools*, **23**, 2, 175–86.
Cohen, P, Kulik, J and Kulik, C (1982) Educational outcomes of tutoring, a meta-analysis of findings, *American Educational Research Journal*, **19**, 2, 237–48.
Cohen, S. and Przbycien, C A (1973) *Modifications in Children's Cognitive Styles: Some Effects of Peer Modeling*, Society for Research in Child Development, March, ERIC No ED 078 906.
Coker, H (1969) An investigation of the effects of a cross-age tutorial program on achievement and attitudes of 7th grade and 11th grade students, *Dissertation Abstracts*, **29**,(10A), 3319.
Coleman, J S et al (1974) *Youth: Transition to Adulthood*, Report of the Panel on Youth of the President's Science Advisory Committee, Chicago and London: University of Chicago Press.
Collier, K G (1980) Peer-group learning in higher education: the development of higher order skills, *Studies in Higher Education*, **5**, 1, 55–61.
Collier, K G (ed) (1983) *The Management of Peer Group Learning*, Syndicate Methods in Higher Education, Guildford: Society for Research into Higher Education.
Community Service Volunteers (CSV) (1971) *School and Community Kits: SACK 2.12*, London: Community Service Volunteers: see Myers, K and Rolfe, J, The Haverstock Tutoring Scheme, Haverstock School, London NW3.
Community Service Volunteers (CSV) (1974) *Tutoring*, London: Community Service Volunteers.
Community Service Volunteers (CSV) (1977) *Working Together in Northern Ireland*, London: Community Service Volunteers, June.
Community Service Volunteers (CSV) (1978) *Study-Service Newsletter No. 1*, P Lewis (ed), London: Community Service Volunteers, November.
Cornwall, M G (1980) *Students as Teachers: Peer Teaching in Higher Education*, COWO, University of Amsterdam.

Conrad, D and Hedin, D (1976) *Action Learning in Minnesota*, Centre for Youth Development and Research, University of Minnesota.

Conrad, D and Hedin, D (nd) *Learning from Service* MS.

Conrad, E E (1975) The effects of tutor achievement level, reinforcement training, and expectancy on peer tutoring, *Dissertation Abstracts*, **36**, 7, 4341–4342A, University Microfilms Number 76, 1407, PhD University of Arizona.

CAEL *Cooperative Assessment of Experiential Learning*, New Jersey: Princeton Educational Testing Service.

Cook, S B et al (1986) Handicapped students as tutors, *Journal of Special Education*, **19**, 4, 483–92.

Cooper, C R et al (1980) *Children's Discourse in Cooperative and Didactic Interaction: Developmental Patterns in Effective Learning*, Texas University, Department of Home Economics.

Core, D and Hall, R (1976) *Storytelling: All About Me, A Tutor Training Mini Course*, Los Angeles: University of South California.

Correll, L (1983) Turning a disruptive study hall into an effective learning center, *NASSP Bulletin*, **67**, 462, 71–4.

Craker, G R and Richardson, J (1981) Helping poor readers in the primary school: a study of a cross-grade tutoring, read-along approach, *Australian Journal of Reading*, **4**, 1, 12–17.

Crone, R, Melroy, H, Strong, H, Wright, J and Campbell, B (nd) *First Form: Reading Development Scheme*, Lisburn, N. Ireland: Laurelhill Secondary School.

Crushon, I U (1977) *Peer Tutoring: A Strategy for Building on Cultural Strengths, Documentation and Technical Assistance in Urban Schools*, Washington DC: National Institute of Education.

Custer, J D (1980) *Improving Social Acceptance by Training Handicapped Students to Tutor their Nonhandicapped Peers*, Utah: Research Report.

Custer, J D and Osguthorpe, R T (1980) *Improving Social Acceptance by Training Handicapped Students to Tutor*, ERIC No ED 217 665.

Cyster, R et al (1979) *Parental Involvement in Primary Schools*, Slough: National Foundation for Educational Research.

Dallas, J D (1974) Cross-age tutoring and the high risk students, *The Clearinghouse*, **48**, 300–2.

Damico, S B and Watson, K J (1976) *Peer Helping Relationships: A study of student interactions in an elementary classroom*, Research Monograph No 18, Gainesville: Florida University, PK Yonge Lab School.

Davis, R J (1978) *Student-to-student Tutoring in Selected English Language Skills at the Island Trees Junior High School, Levittown, New York*, University Microfilms No 68–1122, PhD St John's University, ERIC No ED 033 136.

Deering, A R (1966) *The Homework Helper Tutor Manual*, New York: Board of Education of the City of New York, ERIC No ED 012 278.

Deering, A R (1975) *Factsheet: High School Peer Tutoring (Homework Helpers) Program 1974-75*, New York: Board of Education of the City of New York.

Delquadri, J (1986) Classwide peer tutoring, *Exceptional Children*, **52**, 6, 535-42.

Department of Education and Science (1974) *Community Service in Education Education Survey 20*, London: HMSO.

De Rosier, C (1971) *You and Your Charge*, Leeward (Ha) Community College, April, ERIC No ED 056 011.

Deterline, W A (1970) *Training and Management of Student Tutors: Final Report*, Palo

Alto, California: General Programmed Teaching, ERIC No ED 048 133.0L1.
Devin-Sheehan, L, Feldman, R S and Allen, V L (1976) *Design and Implementation of Field Research on Tutoring Programs: Some Alternatives*, MS.
Devries, D L and Edwards, K J (1972) *Learning Games and Student Teams: Their Effects on Classroom Processes*, Baltimore: Johns Hopkins University, ERIC No ED 070 019.
Diamond, B (1976) Effects of Cross-Age Tutoring on Self-Esteem and Reading Achievement of Low Self-Esteem Fifth Grade Males, *Dissertation Abstracts*, **37**, 2, 877A, University Microfilms No 76–17,895, PhD, Fordham University.
Dickson, A (1972) Each one, teach one, *Frontier*, June, 99–103.
Dickson, A (1975) Tutoring – service within the community of the school itself, *Community Development Journal*, January, 44–9.
Dickson, A (1980) *Study Service: Problems and Opportunities*, Paris: UNESCO.
Dickson, M (1986) *Teacher Extraordinary: Joseph Lancaster 1778–1838*, Lewes: The Book Guild Ltd.
Dillner, M (1971) Tutoring by students: Who benefits? *Research Bulletin of the Florida Education Research and Development Council*, ERIC No ED 061 150.
Dobbs, M E (1975) A study of certain effects of cross-age tutoring, *Dissertation Abstracts*, **35**, 12, Pt 1.7783A, University Microfilms No 75–13, 669, EdD North Texas State University.
Doggett, J (1976) Senior citizens and children bridge the age gap, *Journal of Educational Communication*, **1**, 6, 12–13.
Dollar, B (1974) *Learning and Growing through Tutoring*, New York: National Commission on Resources for Youth.
Dowds, M M, Kullik, J A and Scheibe, K A (1969) Effect of mental hospital volunteer work on career choice, *Psychological Reports*, **25**, 35–40.
Dreyer, H B (1971) Utilizing students as tutors to individualize instruction, *Minnesota Reading Quarterly*, **15**, 4, 132–5, 176.
Duff, R E (1973) *Effects of Pupil-tutoring on Self-perception and Academic Achievement of Primary Grade Tutors and Tutees*, University Microfilms No 74–6262, PhD Southern Illinois University.
Durrell, D D (1960) Implementing and evaluating pupil-team learning plans, *Journal of Education Sociology*, **34**, 360–5.
Durrell, D D and Palos, V A (1956) Pupil study teams in reading, *Education*, **76**, 552–6.
Eagleton, C J (1973) *Reciprocal Effects of Eleventh and Twelfth Graders as Tutors to Sixth Graders in Reading, Written Expression, and Attitude Modification*, University Microfilms No 74–13,721, PhD American University.
Ebersole, E H and Dewitt, D (1972) The solo pupil – team program for reading: an experiment in structured tutoring, *Improving Human Performance*, **1**, 4, 39–42.
Edler, L A (1967) The use of students as tutors in after-school study centres, *Dissertation Abstracts*, **28** (1-A), 74, University Microfilms No 67, 8498, EdD Berkeley: University of California.
Edwards, S S (1976) Student helpers: a multilevel facilitation program, *Elementary School Guidance and Counselling*, **11**, 1, 53–8.
Ehly, S W (1980) *Experimental Analysis of some Process Variables in Peer Tutorial Learning*, Paper presented at the Annual Convention of National Association of School Psychologists.
Ehly, S W and Eliason, M (1980) *Peer Tutoring References from the Education and Psychology Literature*, Iowa, USA.
Eisenberg, T, Fresko, B and Carmeli, M (1981a) *Perach Tutorial Project*, Rehovot, Israel:

The Weizmann Institute of Science.
Eisenberg, T, Fresko, B and Carmeli, M (1981b) An assessment of cognitive changes in socially disadvantaged children as a result of a one to one tutoring program, *Journal of Educational Research*, **74**, 311–14.
Eisenberg, T, Fresko, B and Carmeli, M (1982) Affective changes in socially disadvantaged children as a result of one to one tutoring, *Studies in Educational Evaluation*, **8**, 2, 141–51.
Eisenberg, T, Fresko, B, and Carmeli, M (1983) A follow-up study of disadvantaged children two years after being tutored, *Journal of Educational Research*, **76**, 5.
Eiserman, W D, Shisler, L and Osguthorpe, R T (1987) Handicapped students as tutors: a description and integration of three years of research findings, *BC Journal of Special Education*, **11**, 3, 215–31.
Elliott, A (1973) Student tutoring benefits everyone, *Phi Delta Kappan*, **54**, 535–8.
Ellis, S and Ragoff, B (1980) *Adults and Children as Teachers*, paper presented at the meetings of the Western Psychological Association, Honolulu.
Ellson, D G (1969) *Report of Results of Tutorial Reading Project: Indiana Public Schools 1968-69* (Mimeographed), Department of Psychology, University of Indiana.
Ellson, D G (1971) *The Effect of Programmed Tutoring in Reading on Assignment to Special Education Classes: A Follow-up after Four Years of Tutoring in the First Grade* (Mimeo), Department of Psychology, University of Indiana.
Ellson, D G (1974) *Programmed Tutoring* (Mimeo), Department of Psychology, University of Indiana, November.
Ellson, D G (1975) *Resumé to 1975 Programmed Tutoring Project*, Department of Psychology, Indiana University.
Ellson, D G (1986) Improving Productivity in Teaching, *Phi Delta Kappan*, October, 111–24.
Ellson, D G, Barber, L W and Harris, P L (1969) *A Nation-wide Evaluation of Programmed Tutoring*, Department of Psychology, University of Indiana.
Ellson, D G, Barber, L, Engle, T L and Kampwerth, L (1965) Programmed tutoring: a teaching aid and a research tool, *Reading Research Quarterly*, **1**, Fall, 77–127.
Ellson, D G and Harris, P L (1970) *Project Evaluation Report: Programmed Tutoring of Beginning Reading New Albany Public School System 1969-70* (Mimeo), University of Indiana, Department of Psychology.
Ellson, D G, Harris, P L and Barber, L (1968) A field test of programmed and directed tutoring, *Reading Research Quarterly*, **3**, 3, Spring, 307–67.
Ellson, D G, Harris, P L, Barber, L and Adams, R (1968) *Ginn Tutorial: Tutors' Guide, Comprehensive Book, World-Analysis and Supervisors' Manual*, Boston, Mass: Ginn & Co.
Entwistle, N (1987) A model of the teaching-learning process, in J T E Richardson, M W Eysenck, and I Warren-Piper (eds) *Student Learning: Research in Education and Cognitive Psychology*, Chapter 2, Milton Keynes: SRHE and Open University Press.
Erickson, M R and Cromack, T (1972) Evaluating a tutoring program, *Journal of Experimental Education*, **41**, 27–31.
Feldman, R S, Devin-Sheehan, L and Allen, V L (1976) 'Children tutoring children: a critical review of research', in V L Allen (ed) *Children as Teachers*, Chapter 15, London: Academic Press.
Fenrick, N J and Peterson, T K (1984) Developing positive changes in attitudes towards moderately/severely handicapped students through a peer tutoring program, *Education and Training of the Mentally Retarded*, **19**, 2, 83–90.
Fisher, F G R and Young, R W (1964) Tutorial Systems, *Conference*, **1**, 2, 13–16.
Fitz-Gibbon, C T (1976) The Role-Change Intervention: An experiment in cross-age

tutoring, *Dissertation Abstracts*, **36**, 10.6529A, University Microfilms No 76-8989, PhD, University of California, Los Angeles.

Fitz-Gibbon, C T (1977a) *Tutoring and ESEA Title 1. CSE Report on Tutoring No 2*, California University, Los Angeles, Center for the Study of Evaluation.

Fitz-Gibbon, C T (1976) *The Learning–Tutoring Cycle: An Overview. CSE Report on Tutoring*, California University, Los Angeles, Center for the Study of Evaluation.

Fitz-Gibbon, C T (1978a) *Tutoring: Some New Ideas. CSE Report on Tutoring, No 121*, California University, Los Angeles, Center for the Study of Evaluation.

Fitz-Gibbon, C T (1978b) *A Survey of Tutoring Projects. CSE Report on Tutoring No 118*, California University, Los Angeles, Center for the Study of Evaluation.

Fitz-Gibbon, C T (1980) *Measuring Time Use and Evaluating Peer Tutoring in Urban Secondary Schools*, SSRC End of Grant Report 6570/2.

Fitz-Gibbon, C T (1983) Peer tutoring: a possible method for multi ethnic education, *New Community*, **X1** 160–6.

Fitz-Gibbon, C T (1985) Peer tutoring projects: social education improves achievement, *Noise*, **4**, 2, 4–10.

Fitz-Gibbon, C T and Reay, D G (1982) Peer tutoring: brightening up FL teaching in an urban comprehensive school, *British Journal of Language Teaching*, **20**, 1, 39–44.

Fleming, J C (1969) Pupil tutors and tutees learn together, *Today's Education*, **58** (7), 22–4.

Foot, H and Chapman, I (1982) A case for child tutors? *Education Section Review*, **6**, 1.

Foster, P B (1972) Attitudinal effects on 5th graders of tutoring younger children, *Dissertation Abstracts*, **33** (5-A) 2235, University Microfilms No 72.28, 142.

Frager, S and Stern, C (1970) Learning by teaching, *Reading Teacher*, **23** (5), 403–5, 417.

Frankel, A D (1981) *Structuring An Adult Learning Environment Part 11: Teaching versus Tutoring Support Services*, Paper presented at the Fall Meeting of New York College Learning Skills Association.

Freedman, A (1984) The Carleton University writing tutorial service, *Carleton Papers in Applied Language Studies*, **1**, Canada.

Fresko, B and Eisenberg, T (1985) The effect of two years of tutoring on mathematics and reading achievement, *Journal of Experimental Education*, **53**, 4, 193–201.

Freyberg, J T (1967) The effect of participation in an elementary school buddy system on the self-concept, school attitudes and behaviors, and achievement of fifth-grade Negro children, *Graduate Research in Education and Related Disciplines*, **7**, 3, 3-29.

Furlong, T and Armstrong, S (1976) *Holland Park School: Supportive English Teaching* (Mimeo), November.

Fussell, D and Quarmby, A (1974) *Study-Service: A Survey*, Ottawa: International Development Research Centre.

Fussell, D and Quarmby, A (1977) *Study-Service: A Tool for Change in Higher Education*, paper presented to a seminar on the problems involved in setting up new types of Higher Education institutions and programmes in developing countries and regions, Paris: UNESCO, ED 77/WS/31, 5–8 October.

Gabron, M and Lawler, R (1971) Ninth-graders teach first-graders, *Independent Schools Bulletin*, **31**, 39-43.

Gartner, A, Kohler, M and Riessman, F (1971) *Children Teach Children: Learning By Teaching*, New York and London: Harper and Row.

Gartska, P (1979) *The Role of Tutoring in Community Colleges*, Pepperdine University, California.

Geiser, R L (1969) Some of our worst students teach! *Catholic School Journal*, June, 18–20.

Goldschmid, B, and Goldschmid M L (1976) Peer teaching in higher education: A review, *Higher Education*, **5**, 9–33.

Goldschmid, M L (1970a) Instructional options: adapting the large university course to individual differences, *Learning and Development*, **1**, February (5).

Goldschmid, M L (1970b) *Instructional Options: Adapting the Large University Course to Individual Differences, Learning and Development*, Centre for Learning and Development, McGill University.

Goldschmid, M L (1986) Teaching and learning in higher education: recent trends, *Higher Education*, **5**, 4, 437–56.

Goldschmid, M L (1988) 'Parrainage': Students helping each other, in Boud, D (ed) *Developing Student Autonomy in Learning* (2nd edn) London: Kogan Page.

Goodlad, S (1975a) Social action shows the path to true education, *Times Higher Educational Supplement*, London, 3 October.

Goodlad, S (ed) (1975b) *Education and Social Action: Community Service and the Curriculum in Higher Education*, London: George Allen & Unwin.

Goodlad, S (1976a) *Conflict and Consensus in Higher Education*, London: Hodder & Stoughton Educational.

Goodlad, S (1976b) The Pimlico Connection, *Imperial College Review: Icon*, 12–14.

Goodlad, S (1977) *Socio-Technical Projects in Engineering Education*, General Education in Engineering (GEE) Project, Stirling: University of Stirling.

Goodlad, S (1979) *Learning By Teaching: An Introduction to Tutoring*, London: Community Service Volunteers.

Goodlad, S (1981) *The Wednesday Thousand: A Report on the Sixth Year of 'The Pimlico Connection' Tutoring Scheme*, London: Department of Electrical Engineering, Imperial College of Science and Technology.

Goodlad, S (1982) Communicating technical information, *Physics Bulletin*, **33**, 238–9.

Goodlad, S (1983) *A Great Aid to Learning. (A Report on the Eighth Year of 'The Pimlico Connection' Tutoring Scheme)*, London: Department of Electrical Engineering, Imperial College of Science and Technology.

Goodlad, S (1984) *Education for the Professions: Quis Custodiet?* Guildford: NFER-Nelson and The Society for Research into Higher Education.

Goodlad, S (1985) Putting science into context, *Educational Research*, **27**, 1, 61–7.

Goodlad, S (1988) Four forms of heresy in higher education, in M Tight (ed) *Academic Freedom and Responsibility*, Guildford Society for Research into Higher Education and Open University Press.

Goodlad, S, Atkins, J and Harris, J (1978) *Undergraduates as School Science Tutors*, London: Department of Electrical Engineering, Imperial College of Science and Technology.

Goodlad, S, Abidi, A, Anslow, P and Harris, J (1979) The Pimlico Connection: undergraduates as tutors in schools, *Studies in Higher Education*, **4**, 2, 191–201.

Gray, W A (1983) *Challenging the Gifted and Talented through Mentor-Assisted Enrichment Projects*, Bloomington, Indiana: Phi Delta Kappan Educational Foundation.

Greater Manchester Youth Association (1977) *An Interim Report of 18 Months' Work Investigating the Literacy Needs of Young People*, October, 1975 – April 1977, Manchester.

Green, J and Anderson, H (1970) *Youth Tutors Youth*, London: Community Service Volunteers.

Greenwood, C R, Dinwiddie, G, Terry B, Wade, L, Stanley, S O, Thibadeau, S and Delquadri, J C (1984) Teacher versus peer-mediated instruction: An ecobehavioral analysis of achievement outcomes, *Journal of Applied Behaviour Analysis*, **17**, 4, 521–38.

Habib, B (1981) *A Multi-Purpose Math Lab: A Place for All Seasons*, paper presented at the conference on remedial and developmental mathematics in college: issues and innovations, New York.

Hagen, J W and Moeller, T (1971) *Cross-Age Tutoring*, University of Michigan, Department of Psychology, ERIC No ED 085 090.

Haggerty, M (1971) The effects of being a tutor and being a counselee in a group on self-concept and achievement level of under-achieving adolescent males, *Dissertation Abstracts,* 1971, **31** (9-A) 4460, University Microfilms No 71/7997, PhD, University of Pittsburgh.

Hall, S and Jefferson, T (1976) *Resistance through Rituals: Youth Subcultures in Post-war Britain*, London: Hutchinson.

Halls, W A (1976) A study of the effects a Structured Tutorial Program has on the reading levels of low-achieving readers in sixth grade, *Dissertation Abstracts*, 1976, **37**, 2.733A-734A, University Microfilms No 76-18, 626, PhD Michigan State University.

Hamblin, J A and Hamblin, R L (1972) On teaching disadvantaged preschoolers to read: a successful experiment, *American Educational Research Journal,* **9**, 209–16.

Hamilton, D et al (1977) *Beyond the Numbers Game*, London: Macmillan.

Hamilton, T et al (1985) *Vocational Recreational Programs for 'Latch Key Kids'*, Illinois State Board of Education.

Hargreaves, D H (1967) *Social Relations in a Secondary School*, London: Routledge and Kegan Paul.

Hargreaves, D H (1972) *Interpersonal Relations in Education*, London: Routledge and Kegan Paul.

Hargreaves, D H, Hester, S K and Mellor, F J (1975) *Deviance in Classrooms*, London: Routledge and Kegan Paul.

Harris, P L (1968) Experimental comparison of two methods of tutoring – programmed versus directed *Dissertation Abstracts* 1968, **28** (8-A) 3072, University Microfilms No 67-16, 405, EdD Indiana University.

Harris, W V and Sherman, J A (1973) Effects of peer tutoring and consequences on the math performance of elementary classroom students, *Journal of Applied Behavior Analysis,* **6** (4), 587–97.

Harrison, G V (1969) *The Effects of Trained and Untrained Tutors on the Criterion Performance of Disadvantaged First Graders*, Los Angeles: University of California, ERIC No ED 031 449.

Harrison, G V (1971a) *Structured Tutoring*, Brigham Young University, Department of Instructional Research and Development, ERIC No ED 053 080.

Harrison, G V (1971b) *How to Organise an Inter-grade Tutoring Program in an Elementary School*, Provo, Utah: Brigham Young University Printing Service.

Harrison, G V (1972a) *Supervisers' Guide for the Structured Tutorial Reading Progam*, Provo, Utah: Brigham Young University Press.

Harrison, G V (1972b) Tutoring: A remedy reconsidered, *Improving Human Performance,* **1**, 4, 1–7.

Harrison G V (1980) *Beginning Reading One: A Professional Guide for the Lay Tutor*, Utah: Metra.

Harrison, G V and Brimley, V (1971) *The Use of Structured Tutoring Techniques in Teaching Low-achieving Six-year-olds to Read*, paper presented at the meeting of the American Educational Research Association, February, ERIC No ED 047 898.

Harrison, G V and Cohen, A M (1969) *Training Students to Tutor*, Los Angeles: University of California, ERIC No ED 038 329.

Harrison, G V and Wilkinson, J C (1973) *The Use of Bilingual Student Tutors in Teaching*

English as a Second Language, Paper presented to the Annual Convention of Teachers of English to Speakers of Other Languages, May, ERIC No ED 086 030.

Harrison, M G (1968) A study to determine the effectiveness of student tutors in promoting achievement gain with slow-learning students in related Math 1, *Dissertation Abstracts* 1968, **29**, 10-A, EdD Texas Technological College.

Hartley, S S (1977) *Meta-analysis of Effects of Individually Paced Instruction in Mathematics*, PhD, University of Colorado.

Hassinger, J and Via, M (1969) How much does a tutor learn through teaching reading? *Journal of Secondary Education*, **44**, 1, 42–4.

Hawkins, E (ed) (1971) *A Time for Growing: A Handbook for Organisers of Summer Projects*, London: Community Relations Commission.

Hawkins, E and Derrick, J (1975) Summer projects for children with language difficulties, in S Goodlad (ed) *Education and Social Action*, Chapter 9, London: George Allen & Unwin.

Hayes, R A (1978) *Implementation of a Peer Tutoring Program*, Introductory Practicum, Nova University.

Hedin, D and Conrad, D (nd) *Citizenship Education through Participation*, MS.

Hedin, D. and Schneider, B (1976) *Action Learning in Minneapolis: A Case Study*, Mimeo.

Helwig, C and Griffin, S (1974) Ninth graders teach arithmetic to fifth graders: an experiment, *School Science and Mathematics*, 13–15.

Hendelman, W J and Boss, M (1986) Reciprocal peer teaching by medical students in the gross anatomy laboratory, *Journal of Medical Education*, **61**, 8, 674–680.

Hendrickson, J M (1982) *Using Low Achievers to Tutor Reading and Mathematics*, paper presented at International Reading Association Conference, Gatlinberg, Dec 1982.

Herman, R (1983) Science students go back to school, *New Scientist* 3 March 1987, 578–80.

Hewison J and Tizard J (1980) Parental involvement and reading attainment, *British Journal of Educational Psychology*, **50**, 3, 209–15.

Hill, A and Helburn, N (1981) Two modes of peer teaching in introductory college geography, *Journal of Geography in Higher Education*, **5**, 2, 145-154.

Hinze, L L (1980) *SPEAC for Nutrition, Final Report*, Minnesota: Minneapolis, ERIC No 133 048.

Hipple, T W (1969) Participatory education: students assist teachers, *NASSP Bulletin* (National Assocation of Secondary School Principals), **53**, 80–9.

Hirsch, F (1977) *Social Limits to Growth*, London: Routledge and Kegan Paul.

Holcomb, T F (1971) The effect of a tutorial–friend relationship on elementary school isolates, *Dissertation Abstracts* 1972, **32**, (8A) 4420, University Microfilms No 72-5449, EdD University of Tennessee.

Holder, B and Lister, B (1982) *Peer Force Tutoring Resource Paper No.13*, June, Task for the improvement of Secondary Special Education in New Hampshire.

Horan, J J, de Girolomo, M A, Hill, R L and Shute, R E (1974) The effect of older-peer participant models on deficient academic performance, *Psychology in Schools*, **2**, 207–12.

Howard, B C (1982) *Mathematics in Content Areas*, paper presented at the 62nd Annual Conference of the Association of Teacher Educators, Phoenix, ERIC No ED 213 694.

Hylton, J A and Quellmalz, E (1974) The training of kindergarten children as instructional tutors, *Educational Technology* **14**, 1, 58–9.

Institute for Educational Development (1973) *An Evaluation of the High School Home*

Work Helper Program 1972-73, July, New York: Institute for Educational Development.
International Business Machines (IBM) (1970) Algebra at Age 6? They love it, *IBM Magazine*, September, 40–1.
Isaacs, L M and Stennett, R G (1979a) *Cross-age Tutoring: Going It Alone*, Research Report 79-06, Ontario, Canada: London Board of Education.
Isaacs, L M and Stennett, R G (1979b) *Increasing 'Time on Task' Through a Multi-Method Approach to Reading Instruction*, Educational Research Services Research Report, Ontario, Canada: London Board of Education.
Iwamura, S (1981) *A Multi-skill Approach to ESL in Bilingual Education*, TESCOL Conference held Detroit, March, ERIC No ED 206 172.
Jackson, M (1974) Attitude tests under attack, *Times Educational Supplement* 23 August, 3091, 4.
Jackson, V C and Riessman, F (1977) A children teaching children program, *Theory into Practice*, **16**, 4, October, 280–4.
Janowitz, G (1965) *Helping Hands: Volunteer Work in Education*, Chicago: University of Chicago Press.
Janowitz, G (1971) Educational roles for volunteer youth, *Teachers College Record*, **73**, 1, September, 81–90.
Jason, L A and Frasure, S (1979) *Establishing Supervising Behaviors in Eighth Graders and Peer Tutoring Behaviors in First Graders*, paper presented at the Annual Meeting of the Mideastern Psychological Association, May.
Jenkins, J.R. and Jenkins, L M (1982) *Peer and Cross-Age Tutoring*, ERIC No ED 238 844.
Jenkins, J.R. and Jenkins L (1985) Peer tutoring in elementary and secondary programs, *Focus on Exceptional Children*, **17**, 6, February, 1–12.
Johnson, M and Bailey, J S (1974) Cross-age tutoring: 5th graders as arithmetic tutors for Kindergarten children, *Journal of Applied Behavior Analysis*, **7** (2), 223–32.
Johntz, W (1967) Innovation and the new concern for the disadvantaged, *CTA Journal*, January 5–6, 30–2.
Johntz, W (1973) *An Introduction to the Evaluations of Project SEED*, Project SEED, Lawrence Hall of Science, University of California, Berkeley, August.
Johntz, W (1975) *A Brief Description of Project SEED*, Project SEED, Lawrence Hall of Science, University of California, Berkeley.
Joseph, S M and Delaloyle, J E (1980) *Never Too Late: Extending Continuing Education to the Elderly Homebound: Manual*, Washington, DC: Administration on Aging.
Kalfus, G R (1984) Peer mediated intervention: a critical review, *Child and Family Behaviour Therapy*, **6**, 1, Spring 17–43.
Kammer, C H (1982) Using peer groups in nursing education, *Nurse Educator*, **7**, 6, Winter 17–21.
Kane, B J (1977) The comparison of peer tutor implementors to LD teacher implementors in implementing a computational mathematics program for incarcerated juvenile delinquents identified as learning disabled in computational mathematics ability, *Dissertation Abstracts*, 1977, **37**, 8.5037A, University Microfilms No 77-2240, EdD University of Kansas.
Kane, B J and Alley, G R (1980) A peer-tutored instructional management program in computational mathematics for incarcerated, learning disabled juvenile delinquents, *Journal of Learning Disabilities*, **13**, 3, March, 39–42.
Kann, U and Mokgethi, N (1981) *An Educating, Broadening, Maturing Experience* (A report of the evaluation of the Pilot Project of 'Tirelo Setshaba', the Community

Service Scheme for Senior Secondary School Leavers, Botswana's National Study-Service Scheme), August.

Keel, L (1984) *Re-searching an Ethnographic Study from a Phenomenological Perspective*, paper presented at the Annual Conference of the Mid-South Educational Association, New Orleans, April.

Keele, R and Harrison, G V (1971) *A Comparison of the Effectiveness of Structured Tutoring Techniques as used by Parents and Paid Student Tutors in teaching Basic Reading Skills*, paper presented at the meeting of the California Educational Research Association, April, ERIC No ED 051 967.

Keller, F S (1968) Goodbye, teacher...! *Journal of Applied Behavior Analysis*, **1**, 79–89.

Keller, F S and Sherman, J (1974) *The Keller Plan Handbook*, Menlo Park, California: W A Benjamin.

Kelly, M R (1972) Pupil tutoring in reading of low-achieving, second-grade pupils by low-achieving fourth-grade pupils *Dissertation Abstracts*, 1972, **32**, (9A) 4881, University Microfilms No 72-9399, EdD University of Kentucky.

Kendall, J C, Duley, J S, Little, T C, Permaul, J S and Rubin, S (1986) *Strengthening Experiential Learning Within Your Institution*, Raleigh, North Carolina: National Society for Internships and Experiential Education.

Kenemuth, G L (1974) An experimental study of the effects on achievement and self-concept of sixth-grade pupils as a result of tutoring younger elementary pupils in selective activities, *Dissertation Abstracts*, 1975, **35**, 11, 7043A, University Microfilms No 75-9793, EdD Pennsylvania State University.

Kerlinger, F N (1973) *Foundations of Behaviour Research: Psychology and Sociological Enquiry*, New York: Holt, Rinehart, & Winston.

Kirklees Metropolitan Council (1987) *The Paired Reading Bulletin*, Spring, 3, Paired Reading Project, Kirklees Psychological Service.

Klaus, D J (1973) *Students as Teaching Resources: A Survey of Teaching Models using Non-professionals (Peer Tutoring)*, Pittsburgh: American Institutes of Research.

Klaus, D J (1975) *Patterns of Peer Tutoring*, National Institute of Education Project No 4-0945, February, American Institutes of Research, Washington, D.C.

Klausmeier H J, Jeter, J T and Nelson, N J (1972) *Tutoring Can be Fun*, Madison, Wisconsin: Wisconsin Research and Development MJ Centre for Cognitive Learning.

Klosterman, R (1970) The effectiveness of a diagnostically structured reading program, *The Reading Teacher*, **24**, 159–62.

Kopp, F S (1972) *Evaluation of the Youth Tutoring Youth Program*, Atlanta Public Schools, ERIC No ED 075 560.

Koury, M (1986) The use of delay to teach sight words by peer tutors classified as moderately mentally retarded, *Education and Training of the Mentally Retarded*, **21**, 4, 252–8.

Kromer, T K (1974) Watching themselves teach, they learn, *Improving College and University Teaching*, **22**, 172.

Kuhn, T S (1962) *The Structure of Scientific Revolutions*, Chicago: University of Chicago Press.

Kulik, J A, Kulik L C and Cohen, P A (1979) A meta-analysis of outcome studies of Keller's personalized system of instruction, *American Psychologist*, April, 307–18.

Kulik, J A, Martin, R A and Schier, K E (1969) Effects of mental hospital volunteer work on students' conceptions of mental illness, *Journal of Clinical Psychology*, **25**, 3, July, 326–9.

Lancaster, J (1805) *Improvements in Education, as it respects the Industrious Classes of the Community, Containing among other important particulars, An Account of the Institution for the Education of One Thousand Poor Children, Borough Road, Southwark; and of the New System of Education on which it is conducted* (3rd edn), London (*See* Salmon *below*).

Land, W A (1984) *Peer Tutoring*, paper presented at Mid-South Educational Research Association Annual Conference, New Orleans, November.

Lane, P, Pollack, C and Sher, N (1972) Remotivation of disruptive adolescents, *Journal of Reading*, **15**, 351–4.

Lawton, D (1972) *Social Class, Language and Education (1968)*, London: Routledge and Kegan Paul.

Lazar, G S (1976) *Peer Teaching Assistants and English Composition in the Community College*, paper presented at the National Conference on Personalized Systems of Instruction in Higher Education, Washington DC, May.

Lazerson, D B (1980) 'I must be good if I can teach': peer tutoring with aggressive and withdrawn children, *Journal of Learning Disabilities*, **13**, 3, March, 152–7.

Le Boeuf, F (1968) Qui docet discit – He who teaches learns, *Science Teacher*, **35**, 53–6.

Levin, H M, Glass, G V and Meister, G R (1987) Cost-effectiveness of computer-assisted instruction, *Evaluation Review*, **7**, 1, February, 50–72.

Levine, K P (1976) The effect of an elementary mathematics tutoring programme upon the arithmetic achievement, attitude towards mathematics, and the self-concept of fifth-grade low-achievers when placed in the role of student tutors, *Dissertation Abstracts*, 1976, **37**, 4, 2039A, EdD Temple University.

Levine, S (1986) *Increasing Sight Vocabulary in Grades 1, 2, and 3 through Cross-Age Tutoring and Game Strategies*, EdD Practicum, Nova University, ERIC No 271 723.

Lieberman, S (1956) The effects of changes in roles on the attitudes of role occupants, *Human Relations*, 9, 385–402.

Liette, E E (1971) *Tutoring: The Effects on Reading Achievement, Standard-setting and Effect-mediating Self-evaluation for Black Male Under-achievers in Reading*, Case Western Reserve University, Department of Education, June, ERIC No ED 059 020.

Light, P H, Colbourn, C J and Smith, D J (1987) *Peer Interaction and Logic Programming*, occasional paper, Department of Psychology, University of Lancaster.

Linton, T (1972) The effects of grade displacement between student tutors and students tutored, *Dissertation Abstracts*, 1973, **33**, (8-A) 4091, University Microfilms No 72-32, 034, EdD University of Cincinnati.

Lippitt, P (1969) Children can teach other children, *Instructor* 78.

Lippitt, P, Lippitt R and Eiseman, N J (1971) *Cross-Age Helping Programme*, Ann Arbor: University of Michigan Press.

Lippitt, R and Lippitt, P (1968) Cross-aged helpers, *National Education Association Journal*, **57**, 24–6.

Lombardo, B S (1976) The effectiveness of retarded and non-retarded tutors for educable mentally retarded children, *Dissertation Abstracts*, **37**, 4, 2113A, University Microfilms No 76-21, 957, EdD University of Missouri, Columbia.

Losch, B M (1981) *Cross-Age Tutoring: Meeting Individual Needs Effectively*, Indiana, USA: June, ERIC No ED 204 004.

Lucas, J A, Gaither, G H and Montgomery, J R (1968) Evaluating a tutorial program containing volunteer subjects, *Journal of Experimental Education*, **36**, 78–81.

Lundblad, H and Smith, C B (nd) *Tutor Trainers' Handbook*, Washington, DC: National

Reading Center Foundation, ERIC No ED 068 459.
McCleary, E K (1971) Reports of results of tutorial reading project, *Reading Teacher*, **24**, 556–9.
McClellar, B F (1971) *Student Involvement in the Instructional Process Through Tutoring*, Gainsville: Florida State Department of Education, ERIC No ED 055 046.
McKellar, N A (1984) *Peer Tutoring: An Evaluation of the Relative Cognitive Benefits*, paper presented at the National Assocation of School Psychologists Convention, Philadelphia.
McMonagle, L (1972) An investigation of attitude change in college tutors toward black children as a function of required tutoring, *Dissertation Abstracts*, **33** (4-A) 1521, University Microfilms No 72–27, 204, EdD Temple University.
MacNamara, M (1972) Group dynamics in university tutorials, *Universities Quarterly*, **26**, Spring, 231–53.
MacVicar, M L A and McGavern, N (1984) Not only engineering: the MIT undergraduate research opportunities programme, in S. Goodlad (ed) *Education for the Professions: Quis Custodiet?* Windsor: SRHE/NFER-Nelson.
Mager, R F (1962) *Preparing Instructional Objectives*, Fearon, San Francisco.
Maher, C A (1982) Behavioral effects of using conduct problem adolescents as cross-age tutors, *Psychology in the Schools*, **19**, 3, July, 360–4.
Maher, C A (1986) Direct replication of a cross-age tutoring program involving handicapped adolescents and children, *School Psychology Review*, **15**, 1, 100–18.
Mainiero, J, Gillogly, B, Nease, O, Sheretz, D and Wilkinson, P (1971) *A Cross-Age Teaching Resource Manual*, California: Ontario-Montclair School District, Ontario.
Malamuth, N M and Fitz-Gibbon, C T (1977) *Tutoring and Social Psychology: A theoretical analysis*, CSE Report on Tutoring No 6, November, Los Angeles: University of California, Center for the Study of Evaluation.
Manus, L A and Zipser, D (1977) *Patterns of Problem Solving and its Peer Teaching Program*, Los Angeles: California University, School of Engineering and Applied Science.
Marton, F, Hounsell, D and Entwistle, N (eds) (1984) *The Experience of Learning*, Edinburgh: Scottish Academic Press.
Mason, B O (1975) The effects of university student tutors on the self-concepts of elementary school pupils, *Dissertation Abstracts*, 1976, **36**, 7, 4245A, University Microfilms No 76–159, EdD Louisiana State University.
Mass, J B and Plesser, B N (1983) When students become teachers, *Behavioral and Social Science Teacher*, **1**, (1), 55–60.
Masterson, Sr H (1971) Learning through teaching: the effects of arithmetic tutoring on high school tutors and their first-grade pupils *Dissertation Abstracts*, **31**, 12-A, University Microfilms No 71-13, 654, PhD New York University.
Medway, F J and Lowe, C A (1980) Causal attribution for performance by cross-age tutors and tutees, *American Educational Research Journal*, **17**, 3, Fall, 377–87.
Melaragno, R J (1972) Intergrade tutoring on a school-wide basis, *Improving Human Performance* **1**, 4, 22–6.
Melaragno, R J (nd) *School-Wide Tutoring Over Time*, Mimeo.
Melaragno, R J (1974) Beyond decoding: systematic school-wide tutoring in reading, *The Reading Teacher*, **28**, 157–60.
Melaragno, R J (1976a) *Tutoring with Students: A Handbook for Establishing Tutorial Programs in Schools*, Englewood Cliffs, New Jersey: Educational Technology Publications.
Melaragno, R J (1976b) The tutorial community, in V L Allen (ed), Chapter 12

Children as Teachers, London: Academic Press.
Melaragno, R J and Newmark, G (1969) A tutorial community works towards specific objectives in an elementary school, *Educational Horizons*, **48**, 33–7.
Melaragno, R J and Newmark, G (1971) A tutorial community concept in J Guthrie and E Wynne (eds), *New Models for American Education*, Englewood Cliffs, New Jersey: Prentice Hall.
Mevarech, R (1985) The effects of cooperative mastery learning strategies on mathematical achievement, *Journal of Educational Research*, **78**, 6, July–August, 372–7.
Meyers, P C (1972) Effects of tutorial relationships on adjustment of fifth-grade pupils, *Dissertation Abstracts*, **33**, 3-B, University Microfilms No 72-22, 845, PhD Illinois Institute of Technology.
Middlesex County (1982) *Project COPS Phase 1, 1981-1982 Final Report*, Trenton, NJ: New Jersey State Department of Education, Division of Vocational Education and Career Preparation.
Midwinter, E (1975) Student help for the educationally disadvantaged, in S Goodlad (ed), Chapter 2, *Education and Social Action*, London: George Allen & Unwin.
Miller, A, Robson, D and Bushell, R (1986) Parental participation in Paired Reading: a controlled study, *Educational Psychology*, **6**, 3, 277–84.
Missouri State Department of Corrections and Human Relations (nd) *Adult Basic Education Learning Center 310 Project Final Report July 1983–June 1984*, Jefferson City: Missouri State Department of Corrections and Human Relations.
Mohan, M (1971) Peer tutoring as a technique for teaching the unmotivated, *Child Study Journal*, **1** (4), 217–25.
Mohan, M (1972) *Peer Tutoring as a Technique for Teaching the Unmotivated*, State University of New York, Teacher Education Research Center, January, ERIC No ED 061 154.
Molen, H H van der *et al* (1983) Pedestrian behaviour of children and accompanying parents during school journeys: an evaluation of a training programme, *British Journal of Educational Psychology*, **53**, 2, 152–68.
Mollod, R W (1970) Pupil-tutoring as part of reading instruction in the elementary grades, *Dissertation Abstracts*, 1970, **31** (4-B) 2260, University Microfilms No 70-18, 835, PhD Columbia University.
Moran, J and Oja, S (1977) *Training Kids to Teach*, Peer Teaching Program, Minneapolis, Minnesota 55455: Institute of Technology.
Morgan, M and Foot, H C (1985) The understanding of learning difficulties: implications for peer-tutoring, *BPS Education Section Review*, **9**, 1, 7–11.
Morgan, R F and Toy, T V (1970) Learning by teaching, *Psychological Record*, **20**, 59–69.
Morita, H (1972) *Effects of Cross-age Tutoring on the Reading Achievement and Behaviour of Selected Elementary Grade Children*, University Microfilms No 72-26, 0641, PhD, University of Southern California.
Morris, J H (1984) *Project Teenager, A Skills Exchange Program: High School Students Volunteering with the Elderly in a Rural Community*, Paper presented at the National/International Institute on Social Work in Rural Areas, July.
Moskowitz, J M *et al* (1981) *A Process and Outcome Evaluation of a Peer Tutoring Primary Prevention Program*, National Institute on Drug Abuse, Rockville, Md, and Pacific Institute for Research and Evaluation, Napa, California.
Mulford, B (1980) *The Role and Training of Teacher Trainer Synthesis Report, In-Service*

Education and Training of Teachers: Toward New Policies, Paris, France: Organisation for Economic Cooperation and Development (OECD), Centre for Educational Research and Innovation.
Murdoch, G and Phelps, G (1973) *Mass Media and the Secondary School*, London: Macmillan.
Murgatroyd, S and Thomas, S (1974) *Education Beyond School*, London: Fabian Society.
Myers, K, Travers, R and Stamford, M (1965) Learning and reinforcement in student pairs, *Journal of Educational Psychology*, **56**, 67–72.
NASSP (National Association of Secondary School Principals) (1974) *25 Action Learning Schools*, Reston, Va 22091.
NCRY *See* National Commission on Resources for Youth Inc.
National Commission on Resources for Youth Inc. (NCRY) (nd) *Youth Tutoring Youth – Why?* NCRY, New York.
National Commission on Resources for Youth Inc. (1968a) *Supervisors' Manual: Youth Tutoring Youth*, NCRY, New York.
National Commission on Resources for Youth Inc. (1968b) *Youth Tutoring Youth: It Worked*, National Commission on Resources for Youth: January, ERIC No ED 030 614.
National Commission on Resources for Youth Inc. (1969) *Youth Tutoring Youth: Final Report*, National Commission on Resources for Youth, January, ERIC No ED 034 246.
National Commission on Resources for Youth Inc. (NCRY) (1970a) *For the Tutor*, NCRY, New York.
National Commission on Resources for Youth Inc. (NCRY) (1970b) *Tutoring Tricks & Tips*, NCRY, New York.
National Commission on Resources for Youth Inc. (NCRY) (1970c) *Youth Tutoring Youth: A Manual for Trainers*, NCRY, New York.
National Commission on Resources for Youth Inc. (NCRY) (1973a) *40 Projects by Groups of Kids*, NCRY, New York.
National Commission on Resources for Youth Inc. (NCRY) (1973b) *What Kids Can Do*, NCRY, New York.
National Commission on Resources for Youth Inc. (NCRY) (1974) *New Roles for Youth in the School and the Community*, New York: Citation Press.
National Institute of Adult Education (nd) *Adult Literacy Resource Agency; Lesson Kit for Trainers of Adult Literacy Tutors*, London: Adult Literacy Resource Agency.
National Student Volunteer Program (NSVP) (nd) *High School Courses with Volunteer Components*, Washington, DC: Action, NSVP.
Neckritz, B (1971) Evaluation Report High School Homework Helper Program 1970–71, New York: Board of Education.
Nevi, C N (1983) Cross-age tutoring: why does it help the tutors? *Reading Teacher*, **36**, 9, May, 892–8.
Newmark, G (nd) *About TCP*, Santa Monica, California: Educational Communications Corporation.
Newmark, G (1976) *Schools Everyone Owns*, New York: Park Publishers.
Newmark, G and Melaragno, R J (1969) *Tutoring Community Project: Report of the First Year (May–June, 1969)*, Report TN 4203/001/01, Santa Monica, California: Systems Development Corporation.

New York City Board of Education (nd) *1986 High School Summer Preparation for Raising Educational Performance*, Program End-of-Year Report, OEA Evaluation Report.

New York City Board of Education (nd) *Project Get Set 1984-1985*, OEA Evaluation Report.

New York City Board of Education (nd) *Project Get Set 1985-1986*, OEA Evaluation Report.

New York High School Homework Helpers. See Cloward, 1967; Deering, 1975; Institute for Educational Development, 1973; Neckritz, 1971 and 1972; Price, 1974; Teaching and Learning Research Corporation, 1970.

Niedermeyer, F C (1970) Effects of training on the instructional behaviors of student tutors, *Journal of Educational Research*, **64**,(3), 119–23.

Niedermeyer, F C and Ellis, P A (1969) *The SWRL Tutorial Program: A Progress Report*, Southwest Regional Educational Laboratory, May, ERIC No ED 031 451.

Niedermeyer, F C and Ellis, P A (1970) *The Development of a Tutorial Program for Kindergarten Reading Instruction*, Southwest Regional Educational Laboratory, May, ERIC No ED 057 994.

Niedermeyer, F C and Ellis, P A (1971) Remedial reading instruction by trained pupil tutors, *Elementary School Journal*, **71**, (7), 400– 5.

Niedermeyer, F C and Ellis, P A (1972) Remedial reading instruction by trained pupil tutors, *Improving Human Performance*, **1**, 4, December, 15–21.

Nott, D L and Williams, E J (1980) *The Experimental Effect of Reflective Teaching on Preservice Teachers' Ability to Identify a Greater Number and Wider Variety of Variables Present During the Act of Teaching*, paper presented at the Annual Meeting of the American Educational Research Association, Boston, April.

Nuttall, D (1971) *Administrator's Manual for Science Attitude Questionnaire*, Slough: National Foundation for Educational Research in England and Wales.

Olsen, C R (1969) The effects of enrichment tutoring upon self-concept, educational achievement and measured intelligence of male under-achievers in an inner city elementary school, *Dissertation Abstracts*, **30**, 6-A, University Microfilms No 69-20, 904, PhD Michigan State University.

O'Neil, A L (1975) An investigation of parent tutorial intervention as a means of improving reading skills in the primary age child, *Dissertation Abstracts*, **37**, 1, 124A, University Microfilm No 76-15, 050, PhD University of Oregon.

Osguthorpe, R T, Harrison, G V and Van Monderans, A P (1975) *The Effect of Pre-remedial Instruction on Low-Achievers' Math Skills and Classroom Participation*, paper presented at the annual meeting of the American Educational Research Association, Washington DC, April 1975.

Osguthorpe, R T (1976) *The Hearing Peer as a Provider of Educational Support to Deaf College Students*, paper presented at the Annual Meeting of the American Educational Research Association, April, San Francisco, California.

Osguthorpe, R T (1984) Handicapped students as tutors for nonhandicapped peers, *Academic Therapy*, **19**, 4, March, 473–83.

Osguthorpe, R T (1985) Trading place: why disabled students should tutor non-disabled students, *The Exceptional Parent*, September.

Osguthorpe, R T and Custer, J D (1982) *Training Handicapped Students to Tutor their*

Nonhandicapped Peers, February, MS.

Osguthorpe, R T and Scruggs, T E (1986) Special education students as tutors: a review and analysis, *Remedial and Special Education,* **7**, 4, July/August, 15–25.

Osguthorpe, R T *et al* (nd) *Handicapped Children as Tutors 1983–84: Final report,* Provo, Utah: Brigham Young University.

Osguthorpe, R T *et al* (1985) Increasing social acceptance: mentally retarded students tutoring regular class peers, *Education and Training of the Mentally Retarded,* **20**, 4, December, 235–40.

Page-Jones, R (1976) The Pimlico Connection, *ILEA Contact* (Inner London Education Authority), **5**, 1, 30 April, 16–18.

Paolitto, D P (1976) The effect of cross-age tutoring on adolescence: an inquiry into theoretical assumptions, *Review of Educational Research,* **46**, 2, September, 215–37.

Paoni, F J (1971) *Reciprocal Effects of Sixth Graders Tutoring Third Graders in Reading,* University Microfilms No 71 - 5435, PhD Oregon State University.

Parker, C and Davis, P (1988) *The Open Doors Report,* London: Community Service Volunteers.

Perry, W G (1970) *Forms of Intellectual and Ethical Development in the College Years: A scheme,* New York: Holt, Rinehart & Winston.

Perry, W G (1981) Cognitive and ethical growth: the making of meaning, in A W Chickering (ed), *The Modern American College,* San Francisco: Jossey-Bass.

Pica, T (1976) *Project STEP,* Easton Redding Regional School District No 8, Connecticut.

Pierson, H (1967) Peer and teacher correction, a comparison of the effects of two methods of teaching composition in grade nine English classes, *Dissertation Abstracts,* **28**, 1350A, University Microfilm No 67-11, 122, PhD New York University.

Pigott, H E *et al* (1986) The effects of reciprocal peer tutoring and group contingencies on the academic performance of elementary school children, *Journal of Applied Behavior Analysis,* **19**, 1, September, 93–8.

Plumb, G (1974) *Structured Tutoring in the Boise Schools,* Idaho: Boise School District.

Plumb, G H (nd) *Evaluation Report: Boise Tutorial Program,* Idaho: Boise.

Pope, L and Crump, R (1965) School dropouts as associated teachers, *Young Children,* **21**, 13–23.

Powell, J V, Wisenbaker, J and Connor, R (1987) Effects of intergenerational tutoring and related variables on reading and mathematics achievement of low socioeconomic children, *Journal of Experimental Education,* **55**, 4, 206–11.

Price, G E (1974) *High School Homework Helpers Evaluation Period 1973-74,* New York: Board of Education.

Pumfrey, P (1986) Paired Reading: Promise and pitfalls, *Educational Research,* **28**, 2, 89–94.

Quicke, J C (nd) Pupil culture, peer tutoring and special educational needs, *Disability, Handicap & Society,* **1**, 2, 147–64.

Quilling, M R (1968) *Controlled experimentation in research and instructional units,* paper presented at the Annual Meeting of the American Educational Research Association February, ERIC No ED 030 685.

Ramirez, J V (1971) Effects of tutorial experiences on the problem-solving behaviour of sixth-graders, *California Journal of Educational Research,* **22**, (2), 80–90.

Rayman, R (1981) Joseph Lancaster's monitorial system of instruction and American Indian education 1815–1838, *History of Education Quarterly,* **21**, 4, Winter 395–409.

Redmon, J (1987) Aids and peer tutoring, *Health Education Journal*, **46**, 4.
Reid, S. (1976) National right to read campaign really on the move, *Times Educational Supplement*, 15 October.
Rendall, B (1987) Lessons of a lifetime, *School and Community Magazine*, Spring, London: Community Service Volunteers (CSV).
Richarson, J T E, Eysenck, M W and Warren-Piper, D (eds) (1987) *Student Learning: Research in Education and Cognitive Psychology*, Milton Keynes: SRHE and Open University Press.
Riley, R D and Huffman, M (1980) *Peer Support During Student Teaching: A Shared Relationship*, North Carolina, USA, ERIC No ED 194 468.
Roach, J C *et al* (1983) The comparative effects of peer tutoring in math by and for secondary special needs students, *Pointer*, **27**, 4, Summer, 20–4.
Robertson, D J (1971) *The Effects of an Intergrade Tutoring Experience on Tutor Self-concept*, paper presented at the Annual Conference of the California Educational Research Association, April, ERIC No ED 059 769.
Robertson, D J and Sharp, V F (1971) *The Effect of Fifth-grade Student Tutors on the Sight-word Vocabulary Attainment of First-graders*, San Fernando Valley State College, ERIC No ED 055 735.
Rogers, E and Manning, A (1978) A link scheme in biology between Edinburgh University and local primary schools, *Journal of Biological Education*, **12**, (4), 279–83.
Rogers, M S (1970) A study of an experimental tutorial reading program in which sixth grade underachievers tutored third grade children who were experiencing difficulty in reading, *Dissertation Abstracts*, **30**, 11-A, University Microfilms No 70-9381, PhD University of Alabama.
Rollins, H, Barnes, J and Letson, J W (1970) *Evaluation of the Youth Tutoring Youth Project Summer 1970*, Atlanta: Atlanta Public Schools, Research and Development Report 4.10.
Rosen, S (1977) *Morale and Performance of Same-age Peer Tutoring Partners as a Function of Relative Status and Equity*, paper presented at Annual Meeting of the Southeastern Psychological Association, May.
Rosenbaum, P S (1973) *Peer-mediated Instruction*, New York: Teachers College Press.
Rosenshine, B and Furst, N (1969) *The Effects of Tutoring upon Pupil Achievement: A research review*, ERIC No ED 064 462.
Rosner, H (1970) *Facets of a Cross-grade Tutorial Program*, Anaheim, California: IRAC, ERIC No Ed 041 721.
Ross, G (1982) *Tutor's Handbook – Highline Indian Tutoring Program*, Washington, DC: Office of Indian Education.
Rossmiller, R and Otto, W (1978) *Wisconsin Research and Development Center for Individualized Schooling Bibliography of Publications: Supplement*, Washington, DC: National Institute of Education.
Rotter, J B (1966) Generalized expectancies for internal vs external control of reinforcement, *Psychology Monographs*, **80**, 609.
Rubin, N (1987) How they're wooing the potential dropout, *New York Times*, 8 February.
Russell, T and Ford, D F (1983) Effectiveness of peer tutors vs resource teachers, *Psychology in the Schools*, 20 October.
SEED Project: *See* Johntz, 1967, 1973, 1975; Boehm, 1970; IBM, 1970; Pica, 1976; Shafter, 1976; Waggoner, 1971.
STEP Project: *See* Pica, T.
Salinas, S A (1986) Valued youth partnership: dropout prevention through cross-age tutoring, *DRA Newsletter*, November.

Salmon, D (ed) (1932) *The Practical Parts of Lancaster's 'Improvements' and Bells' 'Experiment'*, Cambridge: Cambridge University Press.
Schermerhorn, S M, Goldschmidt, M L and Shore, B H (1976) Peer tutoring in the classroom, *Improving Human Performance Quarterly*, **5**, 1, 27–34.
Schools Council (1968) *Community Service and the Curriculum*, Working Paper No 17, London: HMSO.
Scoble, J, Topping K and Wigglesworth, C (nd) Training family and friends as adult literacy tutors, *Journal of Reading*, **32**, 5, 411–16.
Scruggs, T E (1985) Behaviorally disordered students as tutors: effects on social behaviour, *Behavioral Disorders*, **12**, November, 36–44.
Scruggs, T E (1986) Peer tutoring with behaviorally disordered students: social and academic benefits, *Behavioral Disorders*, **10**, 4, August, 283–94.
Scruggs, T E and Osguthorpe, R T (1986) Tutoring interventions within special educational settings: a comparison of cross-age and peer tutoring, *Psychology in the Schools* April, 23.
Scruggs, T G, Mastropieri, J and Richter, L (1985) Peer tutoring with behaviorally disordered students: social and academic benefits, *Behavioral Disorders*, **10**, 4, 283–94.
Seaborne, M (1966) *Education: The History of Modern Britain*, London: Studio Vista.
Selig, S M and Perlstadt, H (1985) An instructional methods for mixed medical sociology classes: paired observations of practitioner–patient interactions, *Teaching Sociology*, **12**, 4, July 463–75.
Shafer, D T (1976) *Comparative Analysis of Previous Evaluations of Project SEED*, University of California, Berkeley, Ms, January.
Shafer, M S, Egel, A L and Neef, N A (1984) Training mildly handicapped peers to facilitate changes in the school interaction skills of autistic children, *Journal of Applied Behaviour Analysis*, **17**, 4, Winter, 461–76.
Sharpley, A, Irvine, J and Sharpley, C (1983) An examination of the effectiveness of a cross-age tutoring program in mathematics for elementary school children, *American Educational Research Journal*, **20**, 1.
Shaver, J P and Nuhn, D (1968) Underachievers in reading and writing respond to a tutoring program, *The Clearinghouse*, **4**, 3, 236–9.
Shaver, J P and Nuhn, D (1971) The effectiveness of tutoring under-achievers in reading and writing, *Journal of Educational Research*, **65**, 107–12.
Shaver, P R and Scheibe, K R (1967) Transformation of social identity: a study of chronic mental patients and college volunteers in a summer camp setting, *The Journal of Psychology*, **66**, 19–37.
Sheibe, K E, Kulik, J A, Hersch, P P and La Macchia, S (1969) *College Students on Chronic Wards*, New York: Behavioral Publications.
Sheley, J (1984) Evaluation of the centralized, structured, after-school tutorial, *Journal of Educational Research*, **77**, 4, 213–18.
Shisler, L *et al* (1986) Behaviorally disordered students as reverse-role tutors: increasing social acceptance and reading skills, *BC Journal of Special Education*, **10**, 2, 101–19.
Showitschek, C E (1982) *Use of a Self-Contained Teacher Training Package to Implement and Manage a Peer Tutoring Program for Behaviorally Disordered Adolescents*, paper presented at the Annual International Convention of the Council for Exceptional Children, Houston, Texas, April.
Shure, M B and Spivak, G (1980) Inter-personal problem-solving as a mediator of behavioural adjustment in pre-school and kindergarten children, *Journal of Applied De-*

velopmental Psychology, **1**, 29–44.
Slavin, R E (1981) Synthesis of research on cooperative learning, *Educational Leadership*, May.
Smith, M (1982) *Bibliogaphy of Publications*, Supplement, January, Madison, Wisconsin, Wisconsin Center for Education Research.
Smith, M E (1975) *Peer Tutoring in a Writing Workshop*, University of Michigan.
Smith, P K (1983) *Tutoring: A National Perspective*, ERIC No ED 228 722.
Snapp, M, Oakland, T and Williams, F C (1972) A study of individualized instruction by using elementary school children as tutors, *Journal of School Psychology*, **10**, 1–8.
South Carolina State Department of Education (1985) *Setting up the School Volunteer Program*, Columbia, South Carolina: South Carolina State Department of Education.
Sprinthall, N A (1974) *Learning Psychology by Doing Psychology*, Minneapolis Public Schools, 1–4.
Stander, A (1973) Peer Tutoring and reading Achievement of Seventh and Eighth Grade Students, *Dissertation Abstracts*, **33**, 11-A, University Microfilms No 73-11, 266, PhD University of Michigan.
Starlin, C (1971) Peers and precision, *Teaching Exceptional Children*, **3**, 129–40.
Stierer, B (1985) School reading volunteers: Results of a postal survey of primary school headteachers in England, *Journal of Research in Reading*, **8**, 1, 21–31.
Strain, P S (1977) An experimental analysis of peer social initiations on the behaviour of withdrawn preschool children: some training and generalization effects, *Journal of Abnormal Child Psychology*, **5**, 4, 445–55.
Strodtbeck, F and Granick, L (1972) *The Youth Tutoring Youth Model for In School Neighbourhood Youth Corps: An Evaluation*, Department of Labour Project 42-0-005-034, New York: National Commission on Resources for Youth, December.
Strodtbeck, F L, Ronchi, D and Hansell, S (1973) *Tutoring and Growth*, The Social Psychology Laboratory, University of Chicago.
Stupka, E (1975) Sacramento students improve reading skills of Valley children, *Synergist*, **4**, 1, 29–31.
Surratt, P R and Ulrich, R E (1969) An elementary student as a behavioral engineer, *Journal of Applied Behavior Analysis*, **2**, (2), 85–92.
Swadener, M (1984) *Personal Computers and Cross-Aged Instruction*, Final Report, 20 February, Colorado University Center for Research in Science and Maths Education.
Swenson, S H (1975) Effects of peer tutoring in regular elementary classrooms on sociometric status, self-concept, and arithmetic achievement of slow learning tutors and learners in a special education resource program, *Dissertation Abstracts*, **36**, 9, 6003A-6004A, University Microfilms No 76-635, EdD Indiana University.
Szynal-Brown, C and Morgan, R F (1983) The effects of reward on tutors' behaviors in a cross-age tutoring context, *Journal of Child Psychology*, **36**, 2, 196–208.
Tannenbaum, A J (1968) An evaluation of STAR: a non-professional tutoring program, *Teachers College Record*, **69**, 5, February, 433–48.
Tate, F (1977) *The Use of Hospitalized Adolescents as Tutors for Hospitalized Children in a Residential Treatment Setting*, paper presented at the Annual Meeting of the American Association of Psychiatric Services for Children, November, Washington.

Tawney, D (ed) (1976) *Curriculum Evaluation Today*, London: Macmillan.
Teaching and Learning Research Corporation (1970) *Final Report of the Evaluation of the Homework Helper Program*, New York: Teaching and Learning Corporation.
Thelen, H A (1969) Tutoring by students, *The School Review*, **77**, (3), 229-44.
Thomas, J L (1972) Tutoring strategies and effectiveness: a companion of elementary age tutors and college age tutors, *Dissertation Abstracts*, **32**, 7-A, University Microfilms No 72-2425, PhD University of Texas at Austin.
Tizard, J, Schofield, W N and Hewison, J (1982) Collaboration between teachers and parents in assisting childrens reading, *British Journal of Educational Psychology*, **52**, 1–15.
Topping, K (1986a) *Paired Reading Training Pack*, 2nd edn, Huddersfield: Paired Reading Project, Kirklees Psychological Service.
Topping, K (1986b) *Parents as Educators*, London: Croom Helm.
Topping, K (1987a) *The Peer Tutoring Handbook: Promoting Co-operative Learning*, Beckenham: Croom Helm.
Topping, K (1987b) Peer tutored Paired Reading: outcome data from ten projects, *Educational Psychology*, **7**, 2, 133–45.
Topping, K (1988) Paired Reading bibliography, *The Paired Reading Bulletin*, **4**, 54–63.
Topping, K and Whiteley, M (1988) Sex differences in the effectiveness of peer tutoring, *The Paired Reading Bulletin*, **4**, 16–23.
Towson, S M J (1972) *Tutor Role Enactment in the Peer Teaching Dyad: the Effects of Tutor-initiated Tutee Evaluation and Reward*, Madison, Wisconsin: University of Wisconsin Research and Development Centre for Cognitive Learning, ERIC No ED 065 491.
Training Materials and Resource Packets *See* Allen, 1976; Bloom, 1976; CSV, 1971 and 1974; Deering, 1966; De Rosier, 1971; Gartner, Kohler, and Riessman, 1971; Hawkins, 1971; Janowitz, 1965; Klaus, 1973 and 1975; Lippitt, Lippitt, and Eiseman, 1971; Melaragno, 1976a; NCRY 1968a and 1970c; Topping 1987a.
Tutorial Community Project, Pacoima, California *See* Melaragno, 1972, 1974, 1976a, 1976b; Melaragno and Newmark, 1969; Newmark, 1976.
Waggoner, K (1971) Higher Math in lower school, *Yale Alumni Magazine*, **34**, 9, June 24–5.
Walker, C (1980) *Academic Tutoring at the Learning Assistance Center*, paper presented at the Annual Meeting of the Western College Reading Association, May.
Webb, N M (1982) Peer interaction and learning in co-operative small groups, *Journal of Educational Psychology*, **5**, 74, October, 642–55.
Weiner, A, Goldman, R, Lev, R, Toledano, U and Rosner, E (1974) Applying the helper-therapy principle; a children teach children project, *Child Welfare*, **53**, July 445–451.
Whitley, P (1980) *An Enquiry into Study Service in Institutions of Higher Education*, Department of Education and Science, London: Community Service Volunteers.
Whitley, P (1982) Study Service in the United Kingdom: a survey, in S Goodlad (ed), Chapter 3, *Study Service: An Examination of Community Service as a Method of Study in Higher Education*, Windsor: NFER-Nelson.
Wilkes, R (1975) *Peer and Cross-age Tutoring and Related Topics: An Annotated Bibliography*, theoretical Paper No 53, Madison, Wisconsin: Wisconsin Research and Development Center for Cognitive Learning.
Williams, R W (1981) *Developing a Peer Tutoring Program: A Self-instructional Module*, Chicago: Malcolm X College, Chicago City Colleges.

Willis, P (1977) *Learning to Labour: How Working-class Kids Get Working-class Jobs*, Farnborough: Saxon House.
Winter, S (1986) Peers as Paired Reading tutors, *British Journal of Special Education*, **13**, 3, September, 103–6.
Woods, D E (1975) *The University and Voluntary Service*, Paris, France: Co-ordinating Committee for International Voluntary Service.
Yogev, A and Ronen, R (1982) Cross-age tutoring – effects on tutors' attributes, *Journal of Educational Research*, **75**, 5.

Index

Abidi, A A   83, 90, 96, 125
Adams, R   59
Adderley, K   125
Adeney, K   97
Adult Literacy Resources Agency   50
ALBSU   50
Allen, V L   9, 60, 63, 69, 80, 133, 135, 138
Althof, J   9
Anslow, P   9, 85, 86, 90, 96, 125
Arbor, A   9
Aspira-Mace   9, 29

Balmer, J   73
Barber, L W   59
Bar-Eli, N   76
Barnes, D   58
Barnett, B   36
Barnett, H   73
Bausell, R B   79
Bean, R   73
Begg, C B   71
Bell, A   14, 23–25, 149
Bell, S   74
Berlin, J A   71
Bernstein, B   59
Berry, D J   10, 97, 102
Best, R   47
Bierman, K L   84
Bligh, D   37
Bloom, S   60, 135–136, 139
Boehm, G A W   45

Bohning, G   133, 145
Boss, M   35
Boud, D   36–37
Bremmer, B L   75
Bridge, W   34
Brimley, V   59
Brown, A   14
Bruner, J S   60

Carnegie Commission   120, 121, 126
Carney, J   9
Carsrud, A L   33
Central Advisory Council for Education   47
Cicirelli, V G   83
Cloward, R A   40, 76, 80, 83, 85
Cohen, A M   59
Cohen, J   60, 84
Cohen, P A   69, 70, 75, 82
Coleman, J S   58
Collier, K G   36, 37, 58
Community Service Volunteers   46
Conrad, D   9, 130
Conrad, E E   86
Cook, S B   52, 53
Cornwall, M G   33
Cottam, F   9
Cromack, T   56, 80, 81
Custer, J D   52
Cyster, R   47

Dallas, J D   73

Davis, P   46
Deering, A R   39, 40
Deggan, B   9
Department of Education &
   Science   50, 126, 129
Derrick, J   123
De Rosier, C   144
Devin-Sheehan, L   69
Dickson, A   9
Dickson, M   26
Dobbs, M E   80, 81
Doggett, J   46

Edler, L A   74
Eisenberg, T   31, 32, 33, 85
Eiserman, W D   52, 54
Ellis, P A   59
Ellson, D G   59, 65, 82, 87
Erickson, M R   80, 81

Feldman, R S   63, 69, 80, 83
Fenrick, N J   52, 81, 139
FitzGibbon, C T   82, 84, 85, 88, 133, 145
Fleming, J C   74
Ford, D F   79
Foster, P B   74
Frager, S   86
Frasure, S   27
Fresko, B   85
Freyberg, J T   75
Furman, W   84
Fussell, D   9, 119, 120

Gabron, M   74
Gartner, A   60
Geiser, R L   58, 74
Goldschmid, B   33
Goldschmid, M L   33, 35, 37, 63
Goodlad, S   16, 37, 83, 90, 96, 97, 102, 118, 121, 122
Granick, L   80, 81, 82, 83
Gray, W A   36, 123
Greenwood, C R   88

Haggerty, M   80
Hall, S   58
Hamilton, T   14, 69
Hansell, S   9
Harris, P L   59, 82, 87
Harrison, G V   59
Harrison, M G   85
Hassinger, J   80, 81
Havighurst, R   9
Hawkins, E   123
Hedin, D   9, 130
Helburn, N   34
Hendelman, W J   35
Herman, R   97
Hewison, J   48
Hill, A   34
Hinze, L L   50
Hirsch, F   149
Holcomb, T F   74
Home Tuition Scheme   51
Horan, J J   83
Huffman M   36

Ingerbrigsten, R   9
Institute for Educational
   Development   40
International Business Machines
   (IBM)   45

Janowitz, G   36
Jason, L A   27
Jefferson, T   58
Jenkins, J R   133
Jenkins, L M   133
Johnson, A   9
Johntz, W   44, 45, 116

Kalfus, G R   69
Kammer, C H   36
Kane, B J   85
Kann, U   119
Keller, F S   34
Kelly, M R   80
Kempwerth, L   59

Kendall, J C 121
Kenemuth, G L 80
Kirkless Metropolitan Council 42–43
Klaus, D J 60, 64, 65, 69, 127, 133, 139
Klausmeier, H J 144
Kleinbard, P 9
Klosterman, R 77, 82, 86
Kohler, M 60
Kuhn, T S 69
Kulik, J A 34
Kulik, L C 34

Lancaster, J 14, 23, 25–26
Lane, P 74
Lawler, R 74
Lawton, D 59
Lazerson, D B 84
Le Boeuf, F 74
Leverhulme Trust 9, 10, 90
Levin, H M 88
Levine, K P 85
Linton, T 84
Lippitt, P 9, 94, 133, 137, 141, 143
Lombardo, B S 85
Long, C 36
Lowe, C A 88
Lucas, J A 71
Luke, C 73

McCleary, E K 82
McClellar, B F 60
McGavern, N 120
MacVicar, M L A 9, 120
Maher, C A 61
Mainiero, J 80, 81, 82, 83, 94, 133, 146
Marton, F 121
Mason, B O 82
Medway, F J 88
Melaragno, R J 9, 40, 133, 137, 139, 141, 142
Mevarech, R 82, 83

Meyers, P C 75
Miller, A 49
Mohan, M 80, 81
Molen, H H 50
Mokgethi, N 119
Morgan, M 80, 81
Moody, W B 79
Moore, D 9
Moran, J 9, 27
Morgan, R R 84
Murdoch, G 58

NASSP (National Association of Secondary School Principals) 126
NCRY (National Commission on Resources for Youth) 37, 39, 141, 142
National Student Volunteer Programme 9, 128, 129
Neckritz, B 40
Nevi, C N 88
Newmark, G 40
New York High School Homework Helpers 39–40
Niedermeyer, F C 59, 86
Nott, D L 36
Nuhn, D 78, 82, 86
Nuttall, D 96

Oja, S 27
Olsen, C R 74
Osguthorpe, R T 51, 52, 53, 61, 82, 85

Page-Jones, R 97
Paired Reading 42–43, 49, 83, 117
Paolitto, D P 69
Parker, C 46
Perach Project 31–33
Perlstadt, H 35
Perry, W G 124
Peterson, T K 52, 81
Phelps, G 58

Pica, T 45
Price, G E 40
Project SEED 43–45, 116
Project STEP 45–47
Project Technology Power 9, 27
Project UNCLE 47
Pumfrey, P 14, 43

Quarmby, A 9, 119, 120

Ramirez, J V 74
Raviv, A 76
Rendall, B 46
Riessman, F 60
Riley, R D 36
Robertson, D J 80, 81, 82, 88
Robinson, G 9
Ronen, R 81
Ross, G 133
Russell, T 79

Salmon, D 23
Schermerhorn, S M 35
Schools Council 126
Scruggs, T E 52, 53, 61, 82
Seaborne, M 23
SEED 43–45, 116
Selig, S M 35
Shafer, D T 45, 52, 87
Sharp, V F 82
Sharpley, A 84
Shaver, J P 78, 82, 86
Sheley, J 14
Sherertz, D 9
Sherman, J A 34
Shisler, L 61
Shure, M B 50
Slavin, R E 58, 117
Smith, P K 14
Snapp, M 82
Soren, G 9
Spivak, G 50
Stecker, B 9
Steinberg, B 9

STEP 45–47
Stern, C 86
Stierer, B 48
Strain, P S 52, 87
Strodtbeck, F L 9, 80, 81, 82, 83
Swenson, S H 75
Szynal-Brown, C 84

Tannenbaum, A J 82
Tawney, D 69
Teaching and Learning Research
    Corporation 40
Thelen, H A 9, 60
Thomas, J L 85
Tizard, J 48
Todd, F 58
Topping, K 14, 42, 43, 47, 50, 83, 133
Toy, T V 80, 81
Tutorial Community Project,
    Pacoima California 40–42
Tyler, R 9, 70

University Grants Committee
    (UGC) 10, 108

Via, M 80, 81

Waggoner, K 45
Walzl, F N 79
Webb, N M 82
Weiner, A 73
Whiteley, M 83
Whitley, P 118
Wilkes, R 69
Wilkinson, J C 59
Williams, E J 36
Willis, P 58
Winfield, D 47
Winter, S 43
Woods, D E 118, 119

Yogev, A 81